Curriculum
Compacting

Second Edition

Curriculum Compacting

A Guide to Differentiating Curriculum and Instruction Through Enrichment and Acceleration

Sally M. Reis, Ph.D.,
Joseph S. Renzulli, Ed.D.,
& Deborah E. Burns, Ph.D.

PRUFROCK PRESS INC.
WACO, TEXAS

Library of Congress Cataloging-in-Publication Data

Names: Reis, Sally M.
Title: Curriculum compacting : a guide to differentiating curriculum and
  instruction through enrichment and   acceleration / Sally M. Reis, Joseph
  S. Renzulli, & Deborah E. Burnes.
Description: Second Edition. | Waco, Texas : Prufrock Press Inc., [2016] |
  Previous edition published in 1992. | Includes bibliographical references.
Identifiers: LCCN 2016003296 (print) | LCCN 2016029532 (ebook) | ISBN
  9781618215444 (Paperback) | ISBN 9781618215451 (pdf)
Subjects: LCSH: Gifted children--Education--Curricula. | Curriculum planning.
Classification: LCC LC399 . R44 2016 (print) | LCC LC399 (ebook) | DDC
  371.95--dc23
LC record available at https://lccn.loc.gov/2016003296

Edited by Lacy Compton

Cover design by Raquel Trevino and layout design by Allegra Denbo

ISBN-13: 978-1-61821-544-4

Printed in the United States of America.

At the time of this book's publication, all facts and figures cited are the most current available. All telephone numbers, addresses, and website URLs are accurate and active. All publications, organizations, websites, and other resources exist as described in the book, and all have been verified. The author and Prufrock Press Inc. make no warranty or guarantee concerning the information and materials given out by organizations or content found at websites, and we are not responsible for any changes that occur after this book's publication. If you find an error, please contact Prufrock Press Inc.

Prufrock Press Inc.
P.O. Box 8813
Waco, TX 76714-8813
Phone: (800) 998-2208
Fax: (800) 240-0333
http://www.prufrock.com

Table of Contents

INTRODUCTION

All students, including those who are exceptional, are entitled to a publicly supported education in which instruction is geared to their needs, interests, and developmental levels.

We have seen and read statements similar to the one above on numerous school district websites, in handbooks, and in policy manuals across the country and the world. We have also read similar statements about the need for teachers to differentiate curriculum and instruction. The use of terms such as *personalized learning*, *differentiated learning*, and even *individualized learning*, is common in mission statements that promote the importance of meeting the needs of all students. Addressing all students' differentiated learning needs is indeed a noble goal, but most teachers have not learned a sufficiently broad and effective repertoire of skills and strategies to *implement* these policies and vision statements. Over the last four decades, we have watched many of our most highly able, academically talented and gifted students remain underchallenged in school. Our research on compacting demonstrates that too many spend most of their time in school in classrooms focused on skills or content that they have already mastered (Reis, Westberg, Kulikowich, & Purcell, 1998). These students and many of their age-mates too often tell us that school is "too easy" and that they spend far too much time during the school day on review and practice activities.

Many parents of high-potential students are also dissatisfied with their children's schools. They frequently mention the various ways in which educators struggle to meet the needs of these young people. Over the last four decades, we have spoken with literally thousands of parents who have told us that their academically talented students are both bored and disinterested in school. These parents frequently wonder when or whether their children's academic needs will

1

be met by the local school district. Unfortunately, even if there is a gifted program in the district, many smart and high-potential students still spend the majority of their time in regular classrooms, where they do not encounter challenging curriculum or instruction.

Many educators want to use innovative curriculum and instructional strategies that can be adapted to the learning needs, rates, and interests of all of their students. These same educators tell us that it is difficult to differentiate curriculum and instruction for all of their students given the broad range of instructional levels in their classroom. It is particularly challenging to differentiate for those who are achieving well above grade level. It is also difficult to meet the diverse needs of this group of students because most teachers do not have a professional background in teaching gifted students and the school curriculum often lacks appropriately challenging content and materials. Teachers consistently explain that differentiation:

- ▶ is difficult and challenging to accomplish;
- ▶ requires an inordinate amount of planning time to implement;
- ▶ must address a widening range of student achievement in the same class;
- ▶ is required for far too many students who are both above and below the grade-level curriculum;
- ▶ needs teachers to have extraordinary organization skills; and
- ▶ receives too little administrative support, materials, equipment, and funding to successfully enrich and accelerate learning.

Although we acknowledge that these challenges are real and that implementing compacting can be somewhat challenging, this updated book introduces new knowledge and techniques to help teachers overcome the obstacles they face.

The major purpose of this book is to help teachers learn how to compact, streamline, and enhance their grade-level curriculum to eliminate repetition of previously mastered material, challenge academically talented and above-average students, and create a differentiated, enriched, and accelerated learning environment for students who have already gained mastery of the regular curriculum, or who can, if given the opportunity, master the regular curriculum at a much faster and deeper pace.

Numerous examples of compacting are included in this second edition. These examples illustrate new approaches teachers can use to compact the curriculum and make instructional and curricular modifications for students. We know that many concerned teachers want to assign both challenging and engaging work, and we have tried to make our suggestions for compacting realistic and practical. It is our hope that curriculum compacting, a sequential, easy-to-follow, and well-researched strategy, will save time for *both* teachers and students.

Our work in compacting and curriculum modification has been carried out as a part of our Schoolwide Enrichment Model (SEM) system. The SEM has been field-tested for the last four decades in various schools and districts throughout our country and internationally. Curriculum compacting is one of the three major components of the SEM, which is proven to be effective in reducing boredom for bright students as well as providing them with more challenging and enriching alternatives to the grade-level curriculum. To implement compacting, teachers must be able to identify the goals and standards within the grade-level curriculum, assess whether or not students have attained mastery of those goals, and provide enriching, challenging, and engaging alternate work for students who demonstrate competency. Compacting can be implemented for individual students or for groups of students who demonstrate high ability and achievement in any academic area, including the arts. In addition, compacting can benefit students who demonstrate strength or expertise in any specific content area, even if they are not formally identified as gifted learners.

In Chapter 1, we provide a history, background, and rationale for curriculum compacting. Chapter 2 includes a thorough explanation of each step in curriculum compacting, along with ideas for completing the process. Chapter 3 offers a series of ideas about replacement activities to use during time compacted by teachers. Chapter 4 offers numerous examples of differentiation strategies and options for enrichment and acceleration. Chapter 5 includes a discussion of the professional strategies that can be used to help teachers implement curriculum compacting. Chapter 6 includes a set of case studies that reflect the challenges frequently encountered when implementing compacting. Chapter 7 focuses on assessment strategies that can be used to plan and prepare for compacting, and Chapter 8 includes the most frequently asked questions and answers about compacting and differentiating.

1

An Overview of Curriculum Compacting

How does compacting help gifted and advanced learners? Ask any academically talented or bright student about his or her school day or experiences and you will often hear the same adjectives: boring, dull, uninteresting, repetitive, and even mind-numbing. What is curriculum compacting? Compacting is a research-based procedure (Reis, Westberg, Kulikowich, & Purcell, 1998) that streamlines and eliminates previously mastered regular curriculum for students who are capable of completing content at a faster pace. It saves time by eliminating content that students have already mastered that can be used to provide alternative learning activities that address enrichment or acceleration.

Many of us remember Mark Twain's humorous commentary: "My education was only interrupted by the twelve years I spent in school." On a more contemporary note, Woody Allen provides a similar epilogue to his years of public education. "My teachers loathed me. I never did homework. I'm amazed they expected me to work on those sleazy projects. To this day I wake up in the morning, clutch on to the bed and thank God I don't have to go to school."

On a more personal note, we all have daughters who are advanced readers in school. When one of our daughters, a very advanced reader, ran away from school as a second grader, we found her trudging down a busy road on her escape route. She begged us to let her stay home to be able to do some work that was interesting, challenging, and just a little bit fun.

Some smart kids will, on occasion, encounter a wonderful teacher who inspires and sparks their interests, making learning enjoyable and interesting while these students are fortunate enough to be in this special classroom. The years spent with inspiring teachers are magical for all kids, and the best teachers continually challenge academically talented students to stretch themselves to higher levels. But, let's face it—*all students*, and in particular, our talented students, deserve to have challenging, enjoyable learning experiences *throughout* their education.

There is little doubt that what smart and high-potential kids tell us about school is not just an anomaly, whether it comes from the students themselves or is stated in research about dropouts or high-achieving students from low-income families (Bridgeland, DiIulio, Morison, 2006; Wyner, Bridgeland, & DiIulio, 2007). The majority of students, whether they are in school or have dropped out, say that school is just too easy, and that they would work harder if more was expected from them. In a national poll conducted by a nonprofit education group (Wolniak, Neishi, Rude, & Gebhardt, 2012), 88% of respondents indicated that school was too easy. Only 31% of respondents said that expectations at their schools were high or that they were being significantly challenged. In the same poll, 92% of students said they wanted a curriculum with more real-world experiences.

Gifted and Advanced Students' Learning Characteristics

Students identified as gifted or as advanced academic learners share some common characteristics. For example, students in this group often demonstrate strong cognitive skills or superior academic achievement. However, when it comes to characteristics such as learning styles, interests, prior educational experiences, specific academic and artistic strengths, and personal mindsets, this is a very heterogeneous group, with individuals who vary greatly. Knowledge of both the general descriptors that identify a student as a gifted learner, and the specific characteristics that define the child as an individual, are essential when making appropriate compacting decisions and plans. Of course, both sets of learner attributes also vary for the same child, depending on their grade or age when compacting is being implemented.

Table 1 contains the learner characteristics that can be used to describe each student's individual profile. It is in the best interests of both educators and students to take these descriptors into consideration during the multiple phases of the compacting process.

What defines and characterizes appropriate instruction for advanced learners varies widely, but it is always aligned to the strengths, needs, experiences, characteristics, and interests of each student.

Students come to school from different types of families and economic situations. Some children are fortunate to have enjoyed a broad array of preschool leaning and enrichment experiences, and others live in homes where no one has

TABLE 1

Learning Differences in Students

Cognitive aptitude
Current achievement within core academic areas
Schooling and educational history
Family and community culture
First language
Mindset (beliefs about the role of effort in relation to learning and achievement)
Learning styles (visual, auditory, tactile, concrete)
Interests
Talent development experiences and expertise
Product preferences
Self-regulation strategies and study skills

the time, resources, or skill set to read, play, converse, create, or explore with them on a regular basis. Children with these personal struggles are just as much in need of talent development opportunities and enriching and challenging school experiences as those fortunate enough to live in families who can provide these opportunities in a home setting.

A theme that has inspired our work for more than four decades is, "Schools should be places for talent and strength development." Enriching, challenging curriculum and instruction for high-potential and academically talented learners should engage and develop the talents of these students through rich and interesting learning experiences, characterized by exposure to the key concepts and principles of a discipline.

Joe's work on the Multiple Menu Model and our work on the Enrichment Triad and the SEM are based on these ideas. All students need interesting, meaningful content that is relevant to their personal preferences and experiences, and that piques their interests, encouraging them to seek more information and further exposure. Students also need learning activities that expose them to *new* ideas, concepts, people, places, and events. (We are so dedicated to this premise that it is a cornerstone of the Enrichment Triad Model; Renzulli, 1977.)

What Do Talented Students Need?

Our most able students need opportunities to identify authentic, real-world problems, grapple with real-world complexity, seek solutions, and create products to solve these problems. They need teachers who regularly expose them to enriching experiences, offer them choices, and encourage them to work independently or in small groups as they stretch themselves to achieve at high levels. Talented students also need time to think, reflect, understand, and experience challenging content. They need to learn to expend effort and employ study skills that enable them to achieve at increasingly higher levels than they previously believed possible.

These types of opportunities should be made available to all students, especially those who are academically talented, but, at a very minimum, we believe that curriculum compacting *must* be implemented for high-potential and gifted learners in order to provide them with academic challenge in school. Indeed, we would argue that good instruction for talented and high-potential learners can and should always begin with the compacting process.

Gifted students and high-potential learners often earn top grades without expending effort in school. Many of these students fail to encounter challenge and never learn how it feels to deal with content that is initially difficult for them. Many who have excelled in school and earned top grades without any real effort come to mistakenly believe that being smart means that they do not have to work very hard. When high-potential students and gifted learners encounter true academic challenge for the first time, they may experience fear and anxiety and may begin to make false assumptions. They sometimes exhibit a sense of panic and draw the inaccurate conclusion that they are not really as smart as they had previously believed. Other students incorrectly assume that their parents and teachers were wrong; they are not really smart or gifted, because for them, being identified as gifted really means that they should be able to excel in school without investing a good deal of time or effort.

Providing students with curriculum compacting, offered early and across as many content areas as possible, heads off these misconceptions and helps all students develop mindsets that support them when learning complex skills and concepts becomes frustrating and causes early failures, incorrect answers, and ineffective solutions. This truth is both important and essential in molding young adults to understand the power of effort, repletion, self-evaluation, resiliency, and resolve.

Curriculum compacting enables both curriculum and instruction to be paced in response to students' individual strengths and past achievements, especially when this mastery is not aligned with the progress and achievement of the average student in a given classroom. Most academically talented students learn more quickly than others of their age and require a more accelerated pace of instruction than their peers. Sometimes, these learners need a chance to think more deeply about one aspect of a lesson than others, as they may, at certain times and under certain circumstances, become passionately engaged with a topic or experience burning desires to thoroughly understand some aspect of the curriculum. Sometimes, students' intense interests will actually slow their progress through a compacted version of the regular curriculum, especially when they choose to explore and investigate topics or interests with a depth or breadth that extends beyond the regular curriculum plan.

Compacting also enables teachers to escalate the curricular challenge for students who absolutely need to engage with tasks and problems that are cognitively complex. This elevated level of cognitive demand is critical for this group of students, for the greatest contributor to the underachievement of gifted and talented students is the lack of challenge that they encounter in elementary and middle school (Reis, Hébert, Díaz, Maxfield, & Ratley, 1995). High-potential and academically talented learners should grapple with curriculum, instruction, and the completion of products that are complex, challenging, and deep. Some students will need support and direction to tackle more difficult work, while other academically talented students may actually need less direction from their teachers, depending on the level of tasks and type of work. The learners who may be able to work more independently are often those with intense interests or the capacity to identify interests that they may want to pursue.

Our work with certain components of the SEM for all students has demonstrated that teachers who encourage students to engage and tackle more advanced content and subsequently "support their struggle" make a difference in the type of challenging work that some students can pursue.

According to Vygotsky's (Vygotsky & Cole, 1978) Zone of Proximal Development (ZPD) theory, students' actual developmental level, as determined by the independent work they can complete, is markedly different than the work they can accomplish with adult guidance and support. In essence, the zone of proximal development ranges from the lower level work a student can perform on his or her own without any assistance, as compared to a student's upper area, defined as those tasks that the student is unable to perform even with adult assistance. Student work within the ZPD consists of challenging tasks that students can complete with assistance from a supportive adult who can help students learn the methods for engaging in more challenging work.

The enrichment example we use most often to illustrate the ZPD is the Renzulli Type III independent or small-group experience. Without adult support and guidance, students' advanced projects would not be as advanced nor might they have even been attempted. All high-potential students deserve the opportunity to participate in schoolwork that is sufficiently challenging to require adult assistance in order to achieve and excel. The role of the teacher is to serve as a guide or coach to help students pursue challenging and engaging work and to support them as they learn to struggle and grapple with tasks that they would not be able to accomplish independently.

How Does Compacting Challenge and Engage Academically Talented Students?

Compacting provides the time necessary to allow high-potential and advanced students to experience challenging work at a young age. If it begins in the primary grades, and is provided often, participating students engage in thought-provoking and complex learning activities, ultimately enabling these students to learn to expend effort and subsequently achieve long-term academic success. In other words, encountering challenge earlier prepares students to deal with later challenges in advanced classes in high school and also in competitive colleges. Compacting precludes and often halts the feelings of fright and dread that they may otherwise feel when first encountering difficult work.

Compacting for advanced learners should avoid asking these students to use their compacted time to serve as tutors or teachers for classmates who have not yet achieved mastery of the related curriculum. In too many classrooms across our country, smart kids are asked to teach or instruct other students, often those who struggle to learn content. This practice happens too often, and teachers must understand that academically talented kids are often the worst candidates to assist other students.

Why? Because some of these students process new concepts and skills more quickly than their peers. They make cognitive "leaps" and see relevant evidence that allows them to make inferences and draw conclusions that must be explained to others. Students who are prime candidates for compacting don't follow traditional learning patterns, and sometimes, they actually can't explain how they have learned something or the steps they have used to solve a math problem, write a cohesive paragraph, improvise a musical segment, or complete an assignment.

Although we want all students to be collaborative learners, academically talented students ultimately should not be used to teach other students for at least two reasons. First, if these students spend their time teaching other students content that they have already mastered, they don't have the opportunity to use that time to expand their own learning and engage with new and advanced content. This is inherently unfair. Second, as we noted, academically talented students can't always explain how to do something that they mastered years earlier, often without any practice or effort. That kind of teaching and tutoring is best left to professional educators.

The curriculum compacting process includes opportunities to identify and eliminate content standards that some students have already mastered. It also helps educators identify the related learning tasks that some students do not need to do. Our research has consistently shown us that most advanced learners are regularly assigned work that asks them to practice skills and concepts they have already learned. These students have to wait for peers to catch up, rather than learning something new. This practice can be prevented if students have their content knowledge assessed before they start any new work. A hallmark of curriculum compacting is that students can be assigned more advanced materials, concepts, and skills if and when they demonstrate competency.

Curriculum compacting stops students from being assigned "more of the same" work. When a student has the opportunity to participate in a unit or subject area preassessment, yet is still asked to participate in the same instruction, tasks, and practice as those students who did not demonstrate prior mastery, that action sends a not-so-subtle message to all of the students in the class: "I am treating everyone in this class as if they were just one person, with the same needs and learning rates. I will teach to the middle." It is also the fastest way to kill the love of learning, dampen intrinsic motivation, and develop the Mark Twain and Woody Allen mindset we mentioned at the beginning of this chapter.

When teachers compact curriculum well, they help students identify work that is interesting and challenging. They provide choices about what students can do with the time saved by compacting. In our national study of curriculum compacting (Reis, Westberg et al., 1998), we found that the biggest challenge teachers encountered was determining what to give students to do during the time saved by compacting. Teachers actually learned very quickly to identify students' strengths and to eliminate previously mastered learning standards, goals, and their related instruction and practice work. But a problem occurred when some teachers then had to identify challenging and engaging replacement work that was either based on students' interests or teachers' decisions. Often, teachers just did not know what to assign. Instead, they used and implemented whatever they had readily available—games, puzzles, nonchallenging writing or reading assignments, or worksheets (in our opinion, the worst of all options).

Curriculum compacting enables students to have some independence and choice about their learning. It also gives them time to learn from their teachers and interact with other students, when possible, at a similar level of learning potential or achievement. Advanced-level learners need to be challenged without simply moving them to the side of the room or to the library to work quietly or alone for a good bit of the time.

Steve, for example, transferred into a school mainly because of its gifted program. In the previous school he attended, a very small religious school, Steve had spent 3 years sitting by himself at the back of the room, doing independent worksheets in math and reading more advanced books. Although he was a brilliant student whose talents were recognized by teachers who wanted Steve to be challenged, he was usually given work to do by himself. This segregation made him feel both isolated and different and denied him the opportunity to work both with his teacher and with other students. Compacting done well guarantees that students like Steve will have the opportunity to be taught in a way that respects their needs for appropriate instruction, academic peers, and peer engagement.

Curriculum compacting provides time for students to pursue their interests or accelerate their learning. Our research has found that opportunities for students to become immersed in enrichment learning make a difference in their education and subsequent lives. For example, Baum, Renzulli, and Hébert (1995) studied students who were underachieving in school. The students were assigned to mentors who supported and guided them as they completed a self-selected Type III (problem and interest-based investigation) study. During the course of the semester in which they had mentors, most completed independent Type III studies, and 82% of these students reversed their underachievement and succeeded in school.

Field (2009) studied the use of Renzulli Learning, an innovative online enrichment program based on the Enrichment Triad Model, for students in both an urban and suburban school. She found that both gifted and nongifted students who participated in various levels of enrichment for 2 or 3 hours each week demonstrated academic growth and significantly higher achievement in reading comprehension than control group students who did not participate in the program. Students also demonstrated significantly greater growth in oral reading fluency and in social studies achievement than those students who served as a comparison group.

Curriculum compacting and enrichment can also reverse underachievement for some able learners. In a longitudinal study conducted in an urban high school, Sally found that approximately 50% of the academically talented students studied underachieved because they repeatedly experienced low-level curriculum that did not provide sufficient challenge. This environment caused lower overall levels of achievement (Reis et al., 1995). The underachievement of these students was heartbreaking, as many of them had previously been strong and committed students who excelled in school and in the gifted programs in which they participated.

Thankfully, there is a way to reverse some underachievement experienced by academically talented students. Over time, and with repeated exposure to enrichment learning and self-selected projects supported by teacher mentors (Baum et al., 1999), students often enhance their motivation for learning and challenge. We consider these findings in light of another study that analyzed a large national database about the characteristics of dropouts (Renzulli & Park, 2000), finding that 5% of identified gifted students have dropped out of high school. This loss of talent emerges as a major loss that could have been ameliorated by implementing both curriculum compacting and enrichment.

So, what should we conclude from all of these studies? Curriculum compacting is a common sense strategy, based on the premise that all students deserve the right to make continuous progress in learning in school. Students deserve the right to learn new content, and be exposed to important ideas and concepts that extend their thinking. Our goal is to have all of our students continually increase their skills and knowledge; we believe that students who enter third grade reading at a sixth-grade level deserve the opportunity to enter fourth grade reading at least at a seventh-grade level. This happens when teachers are innovative, flexible, reflective, and commit to the notion of instruction that responds to students' needs and the importance of continuous progress in learning for all students.

What Is Curriculum Compacting?

For almost four decades we have been involved in efforts to introduce the concept, process, and rationale for compacting and to provide related professional development. Compacting is a procedure used to streamline the regular curriculum for students who are capable of mastering it at a faster pace. It saves time that can be used to provide alternative learning activities that address enrichment or acceleration. As mentioned earlier, curriculum compacting helps prevent our academically talented and high-potential students from repeating academic content that they already learned, a practice that often leads to frustration, boredom, and, ultimately, underachievement. Adapting the regular curriculum for high-achieving students requires that teachers learn how to preassess standards and learning goals in various content areas, measure mastery, address situations that arise when not all learning standards can be compacted, and streamline or "compact" teaching and learning tasks when standards and content has been mastered. Next, they need to learn how to manage the multiple student grouping formats that arise when compacting is implemented in a given classroom. When they have mastered those skills and processes, they also need to make decisions and plan the related enrichment and acceleration options that either accelerate or broaden the regular curriculum or enable students to pursue interests that extend well beyond what is being taught in their classrooms.

A Brief History of Curriculum Compacting

Curriculum compacting has been field-tested and researched since the early 1970s and is one research-based way to differentiate, personalize, and individualize educational programs. Although Joe coined the term *compacting* in the 1970s, the concept has a much longer history. As early as the 1860s, St. Louis,

MO, schools offered above-average students the opportunity to "compress" their academic requirements by participating in an accelerated track of courses that would allow them to graduate at least one semester earlier than their peers. The terms *enrichment*, *acceleration*, *ability grouping*, and *compression* have been found repeatedly in the early literature on gifted education. These terms were used to describe a variety of options that allowed academically talented students to participate in advanced-level learning options or to progress through the academic curriculum at a pace that is appropriate for their potential.

Researchers who have conducted reviews of the compacting/compression literature found that early educators and practitioners defined the terms acceleration or compression in a variety of ways. In some cases, the term acceleration has been used interchangeably with compression and included grade skipping and early entrance into college, high school, or elementary school (Clark, 1985; Rogers, 1991; Tannenbaum, 1983).

As historically defined, compression enabled students to be educated from out-of-level texts while enrolled in a grade level associated with their chronological age. Able students had the option of participating in independent study, small-group instruction, programmed instruction, cross-grade groups for math or reading instruction, or credit by examination. These provisions were made in order to provide them with a course of study that was suited to the rapid pace with which many were capable of learning new skills or concepts.

Whether the term used is compression, compacting, or acceleration, strategies to modify curriculum are referenced repeatedly in the early literature on gifted education. Compacting is considered one type of acceleration (Assouline, Colangelo, VanTassel-Baska, & Lupkowski-Shoplik, 2015; Colangelo, Assouline, & Gross, 2004) along with many others, including grade skipping; early entrance into college, high school, or elementary school; the opportunity to complete two semesters of work in one; and the option to take part in independent study or small-group projects. Acceleration may begin with or result from the compacting process, but compacting, the way we have defined and developed it, incorporates a combination of acceleration and enrichment opportunities.

Compacting has been used in many ways: with individuals, with groups of students who have high potential or are identified as academically talented, and even with an entire class. It has been proven to be beneficial for high-potential and academically talented students in several research studies, conducted both by us and others (Reis, Westberg et al., 1998), where we have learned that compacting can dramatically reduce redundancy and challenge students to work at an accelerated pace in areas of interest as well as with advanced content.

How Does Compacting Relate to the SEM and the Enrichment Triad Model?

Compacting is one of the major components of the Schoolwide Enrichment Model (SEM; Renzulli, 1977; Renzulli & Reis, 1985, 1997, 2014), our widely implemented enrichment program used with academically gifted and talented students and for all students in schools using a theme related to talent development, enrichment, or creativity. The SEM is implemented in thousands of school districts across the country and the world. Within the SEM, educators provide children with enriched learning experiences and expose them to advanced learning standards. These educators also develop the talents of all children, providing a broad range of advanced-level, in-depth enrichment experiences for high-potential and academically talented students. They follow exploratory experiences with more intense learning opportunities for all students based on their developing interests. The SEM emphasizes engagement and the use of enjoyable and challenging learning experiences that are constructed around students' interests, learning styles, and expression/product styles.

The goal of the SEM is to develop educational programs for talented and high-potential students as well as to enable all children to participate in opportunities for talent development. The SEM draws upon almost 40 years of research and field-testing (Renzulli & Reis, 1994; Reis & Renzulli, 2003) that suggests that the SEM promotes engagement through its three types of enrichment experiences—experiences that are enjoyable, challenging, and interest-based. Separate studies on the SEM, conducted over the last few decades, have demonstrated its effectiveness in schools with widely differing socioeconomic levels and program organization patterns. The SEM has been shown to be effective in increasing student creative productivity, enhancing personal and social development, encouraging talent development in culturally diverse and/or special needs populations, and as a curricular framework. This research on the SEM also suggests that the model is effective in serving high-ability students and providing enrichment in a variety of educational settings, including schools serving populations of low socioeconomic status families.

Renzulli's (1977) Enrichment Triad Model is the curricular core of the SEM. The Triad was developed in the mid-1970s and initially implemented as a gifted and talented program in school districts in Connecticut and the Northeastern United States. The model eventually began to be used in schools across the country and the world. Triad programs were designed and implemented by classroom, gifted education, and enrichment teachers in all kinds of settings. The programs varied tremendously, but in all of the ones we visited, a similar focus emerged related to providing different types of enrichment, increasing student creative productivity, and differentiating instruction and learning opportunities for all students.

The SEM focuses on the development of both academic and creative-productive giftedness. Creative-productive giftedness places a premium on the development of original material and products designed to have an impact on one or more audiences. In the SEM, academic gifts are developed when the student is transformed from that of a learner of lessons to one in which she or he uses the modus operandi of a firsthand inquirer to experience the joys and frustrations of creative productivity.

How does compacting fit into the SEM? An example might help. Two afternoons a week Colleen participates in an enrichment program in her elementary school in Hartford, CT. Colleen's family lives in subsidized housing and survives on a monthly welfare check and food stamps. Colleen's strongest academic area is reading, and through curriculum compacting, she was provided with some choice-based reading material that is two grade levels above the level of reading being covered in her classroom. Colleen was once identified as an underachieving student but now she finds school a much more inviting place. She is considering a career in journalism and with the help of the enrichment specialist at her school, she applied for a special summer program in writing and attended it on an academic scholarship.

"School," explained Colleen, "is a place where you have must-dos and can-dos. I work harder on my must-dos so I can spend more time working on my can-dos." The enrichment program in which Colleen participates is a key focus of our talent development approach in the SEM. The SEM identifies a broad range of talent potentials, by focusing on student interests and learning style preferences, as well as their academic strengths.

The Three Components of the SEM

The Total Talent Portfolio

The Total Talent Portfolio (TTP), one component of the SEM, focuses on helping teachers learn more information about the abilities, interests, and learning styles of students in their classrooms. This information focuses on strengths rather than deficits, is compiled in a student's TTP, and is used to make decisions about talent development opportunities in regular classes as well in the enrichment experiences we recommend. Curriculum compacting is one type of talent development opportunity that may be documented on a student's TTP (see Appendix A for a TTP that includes compacting).

Curriculum Compacting

Compacting is the second service delivery component of the SEM. It includes curriculum modification techniques designed to eliminate repetition of previously mastered material so that all students are challenged. It also provides time for and increases the number of in-depth learning experiences and introduces various types of enrichment into regular curricular experiences.

Enrichment Learning and Teaching

The third service delivery component of the SEM is enrichment learning and teaching, usually delivered as the Enrichment Triad Model is implemented. Enrichment learning and teaching is a method in which teachers learn more about the abilities, interests, and learning styles of their students, identify learning experiences that give students choices, and help them identify problems or issues about which they want to know more. The ultimate goal of learning guided by the SEM philosophy is to challenge and engage all students, replacing dependent and passive learning with independent and engaged learning.

The Enrichment Triad Model (Type I, Type II, and Type III Enrichment) is used for this purpose. Type I Enrichment includes general exploratory experiences such as guest speakers, field trips, demonstrations, interest centers, and the use of audiovisual materials and technology (such as webinars) designed to expose students to new and exciting topics, ideas, and fields of knowledge not ordinarily covered in the regular curriculum.

Type II Enrichment includes instructional methods and materials purposefully designed to promote the development of thinking, feeling, research, communication, and methodological processes. Type II training, usually carried out both in classrooms and in enrichment programs, includes the development of creative thinking and problem solving, critical thinking, and affective processes; a variety of specific learning-how-to-learn skills; skills in the appropriate use of advanced-level reference materials; and written, oral, and visual communication skills.

Type III Enrichment is the most advanced level in the Enrichment Triad Model. Although Types I and II Enrichment and curriculum compacting should be provided on a regular basis to Talent Pool students, the ability to revolve into Type III Enrichment depends on an individual's interests, motivation, and desire to pursue advanced-level study. Type III Enrichment is defined as investigative activities and artistic productions in which the learner assumes the role of a first-hand inquirer thinking, feeling, and acting like a practicing professional, with involvement pursued at as advanced a level as possible given the student's level of development and age.

The most important feature of the model is the connection among the experiences (see Figure 1). Each type of enrichment is viewed as a component part of a holistic process that blends present or newly developed interests (Type I) and advanced-level thinking and research skills (Type II) with application situations based on the modus operandi of the firsthand inquirer (Type III).

Too often, enrichment has been regarded as something extra, a nonessential frill that does not belong in serious discussions about student achievement. Yet ignoring this critical component of instruction means ignoring student engagement and motivation to learn. Special things can happen in the learning environment when students are interested in learning. When students' interests and choices help determine their work and paths to learning, engagement in learning is enhanced and achievement is increased. Many children in our schools want to make connections between their learning environment and their future interests and education.

Desire to learn and engagement also affect the successful implementation of curriculum compacting. The SEM has embraced the concept of compacting by replacing compacted curriculum with content based on students' talents and interests, using those strengths to extend, expand, and accelerate learning. In fact, the SEM has been used to turn around struggling schools with low achievement through our strength-based enrichment approach and the elimination of content that students have already mastered: exactly the core service delivered by compacting.

A Multipronged Rationale for Curriculum Compacting

Several reasons exist for compacting curriculum for our most able students, as summarized in research (Reis, Westberg et al., 1998). Before beginning the compacting process, teachers should understand its rationale and purpose. The following series of bolded research findings summarize our rationale and provide pertinent references for teachers.

Many academically talented students already know much of their text's content before "learning it." Our research about compacting (Reis, Westberg et al., 1998) tells us that elementary and middle school teachers who implement compacting can eliminate as much as 40%–70% of the regular curriculum for approximately 10%–15% of all students in their heterogeneous classes. In language arts and mathematics programs, advanced students may have 70%–80% of the curriculum eliminated. Field tests of compacting at the elementary and middle school level show that grouping students by their prior knowledge *of*

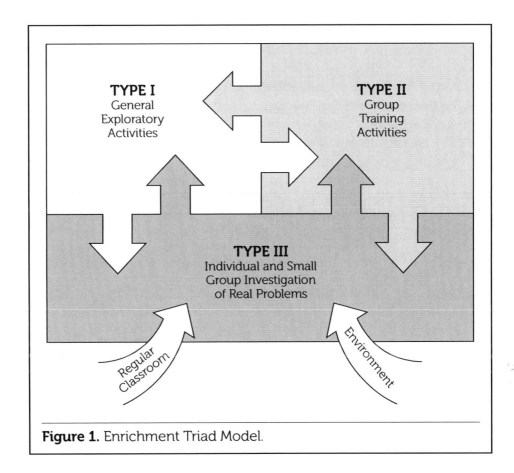

Figure 1. Enrichment Triad Model.

and their interest *in* the subject often allows a teacher to eliminate approximately 50% of the regular curriculum.

School is too easy for many of our most able students, and a continuing absence of challenge continues to exist for gifted and talented students. James Michener, a prolific novelist once worked as a textbook editor, an experience he wrote about in his book *This Noble Land*, published in 1996. In this segment, he referred to the mandatory use of a list of words compiled by a highly regarded educator and psychologist, Edward Lee Thorndike. It was this list, Michener believed, that began the process known as "dumbing down the curriculum." As he explained,

> what I had once helped write as a book suitable for students in the sixth grade gradually became a book intended for grades seven through eight. Texts originally for the middle grades began to be certified as being appropriate for high school students, and what used to be a high school text appeared as a college text. The entire educational process was watered down, level by level. (p. 62)

More than two decades ago, an important federal report entitled *National Excellence: A Case for Developing America's Talent* (U.S. Department of Education, 1993), summarized the status of education for our nation's academically talented students. In this report, the education of talented students in the United States was described as a quiet crisis. The *National Excellence* report eloquently summarized the absence of attention paid to this population and the absence of challenge that gifted and talented students experience:

> Despite sporadic attention over the years to the needs of bright students, most of them continue to spend time in school working well below their capabilities. The beliefs espoused by school reforms who strive to help children from all economic and cultural backgrounds reach their full potential has not been extended to America's most talented students. They are under-challenged and therefore underachieve. (p. 5)

The report further argued that our nation's talented students read fewer demanding books, and are less prepared for work or postsecondary education than top students in many other industrialized countries. Talented children from economically disadvantaged homes or from culturally or linguistically diverse groups were found to be especially neglected and the report indicated that many of them will not realize their potential without some type of intervention.

Unfortunately, inattention to the needs of academically able students continues in American schools today. A 2015 book, *Failing Our Brightest Kids: The Global Challenge of Educating High-Ability Students*, by Chester Finn Jr. and Brandon Wright addressed this issue and reached the same conclusion that high-achieving, talented students are being neglected in many if not most of our schools. Finn and Wright argued that the United States does not produce enough outstanding students. Secondly, children from disadvantaged backgrounds are severely underrepresented among our most talented students. But these types of findings are not new. A long history chronicles the increasing levels of antiintellectualism and the dumbing down of America, first discussed by Richard Hofstadter, who won a Pulitzer Prize in 1964 for his 1963 book, *Anti-Intellectualism in American Life*. The trend continued with the Finn and Wright text. Reading these books has reminded us of what our friend James Gallagher once said, that the citizens of the United States love the products of gifted individuals, even if they don't like the individuals themselves.

A 2009 book by Mark Bauerlein, entitled *The Dumbest Generation: How the Digital Age Stupefies Young Americans and Jeopardizes Our Future (Or, Don't Trust Anyone Under 30)*, described what we ourselves have begun to notice and fear: that the youngest generation of school-aged students have a growing distaste of reading texts of any depth and substance, at the same time that they are increasing their addiction to lighter reading via the hours that they spend each day with social media.

Another reason that compacting is important is that students need to interact with content and books that both challenge and engage them so they can develop the skills needed to react positively to challenge throughout their lives. When this doesn't happen, a pattern of underachievement may result as academically talented students earn top grades with minimal effort. Many falter when they reach secondary school or college, simply because for the first time they are enrolled in difficult classes with peers who are just as capable as they. As expectations rise, so does the effort needed to meet these increased demands. As noted earlier, without early encounters with challenge, students find themselves lacking, and may be unable to learn the study habits and perseverance that are essential for academic success.

Compacting provides time for more challenging learning experiences. One of the greatest benefits of curriculum compacting is the time saved to do alternate work, often based on students' choice and interests. Students whose curriculum is compacted may have their curriculum accelerated, participate in enrichment or gifted programs, pursue independent studies, read self-selected materials, or pursue one of many other options. How much content can be eliminated and for how many students? We (Reis, Westberg et al., 1998) found that teachers using curriculum compacting could eliminate 40%–70% of the regular reading curriculum for advanced learners with no decrease in standardized achievement test scores.

In a follow-up study, we found that teachers could also use curriculum compacting with students who were not identified as academically talented and with some students with learning disabilities. Both student groups achieved similar positive outcomes. This research demonstrated that our most talented students, whose reading or math curriculum might be compacted by up to 50%–70%, then have up to 8 hours each week to work on more challenging content, delve into areas of self-selected interest, and investigate a new topic that they may learn to love with passion and vigor.

Compacting gives students (and their teachers) time to pursue work that we are often told there is *no* time to pursue in school—time for things such as creating a class newspaper, participating in a class drama, writing fiction or poetry, completing an advanced science fair project or a historical investigation for History Day, practicing for geography or spelling bees, participating in Future Problem Solving Program International, starting a debate club, or diving into any other creative pursuit.

Teachers can modify and increase the pace of instruction and practice time can reduced. Because repetition and extended practice opportunities are built into nearly all curriculum, whether provided by a publisher or created locally, many advanced students spend their time in school practicing skills and reading content they have already mastered. In too many schools, no grouping or acceleration policies exist to challenge these students, so academically talented students spend a great deal of their time in heterogeneous classrooms, doing the same work as every other student in the class. But, here is the good news: Most teachers can learn to implement curriculum compacting fairly quickly and when they have mastered this differentiation strategy, they can eliminate work that students have already mastered and identify and assign appropriate content to engage and extend learning beyond the regular grade-level curriculum.

In the national research study we conducted on compacting, more than 90% of participating teachers learned quickly how to identify major learning outcomes and eliminate content that students had already mastered. The challenge has been finding replacement activities. Fortunately, this task that has become so much easier with the advent of the Internet and the proliferation of easy-to-use, free, high-quality activities described in Chapter 3.

Unfortunately, most teachers don't know how to or just don't compact or differentiate curriculum or instruction. A great number of research studies have found that high-potential students are often unchallenged in their classrooms and that their teachers fail to differentiate instruction, sometimes because they don't know how to juggle multiple responsibilities and other times, because they simply "don't get it done" (Archambault et al., 1993; Loveless, Parkas, & Duffett, 2008; Moon, Tomlinson, & Callahan, 1995; Reis et al., 2004; Reis & Purcell, 1993; Westberg, Archambault, Dobyns, & Salvin, 1993). Some of this research, conducted by researchers at the National Research Center on the Gifted and Talented, involved patterns of teachers' inattention toward high-ability students, and others focused on solutions, such as curriculum compacting. The Classroom Practices Survey was conducted to determine the extent to which gifted and talented students receive differentiated education in regular classrooms. Thousands of classroom teachers, responding to this survey, reported making only minor modifications in curriculum and instruction on a very irregular basis to meet the needs of gifted students (Archambault et al., 1993). The Classroom Practices Observational Study (Westberg et al., 1993) examined instructional and curricular practices for high-ability students in 46 regular elementary classrooms throughout the United States. Results indicated little differentiation in the instructional and curricular practices. In fact, targeted academically talented students experienced no instructional or curricular differentiation in 84% of the instructional activities in which they participated.

In our national study on curriculum compacting, after just a few hours of training, classroom teachers learned how to compact and differentiate curriculum and instruction and were able to eliminate between 40%–50% of previously mastered regular curriculum for high-ability students. However, they were less effective at replacing what they eliminated with high-quality, challenging curriculum and instruction (Reis et al., 1993). No differences were found in the achievement scores of gifted students whose work was compacted when compared with the achievement scores of students who did *all* of the work in reading, math computation, social studies, and spelling. In science and math concepts, students whose curricula were compacted actually scored significantly higher on achievement tests than students in the control group whose curricula were not compacted (Reis, Westberg et al., 1998).

Other research on this topic reinforced earlier findings, suggesting not much has changed over the last decade or so. For example, we studied talented readers, finding that teachers provided little to no differentiation in reading for third- or seventh-grade gifted readers who read several grade levels ahead (Reis et al., 2004). Research conducted in 12 different third- and seventh-grade reading classrooms in both urban and suburban school districts over a 9-month period revealed that little purposeful or meaningful differentiated reading instruction for talented readers was available in any of the classrooms (Reis et al., 2004). The absence of purposeful differentiation in this study and others (Moon et al., 1995) suggested that advanced students continue to remain underchallenged in many classrooms in the United States.

Some research shows that the trends are worse now than they were when we published our first book on compacting. A report by the Fordham Institute (Loveless et al., 2008) indicated that while some low-achieving students made gains under No Child Left Behind (NCLB), most advanced learners did not, and these students failed to make progress because their teachers spend the majority of their time with struggling students, even though they know that others in the classroom need attention and advanced instruction as well.

In our research on talented readers (Reis et al., 2004), for example, teachers did not even do the minimum differentiation that might be expected. One might hope that very talented readers would, at the very least, be encouraged and supported to read more challenging books, but we found that above-grade level books were seldom made available for these students and they were often not encouraged to select more challenging books from the school or classroom library. Talented readers seldom encountered challenging reading material during regular classroom instruction.

The range of achievement in today's classrooms makes compacting even more necessary. In another recent study, Sally and colleagues (Firmender, Reis, & Sweeny, 2013) examined the range of reading fluency and comprehension scores of more than 1,000 students in five diverse elementary schools, including a gifted and talented magnet school. We found an enormous range in reading comprehension across all schools. For example, the reading level range was 9.2

grade levels in grade 3, 11.3 in grade 4, and 11.6 in grade 5. A similar wide range of oral reading fluency scores was found across all elementary schools, as students scored from below the 10th percentile to above the 90th percentile. These wide ranges of reading achievement levels across all students suggest that the need for teachers to compact content and instruction is pressing—indeed, it is absolutely necessary if we are to enable all students to make continuous progress in their learning. This wide range of achievement levels makes it even more important to examine how and when we can most effectively differentiate for all students, especially for those at the highest and lowest ranges of achievement.

Compacting works well with some forms of grouping and it is clear that grouping academically talented students together benefits them and does not harm other students. Many and varied forms of grouping can be used to teach students at a level that is both engaging and challenging. A full description of the research on grouping is beyond the scope of this book, but we summarize some of the most relevant research in subsequent chapters. We also recommend using some form of cluster grouping (Gentry & Owen, 1999) to accompany curriculum compacting, as it makes the process easier for teachers. We include a broader discussion of cluster grouping in Chapter 4, but it is essentially the intentional placement of a group of high-achieving students in an otherwise heterogeneous classroom with a teacher who has both the skills and willingness to provide appropriate challenges for these students. Cluster grouping is a popular and often recommended strategy for meeting the needs of high-achieving students in the regular classroom. Cluster grouping has gained more popularity recently as heterogeneous grouping policies have created more challenges for teachers and as financial cutbacks in states have eliminated some special programs for gifted and talented students, and it works extremely well with curriculum compacting.

Compacting can be embedded into many other types of services for gifted and talented students. Several strategies exist that enable teachers to combine more than one differentiation technique. Suggestions for doing this effectively are made throughout this book, but one example of how compacting, enrichment, and acceleration can be combined is through the use of the Schoolwide Enrichment Model Reading (SEM-R) framework, an enriched and accelerated program implemented in regular and gifted classrooms that compacts reading and language arts instruction that students have already mastered (Reis et al., 2009). Research using stringent experimental designs compared the performance of students whose teachers used the SEM-R enrichment approach to reading instruction to a control group of students who participated in basal or standard reading programs. Students who participated in this differentiated reading approach scored as well or higher in reading fluency, comprehension, and attitudes toward reading than students in the control group (Reis et al., 2007; Reis, Eckert, McCoach, Jacobs, & Coyne, 2008). Results demonstrated that talented readers, as well as average and below average readers, benefited from the SEM-R (Reis et al., 2007; Reis et al., 2008; Reis & Housand, 2009). In a recent study, for example, we (Reis et al., 2011) found that when differentiated, enriched reading instruction was implemented, students' reading fluency and comprehension was as high or higher than a control group that used a traditional whole-group instructional standardized reading approach. *In fact our research has consistently demonstrated that teachers can eliminate up to 4 to 5 hours a week of grouped reading instruction and replace it with approximately 10 minutes a week of differentiated, individualized reading instruction based on the SEM-R and their students do as well or better on standardized assessments when they do so.*

Compacting guarantees educational accountability. Educational accountability matters, and the use of compacting procedures can guarantee that students who are allowed to skip assignments or be excused from participating in lessons in which they know the content are doing so because the teacher can document the appropriateness of this decision.

The research studies summarized in this book suggest that that gifted and high-potential students in American schools are underchallenged. In a data-based longitudinal study (Reis et al., 1995) conducted with gifted, urban high school students, half of these students were found to be underachieving in high school. These students provided insight about why they did poorly, blaming an elementary and middle school program that was too easy. The problem of systematically learning not to work exists in rural, suburban, and urban areas and seems to be an area of increasing importance in the education of gifted and talented students. Compacting works and provides accountability for teachers who decide to use this strategy to increase challenge for all students, including our academically talented population.

Achievement increases occur when accelerated and enriched programs are implemented. The use of enrichment, differentiation, acceleration, and curriculum enhancement results in higher achievement for students who score across the spectrum, from gifted and talented learners to average and high achievers (Colangelo et al., 2004; Field, 2009; Gavin et al., 2007; Gentry & Owen, 1999; Gubbins et al., 2008; Kulik, 1992; Reis et al., 2007; Rogers, 1991; Tieso, 2002). For example, teachers who used curriculum compacting and enrichment for gifted and high-ability students demonstrated that elimination of up to 40%–70% of the work already mastered by gifted and talented students followed by the replacement of enriched learning opportunities such as self-selected independent study resulted in higher or similar achievement scores than a similar population of students in the control group who completed every assignment (Reis, Westberg et al., 1998).

Colangelo, Assouline, and Gross (2004), in the most comprehensive meta-analysis of acceleration to date, studied many forms of acceleration practices, summarizing research over decades that demonstrates that accelerative practices result in both higher achievement and higher standardized test scores for high-potential and gifted and talented learners. Students whose grade level was accelerated tended to be more ambitious and earned graduate degrees at higher rates than other students. Interviewed years later, accelerated students were uniformly positive about their experiences, reporting that they were academically challenged, socially accepted, and did not fall prey to boredom, as do highly capable students who are forced to follow the curriculum for their age-peers (Colangelo et al., 2004).

Gavin et al. (2007) used quasiexperimental methods in intact classrooms to investigate the use of more challenging math curriculum for gifted students; findings showed that talented third-, fourth-, and fifth-grade math students achieved significant gains in achievement in math concepts, computation, and problem solving each year over a 3-year period. As summarized earlier, Reis and her colleagues (Reis et al., 2007; Reis et al., 2008, Reis et al., 2011), using experimental research methods, found that a broad range of students, including academically talented students, benefitted from an enriched and accelerated reading intervention. A broad range of studies have demonstrated that enrichment pedagogy (Field, 2009; Reis et al., 2007, 2008), differentiation (Gentry & Owen, 1999; Reis et al., 1993; Tieso, 2002), acceleration (Colangelo et al., 2004), and curriculum enhancement and advanced lessons (Gavin et al., 2007; VanTassel-Baska, Zuo, Avery, & Little, 2002) have resulted in higher achievement for gifted and talented learners as well as other students when they are applied to both gifted and other lower achieving students.

2 How to Compact Curriculum for Students

Many academically talented students spend much of their time in school doing work that they have already mastered. Imagine what it must be like to spend hour after hour completing exercises and tasks that practice things you have known for years! Most adults would never tolerate the type of repetitiveness that many of our brightest students face every day in school. Quite often, our smartest and most advanced students find so much repetition and low-level thinking in school that they never really learn how to work. Unfortunately, unless the regular curricular work assigned to these students is significantly altered, what many of them will learn about going to school is how to expend minimum effort.

If students are consistently bringing home papers with perfect scores, the work being assigned to them is most likely too easy. By initiating curriculum compacting, teachers can increase the challenge level of the work that students are expected to complete and also provide enrichment, extension, and acceleration experiences that challenge their abilities. In this chapter, we describe curriculum compacting in detail and discuss how to implement this procedure. When teachers compact curriculum, they begin by preassessing above-average-ability students' skills or knowledge about content prior to instruction. Next, they document the learning goals or standards that these students already understand, and then use this information to modify and differentiate curriculum. As we have defined it, compacting enables teachers to:

- ▶ select the relevant learning objectives/standards in a subject area or grade level;
- ▶ identify students who may benefit from curriculum compacting and should be assessed;

- ► pretest students on one or more of these objectives/standards prior to instruction;
- ► eliminate instruction, practice, and/or assignments for students who have demonstrated prior mastery;
- ► streamline instruction of those objectives and standards students have not yet mastered, but are capable of mastering more quickly than their classmates;
- ► offer engaging, and when possible, interest-based enrichment or acceleration options for students whose curriculum should be compacted;
- ► maintain records of this process and the instructional options available; and
- ► when possible, extend compacting to additional students in the class.

A high-quality education for high-ability and academically talented students means more than simply providing an arbitrary collection of mini courses, speakers, or individual research opportunities. A tally of the phone calls to our national research center over the last few decades suggests that problems associated with the regular curriculum are parents' greatest concerns. In order to meet all of the learning needs of all of our high-ability students, we must provide an appropriate content curriculum as well as an opportunity for a student to explore interests and develop self-directed learning habits. If having high academic potential means that a student either knows more or has the potential to learn faster than peers, curriculum compacting can ensure that a challenging curriculum be delivered for these students.

As we have noted, one of the greatest benefits of curriculum compacting is the time it creates for alternate learning experiences. Students may participate in the gifted program, pursue independent studies, read self-selected materials, or pursue one of many other options, as suggested in this chapter. We should also note that in our many decades of working on this strategy, we have found that parents of academically talented students love compacting because they are often disturbed about the amount of whole-class instruction that they find in their children's classrooms. Seatwork assignments that are too easy and unchallenging homework frequently confirm parents' fears that whole-group instruction is forcing their child to practice skills and concepts that had initially been mastered 2 or 3 years earlier. Imagine the surprise of a father (whose first-grade child is reading the Harry Potter series at home) when he finds that his daughter is still being asked to complete phonics worksheets that practice phonemic awareness of short vowel sounds!

Consider the added frustration of parents when they witness countless school administrators ignoring—or worse yet, misrepresenting—the research on the effects of grouping on students' abilities and self-esteem. In a misguided attempt to provide equal educational opportunities to all students, some officials have mandated an end to any form of instructional grouping or acceleration for fear of damaging the achievement or self-esteem of students in the lower ability groups. These policies are at odds with the research that demonstrates the positive outcomes of flexible grouping arrangements for all students, discussed in Chapter 4.

Talented students should not have to participate in curricular activities that they have previously mastered, but we cannot automatically assume that all high-ability students can or should be excused from all assignments in all content areas. This "batch" approach to acceleration or compacting can produce gaps in students' education just as the practice of grade skipping often does. When students are allowed to skip an entire grade level, a new teacher may assume, often erroneously, that all material covered in the skipped grade was mastered by the accelerated student. Yet the student may not have a good grasp of some material, such as punctuation or multiplication tables, because those were taught in the grade skipped and no effort was made to assess gaps or skills.

In this age of educational accountability, the use of compacting procedures can guarantee that students who are allowed to skip assignments or be excused from participation in lessons or lectures are doing so because the teacher can document the professional appropriateness of this decision. Teachers who use the compacting techniques described in this chapter will undoubtedly find that some of their above-average-ability students perform well in one subject area and not another, while others demonstrate advanced abilities in several content areas, and that is where curriculum compacting most often makes a difference in accountability procedures.

Steps for Getting Compacting Done: Name It, Prove It, and Then Change It

Imagine the frustration faced by a precocious reader who independently reads two or three grade levels above his or her age or class. When a 6-year-old who loves to read and is accustomed to reading several books a day encounters the typical basal reading system, it can be the beginning of the end of a love affair with reading. As noted, many bright students are engaged with content that is well below their ability level and this lack of challenge promotes apathy, negative attitudes toward learning, and poor work habits. Students who are not provided with a challenging learning environment often find school too easy and are therefore unlikely to learn how to deal with the challenge that is frequently experienced when learning new and difficult skills or concepts.

Differentiation of Curriculum and Instruction

In order to meet the needs of students of varying levels of academic achievement, teachers often try a variety of within-classroom strategies collectively referred to as differentiated instruction. *Differentiation* addresses the variation of learners in the classroom through multiple approaches that modify instruction and curriculum to challenge all students (Tomlinson, 2000). When teachers differentiate curriculum, they stop acting as dispensers of knowledge and, instead, serve as organizers of learning opportunities. Differentiation of instruction and curriculum suggests that students can be provided with materials and work of varied levels of difficulty with scaffolding, diverse kinds of grouping, and different time schedules. It is interesting to note that compacting is one of the oldest forms of differentiation strategies.

PURPOSES OF DIFFERENTIATION

1. Enhance learning to improve match between student and curriculum.
2. Change depth or breadth of student learning.
3. Use varied learning strategies, appropriate grouping, and management.
4. Enable all students to make continuous progress in all content areas.

We have been pioneers in the area of differentiation, piloting curriculum compacting since the 1970s (Renzulli, 1977; Renzulli & Smith, 1979) and subsequently defining differentiation as encompassing five dimensions. These dimensions include content, process, products, classroom organization and management, and the teacher's own commitment to change him- or herself into a learner (of differentiated instruction and curriculum) as well as a teacher of students who need this service (see Figure 2).

The differentiation of *content* involves adding more depth to the curriculum by focusing on structures of knowledge, basic principles, functional concepts, and methods of inquiry in particular disciplines. The differentiation of *process* incorporates the use of various instructional strategies and materials to enhance learning and motivate students by addressing learning styles. The differentiation of *products* enhances students' communication skills by encouraging them to express themselves in a variety of ways. To differentiate *classroom management*, teachers can change the physical environment and grouping patterns they use in class and vary the allocation of time and resources for both groups and individuals. Classroom differentiation strategies can, of course, be expanded and enhanced by using the Internet in a variety of ways. Last, teachers can differentiate *themselves* by modeling the roles of athletic or drama coaches, stage or production managers, promotional agents, and academic advisers. All of these

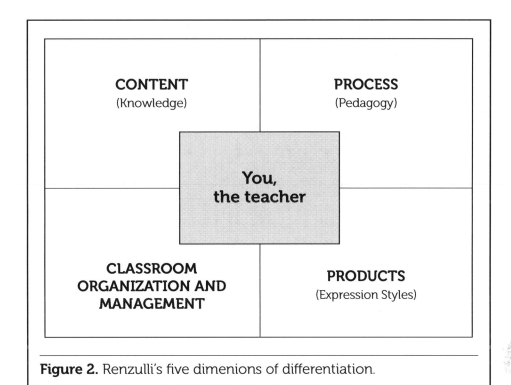

Figure 2. Renzulli's five dimenions of differentiation.

roles differ qualitatively from the role of teacher-as-instructor. Teachers can also "inject" themselves into the material through a process called *artistic modification* (Renzulli, 1988), guiding teachers to include direct, indirect, and vicarious experiences related to personal interests, travel experiences, collections, hobbies, and teachers' extracurricular involvements that can enhance content.

Curriculum compacting is one differentiation strategy that incorporates all five dimensions—content, process, products, classroom management, and teachers' personal commitment to accommodating individual and small-group differences. Teachers can compact curriculum in all grade levels and in any content area, addressing the demand for more challenging learning experiences designed to help all students make continuous progress and realize their potential. Simply put, the goals of compacting are the following:

- ▶ Create a challenging learning environment in the classroom and the enrichment program for all children.
- ▶ Define objectives and guarantee proficiency in basic curriculum.
- ▶ Find time for alternative learning activities based on advanced content *and* individual student interest.

Curriculum Compacting: Definition and Steps for Implementation

Curriculum compacting streamlines and eliminates the regular grade-level curriculum for high-potential students to find time for more challenging, engaging, and interesting work. This differentiation strategy was specifically designed to make appropriate curricular adjustments for students in any curricular area in which they demonstrate strengths. The procedure involves

- defining the goals and learning standards within a particular content area, or unit of instruction;
- selecting students for preassessment and documenting the mastery levels of those students who demonstrate grade-level proficiency; and
- providing replacement resources and tasks that give more challenge and address individual interests, curiosities, and strengths.

Most teachers who use compacting learn to streamline or "compact" curriculum through their use of a simple, step-by-step protocol. Practical issues such as record keeping and how to use the compacting form are also necessary to help guide teachers toward implementing this strategy. Once learned, these guidelines can help to save valuable classroom time for both teachers and students.

Curriculum compacting can be implemented with individuals and groups of students with above-average ability in any academic, artistic, or even vocational area. Most important, as noted in Chapter 1, our research demonstrates that compacting can dramatically reduce redundancy, challenge gifted students to reach new heights of excellence, and reduce underachievement because it provides one clear way to streamline work that is too easy, replacing it with more challenging work and with self-selected opportunities in that area or in another area of interest.

Many educators want to modify the regular curriculum for high-achieving students. Accomplishing this, however, requires effort and time. Too little time, too many curricular standards, and a curriculum based on resources and tasks instead of mastery all take their toll on even the most dedicated professionals. Curriculum compacting is designed to help teachers overcome those obstacles.

Targeted for both elementary and secondary educators, "compacting" curriculum is a practical procedure that enables teachers to modify curriculum, as well as to learn to pretest students and to prepare a variety of acceleration and enrichment options. Practical issues such as record keeping and administrative support are also included in this chapter to help curriculum compacting save valuable classroom time for both teachers and students.

The Compactor Form

The curriculum compacting process is easily introduced through the use of the Compactor Form presented in Figure 3.

This form can serve as both an organizational and a record-keeping tool that teachers may complete for an individual student, or in some cases, for a group of students with similar curricular strengths, such as advanced reading skills. Completed compactors (whether paper-based or electronic) can be kept in students' academic files and updated regularly. The form can also be used for small groups of students who are working at approximately the same level (e.g., a reading or math group), and as an addendum to an Individualized Education Plan (IEP) in states in which services for gifted students fall under special education laws.

The Compactor is divided into three columns:

▶ The first column includes information on a curriculum unit's learning goals and standards. It also provides space to indicate the initial observations that lead a teacher to suppose that a given student might benefit from compacting. These observations might include data on students' prior knowledge, proficiencies, test scores, behavioral profiles, and past academic records.

▶ In the second column, teachers document the ways in which they will preassess whether students already know the concepts and skills that will be taught in the unit, course, or class. The pretest or preassessment strategies they select, along with the results of those assessments, should be recorded in this column. The assessment instruments can be formal measures, such as tests, or informal measures such as performance assessments based on observations of class participation and written assignments. It is important to specify which content and skills have been learned; recording an overall score of 85% on 10 outcomes, for example, sheds little light on which of the learning standards can be compacted, because students might show limited mastery of some outcomes and high levels of mastery of others.

▶ Column Three is used to record information about acceleration or enrichment options, based on students' individual preferences, interests, and learning styles. Teachers understand that they should not replace compacted regular curriculum work with harder, more advanced material that is solely determined by the teacher. Many years of research and field-testing have helped us to learn that when teachers do this, students will learn a negative lesson: If I do my best work, I am rewarded with harder work and more work. Instead, we recommend that students' interests should be considered. If a student loves working on science fair

Individual Education Program Guide

The Compactor

Student Name(s):   Grade: School:

Participating Teachers:

Name it.	Prove it.	Change it.
Curriculum Area	**Assessment**	**Enrichment/Acceleration Plans**
Name or insert the subject area, unit or chapter, or learning standards that are the focus for compacting.	List the assessment tools and related data that indicates student strengths or was used for preassessment, the results of the preassessment data, and learning standards that have not yet been mastered. Identify pertinent student interests that emerged from inventories or interviews.	Briefly describe the enrichment or acceleration tasks that will be substituted for the compacted curriculum, and any strategies used to ensure student mastery of learning standards and objectives that have not been met through enrichment and acceleration. Explain which strategies will be used to support, or coach student learning at more advanced levels.

Figure 3. The Compactor.

projects, time working on these projects can replace the time that would have been spent working on skills and concepts that the student has already mastered in a different content area. Teachers should monitor the challenge level of the material being substituted and help talented students come to an understanding about the importance of mindset and effort when compacted material is replaced with work that is more interesting, engaging, and cognitively challenging.

How to Implement the Compacting Process: Take Two!

Like us, our colleague and friend Alane Starko conducted hundreds of workshops on curriculum compacting and developed this simple way to explain the process, using the three columns of the compactor as described in Figure 4. Her titles of each of the columns can also help guide teachers in trying this process.

Defining Learning Outcomes and Goals (Name It)

The first of three phases in the compacting process includes defining the goals and learning standards in a given curriculum unit or segment of instruction within a content area. This information is readily available in most subjects because specific goals and learning standards are included in teachers' manuals, curriculum guides, scope-and-sequence charts, and some of the new curricular frameworks that are emerging in connection with the Common Core State Standards as well as proficiency-based or mastery-based teaching and learning models. Teachers should examine these learning goals and outcomes to identify those that address new concepts and skills or thinking skills as opposed to a review of standards and learning goals from previous units or grade levels. The scope and sequence charts prepared by state departments of education, school districts, or textbook publishers can be used to start this process. A major goal of this phase of the compacting process is to enable teachers to make individual programming decisions; the larger professional development goal is to help teachers become more savvy, critical analysts of the curriculum and content standards they are teaching and better consumers of standards, textbooks, and published curriculum.

The Common Core State Standards are a useful starting point for this analysis. These K–12 standards are well-written, well-sequenced, and align well with the National Assessment of Educational Progress's expectations. These 2010 standards were drafted by experts and teachers from across the country and were

Individual Education Program Guide The Compactor		
Student Name(s): Grade: School:		
Participating Teachers:		
Name it.	**Prove it.**	**Change it.**

Figure 4. Blank Compactor.

designed to ensure students are prepared for college and careers, by focusing on critical thinking, problem solving, and analytic thinking, as well as important concepts and skills in reading, writing, math, listening, speaking, and research. Forty-two states, the District of Columbia, and four territories voluntarily adopted and implemented these standards. The use of these standards provides an excellent way for teachers to measure student progress on learning outcomes throughout the school year and further ensure that students are on the pathway to success in their academic careers.

The National Association for Gifted Children (NAGC) has also written its own set of standards and expectations. Its standards provide support for policy changes that address the critical needs of gifted students. These standards also provide guidance and direction for curriculum compacting at the local level. In particular, the NAGC curriculum standards are a helpful resource for planning compacted curriculum that provides advanced, conceptually challenging, in-depth, distinctive, and complex content. These standards may be found at http://www.nagc.org/resources-publications/resources/national-standards-gifted-and-talented-education/pre-k-grade-12.

Prove It

The second phase of the curriculum compacting process asks educators to name and measure students' mastery level with the content and skills identified in Phase One. Although standardized achievement tests can serve as a general screening to identify potential students for future compacting, the Phase Two process asks teachers to verify mastery of specific grade-level standards within specific curriculum units.

Being identified as a candidate for compacting does not necessarily mean that a specific student has mastered all of the grade level or curriculum unit learning standards. Therefore, the second phase involves the use of assessment techniques to evaluate specific standards and mastery levels.

It is usually fairly easy for teachers to identify students who should be considered for compacting by the behaviors and characteristics that they exhibit as suggested in Figure 5.

Unit pretests, end-of-unit tests, and performance tasks are especially useful during Phase Two. An analysis of pretest results enables the teacher to document proficiency with specific skills and concepts aligned to targeted and essential learning standards. This preassessment process also allows the teacher to identify "gap" standards and make plans for their mastery.

The Phase Two assessment process is slightly different in subject areas such as social studies that focus on concepts as opposed to a skills-based subject area like reading. In the former situation, a teacher is likely to find that even the most academically talented student has not yet had the opportunity to learn all of the concepts and knowledge deemed essential in a course such as British literature or anatomy and physiology. In these instances, the Phase Two process usually incorporates performance tasks, written reflections, and oral conferences, all in an attempt to select the students who could benefit from a more rapid pace, greater depth, or more cognitively challenging tasks.

It is important to note that before a teacher begins the compacting process, student candidates should be informed of this option and the process explained to them. When this happens, teachers are likely to find that even the chronically underachieving gifted education students relish the thought of having learning options and being part of the decision-making process as it relates to their learning goals and tasks.

Change It: Providing Acceleration and Enrichment Options for Talented Students

The third and final phase of the compacting process is both exciting and motivating for students because it involves cooperative decision making and creativity between teachers and students. Time saved through curriculum compacting can be used to provide a variety of enrichment and acceleration opportunities for the student. Enrichment strategies might include those described in the Enrichment Triad Model (Renzulli, 1977) and the Schoolwide Enrichment Model (Renzulli & Reis, 1985, 1997, 2014); opportunities that expose interested students to new topics and ideas, methods training, creative and critical thinking activities, and opportunities to pursue advanced independent or small-group creative projects.

- Consistently finishes tasks quickly
- Completes reading assignments first in the class
- Appears bored during instruction
- Brings outside reading material to use in class
- Creates diversions in class and may misbehave or ask for attention
- Asks for simple enrichment—activities, online work, puzzles, kits, etc.
- Consistently daydreams or appears bored in class
- Has consistently high performance in one or more academic areas
- Achieves high tests scores consistently
- Asks questions that indicate advanced familiarity with material
- Is sought after by other students for assistance
- Uses vocabulary and verbal expression advance of grade level
- Expresses interest in pursuing alternate or advanced topics

Figure 5. Student behaviors suggesting that compacting is necessary.

This aspect of the compacting process should also be viewed as a creative opportunity for teachers to serve as mentors to one or two students who are not working up to potential. We have observed an interesting occurrence that sometimes results from curriculum compacting. When some bright but underachieving students realized that they could both economize on regularly assigned material and "earn time" to pursue self-selected interests, their motivation to complete regular assignments increased. As one student put it, "Everyone understands a good deal!"

Several strategies have been suggested for differentiating instruction and curriculum for talented or high-potential students. They range from substitution of grade-level standards and tasks for more advanced standards and activities to options such as independent study, research, or specific-content instructional strategies such as literature circles, coding, and scientific inquiry. Many of these strategies can be used in combination with compacting or as replacement options after the students' curriculum has been compacted. Acceleration, which enables students to learn standards, skills, and content designed for higher grade levels, can also be pursed as a result of compacting. This accelerated work can occur in cross-grade groupings or within the same grade-level classroom.

Document It: Completing the First Column of the Compactor

The first column of the Compactor documents the first steps in the compacting process, naming the standards(s) being considered for compacting and citing information that indicates that a student is a good candidate for compacting with respect to these standards. Teachers can reduce the time needed to complete the form by using brief notes to record the relevant information.

The first sentence in this column might look like these examples:

- John's achievement test scores in math (99th percentile) indicate curriculum compacting is necessary.
- Tamara's grades in English have been A's for the last 4 years.
- Liza's instructional reading level is 4 years above her grade placement.
- Sasha is an amateur ornithologist with the local Audubon association whose science curriculum may be able to be compacted, due to her advanced interests and knowledge.

In each of these cases, the teacher has provided the reader with evidence of above-average ability in the subject area. Information from tests scores, classroom behaviors, and notes on performance assessment can also be used to document curriculum strength.

The second part of Column One provides information about the standard(s) being considered for compacting. Here are a few examples:

- John will be pretested on the math standards in grade 4 that address numbers and operations in Base Ten.
- Tamara's written work appears to demonstrate above-grade-level proficiency. She scored 4/4 on each of the five criteria used to score her last three writing assignments.
- It is likely that Liza can be compacted from vocabulary and comprehension objectives for this and the next grade level.
- Sasha will be pretested on the next seven standards in our science curriculum.

The teacher does not need to identify *all* possible standards or curricular areas to be considered for compacting during the first week of the school year. It is more likely that the process will start slowly with one student or in one content area. As the teacher and students become more proficient with the process, additional standards will be identified and additional notes can be added in the remaining space in Column One of the Compactor. In most cases, compacting activities will vary during the course of the school year as students' proficiency or the availability of assessment data increases or decreases.

Completing the Second Column of the Compactor

Information about which standards will be assessed and how they will be measured should be documented in the second column of the Compactor. In addition, the second column is used to describe how the student will learn the "gap" standards in the unit that have not yet been mastered. For example, if a student has shown mastery of seven of the 10 standards in a unit, the teacher must decide how to provide instruction and practice with the remaining three standards. The teacher may require that the student participate with the rest of the class, learn the standard through an individual tutorial, or become responsible for independent mastery of the unmet objectives. (Sample entries from this second column of the Compactor are included in subsequent case study examples in Chapter 6.)

The second column of the Compactor Form should also document how much time has been saved for enrichment or acceleration activities and just what is being eliminated from the classroom curriculum as a result of student mastery of assessed standards. If, for example, math pretests indicate that a student has mastery of six of the next eight units in the math curriculum, the writer might indicate the dates, the times of day, or the days of the week when the six units are to be taught.

Column Two of the Compactor documents the standards and pretest results. First, the teacher should indicate which standards were pretested for the student. The use of codes, numbers, or a reference to standards are all appropriate. The parent or teacher who sees the Compactor should be able to understand the extent of the pretest and the specific standards on which it is based. The teacher should record this information as succinctly as possible, including the use of scanned copies of the assessments and standards. When documenting student performance on the pretest, it is important to be precise about which standards were mastered and which still need to be mastered by documenting the scores for *each standard*.

Completing the Third Column of the Compactor

The third column, "Acceleration and/or Enrichment Activities," includes documentation about how time is to be spent once it has been provided by the compacting process. Many different enrichment options are included in Chapter 3. This column can be enhanced and added to as more options emerge based on students' interests and increasing knowledge of student strengths.

Alternatives to the Compactor Form

Some teachers might find that using the Compactor is redundant in light of the other record-keeping devices already being used. The decision to use or amend the Compactor is one that can and should be made by individual teachers or a committee of teachers within the building or school district. The use of the form enables the teacher to document all instances of change from the regular curriculum. If you work in a state that has a mandate for gifted education, the Compactor might also be used to reduce some of the paperwork required for students who are receiving special, state-funded services.

In many of these cases, gifted education is classified within special education, and due process procedures are required. In these cases, the Compactor has often been used as a substitute for the Individualized Education Plan (IEP). Because the Compactor documents all instances of curricular modification, it records the assessment information that led to compacting. It also provides information about the enrichment or acceleration options that were offered to students who took advantage of the compacting procedure.

Some teachers prefer to keep track of students' pretest scores using a matrix in which every student is listed, as are standards that must be mastered. Teachers might use checklists or matrices that are provided with their district curriculum maps or adapt existing forms for their own purposes. Others prefer to keep records for each student in the class. The latter approach can also be combined with an individual student record (for the student's file) and a contract that describes required assignments and optional activities.

The Importance of Documentation

Whether you choose to use the Compactor, to modify it, or to use your own record keeping devices, we strongly recommend documentation. Such accountability is useful during parent-teacher conferences or to support teachers' decisions in future grade levels. Students who transfer to a new school system should also have access to the documentation, for without this information the student is likely to repeat inappropriate grade-level material. The use of the Compactor will enable teachers in the new school to identify the student's strengths without the need to repeat extensive assessment procedures. Teachers in the new school can analyze these strengths and compact related standards and tasks within the curriculum at the new school.

Documentation is also critical for teachers who are trying to use the compacting process in a less-than-supportive situation. Consider a primary grade teacher who has been attempting to compact curriculum for her precocious readers during the last 2 years. Her efforts have been thwarted several times by the district's reading supervisor who believes that repetition breeds mastery. When the teacher asked for preassessment resources aligned with the district's reading standards, she was told by the supervisor that the pretests were not to be used and that the posttests were only to be given to the class as a large group after finishing each of the two required reading texts for their grade level. Teachers in the district were told to teach the reading series to the whole group and that no student should be compacted or allowed to read an out-of-level text. The situation was extremely frustrating for the teacher, and finally, the teacher located a norm-referenced, diagnostic reading test that gave her the ammunition she needed to confront the supervisor about the policy of large-group instruction in the district's reading program. Armed with the objectives for the grade-level reading program and a set of tests scores from the diagnostic reading test, the teacher called a conference with the reading supervisor and her principal. As she expected, when she showed the supervisor the actual test scores for the able readers in her classroom and suggested that these students were wasting their time by participating in needless instruction and practice, the reading director backed down. Although the teacher has still not been allowed to use out-of-level basal readers, she has been given permission to substitute trade books for the precocious readers who have demonstrated skill mastery.

This teacher proved her case by using documentation to substantiate her students' content strength. This situation is not rare. Parents, fellow teachers, and administrators may question a decision to modify the standard curriculum. Through attempts to define, preassess, and document learning standards, teachers can better explain why some students can be excused from selected instruction or practice. In the end, this documentation may even convince others to compact curriculum as well.

Eileen: A Sample Compactor Form

Eileen is a fifth grader in a self-contained classroom. Her school is very small and is part of a lower SES urban school district. While Eileen's reading and language scores range between 2–5 years above grade level, most of her 25 classmates are reading 1–2 years below grade level. This presented Eileen's teacher with a common challenge about how to teach Eileen and the ways he could compact and differentiate her curriculum. Taking the easiest approach possible, he administered all of the unit and level tests in the language arts program, and excused Eileen from completing the activities and worksheets in the units where she showed proficiency (80% and above). If Eileen missed one or two questions, the teacher would quickly check for trends in those items; if an error pattern emerged, instruction would be provided to ensure concept mastery. Eileen usually took part in language arts lessons 1 or 2 days a week. The balance of the time she spent with alternative language arts work, some of which was accelerated content and projects that her teacher and she selected, and some of which she selected on her own. This strategy spared Eileen up to 6 or 8 hours a week of learning language arts skills that were simply beneath her level. She joined the class instruction only when her pretests indicated she had not fully acquired the skills.

During time saved through compacting, Eileen engaged in a number of enrichment and accelerated learning activities. First, she enjoyed as many as 5 hours a week in a resource room for high-ability students. This time was usually scheduled during her language arts class, benefiting both Eileen and her teacher; he didn't have to search for enrichment options because Eileen went to the resource room, and she didn't have make-up assignments because she was not missing essential work. Eileen also visited a regional science center.

Science was a secondary strength and interest area for Eileen, and based on the results of her Interest-A-Lyzer, famous women were a special interest. Working closely with her teacher, Eileen chose seven biographies of noted women in the science field. All of the books were extremely challenging and locally available. Three were even adult level, but Eileen had no trouble reading them.

Eileen's Compactor, which covered an entire semester, was updated in January. Her teacher remarked that compacting her curriculum had actually saved him time—time he would have spent correcting papers needlessly assigned, as well as teaching Eileen skills she had already mastered. The value of compacting for Eileen also convinced him that he should continue the process.

Providing More Sequential Support for Teachers to Implement Compacting

In our experiences with professional development on curriculum compacting and differentiation, we have learned that most teachers can implement compacting, but this process is easier for some teachers than for others. Some teachers see the form and read the explanation above and are ready to get started. Others require more coaching and help, and for that reason, we provide a five-step process to accomplish compacting below that we have used with teachers over the last two decades and modified slightly in this updated book for ease of implementation.

Step One: Select Relevant Learning Standards Within a Content Area and Grade Level

When selecting curricular content and learning standards, teachers may refer to the formal curriculum guides issued by school districts or states or the informal guides provided by textbook publishers. After identifying the range and sequence of learning goals or standards, teachers should select those that are essential for their students. Oftentimes, there's a discrepancy between the number of standards or goals listed in the curriculum guides and those actually required and important for students to learn. Other goals and standards may be redundant or overly ambitious, and so teachers should ask:

1. Which of these goals and standards represent new learning for this subject area and grade level?
2. Which of these goals and standards incorporate higher level thinking?
3. Which of these goals and standards will help my students?
4. Which of these goals and standards can be applied to real-world situations?
5. Which goals and standards cannot be learned without direct instruction and guided practice or sustained instruction?
6. Which goals and standards are priorities for my school district or state department of education?

After the relevant learning goals and standards are selected, they should be sequenced by priority. The higher-ranked items become the standards and goals teachers address first, with the entire class, while the less relevant standards are prime candidates for compacting.

Simply having a set of learning standards doesn't tell a teacher how or if these goals can be adapted to meet students' individual needs. Teachers must know the subject matter, as well as their students' learning styles. Step Two in the compacting process can help teachers make these evaluations.

Step Two: Find an Appropriate Way to Preassess the Learning Goals/Standards

Pretesting or preassessment, as the name implies, is intended to measure students' skills and prior knowledge before instruction begins. It should provide teachers with precise information that answers these questions:

1. Which student learning standards have already been met?
2. Which standards have not yet been mastered?
3. What challenges may slow or impede student progress?

Ideally, preassessments should demonstrate whether a student has full, partial, or little mastery of a learning goal. Objective-referenced tests can do that effectively, as they usually assess one objective/standard at a time using selected response formats. On a practical level, these kinds of assessments appeal to teachers because they can be administered in large group settings, require little time to oversee or correct, and are often readily available from publishers or testing companies and allow teachers to keep succinct records of students' progress.

Performance-based assessment. Performance-based assessment is a popular alternative to objective-referenced or standards-based tests. By asking students to complete oral, written, or manipulative tasks, teachers can observe and evaluate the process students use to arrive at their response. This procedure is especially successful with younger children who are not yet ready for paper-and-pencil tests. Students may be evaluated individually or in small groups through conferences, interviews, or portfolios of completed work. As with objective-referenced tests, this requires preplanning. Teachers must take the time to locate or create the performance tasks, making sure that they're aligned with the desired learning goals and outcomes.

Step Three: Identify Students to Be Involved in the Preassessment Opportunities and Pretest Students to Determine Mastery Levels

First, teachers must identify students who should participate in the preassessment activity. To do this, teachers identify students' specific strengths. This step is important for two reasons. First, it ensures that when students are excused from class for various enrichment activities, they have the opportunity to work on those tasks during curricular strength times. Second, it eliminates the need to assign make-up work when the students return to the classroom. Academic records, standardized tests, class performance, and evaluations from former teachers are all effective means of pinpointing candidates for pretesting.

Another method for identifying candidates for compacting involves performance assessment and classroom observations. Teachers carefully monitor students who complete tasks quickly and accurately, finish assignments ahead of their peers, or seem bored or lost in daydreams. Some students will even tell their teachers that the work assigned is too easy.

Achievement and aptitude tests can also be a valuable way to assess academic ability. By comparing students' subtest scores with local or national norms, educators can identify those whose scores fall within the above-average ranges. Because these students usually know more or learn faster than their peers, it's safe to assume that they may benefit from pretesting.

National assessment results confirm that academically talented and high-potential students do not necessarily excel in all subject areas. For example, those who score well in math will not always show similar superior ability in vocabulary or social studies. Likewise, students with strong vocabulary skills are not always those who excel in reading comprehension. This finding underscores the importance of using more than one assessment and relying on data to evaluate students' strengths and weaknesses in specific content areas. Teachers must consider the whole child and remember that a broad range of information will most often be used to identify candidates for compacting. In other words, just because students perform well in a given area doesn't mean they've mastered all of the learning goals in that area. What's more, all tests are flawed to some degree, and establishing "cut-off" scores is not an exact science.

When it comes to measuring achievement, the debate still rages over "how high is high?" Overall, students who place above the 80th percentile or achieve higher percentiles on subtests of norm-referenced achievement tests may be considered viable candidates for compacting. Some teachers may decide that they want to pretest all students in the classroom. These preassessment results can be used to organize small groups of students with common instructional profiles and ranges of achievement.

Preassessment, both formal and informal, helps teachers determine student mastery of course material. But what constitutes mastery? Because definitions of mastery vary, teachers within the same school, or at least grade level, should strive to reach a consensus.

It is important to decide how and when to pretest students, because pretesting can be a time-intensive exercise. One shortcut is to increase the number of students or standards examined at one time; for example, if a chapter in a math text covers 10 standards, a small group of students or the entire class could be tested on all 10 standards in one sitting. If small-group testing is not feasible, teachers can follow the same procedure with individual students.

Some educators also allow their students to score and record their own test results to save time. In the beginning of the year, we recommend that the entire class participate in the preassessment process, as teachers can learn a great deal about overall student performance from the results of these types of assessment.

Performance-based testing. Some teachers may choose to use performance-based assessment. If they select this form of pretesting, they should observe students closely, by reviewing assignments, monitoring patterns of critical and creative thinking activities, and posing open-ended questions to assess proficiency with the goals and standards. Let's assume, for example, that the learning standards expect students to be able to write a well-sequenced, logical, and evidence-based argument. The preassessment task and instructions ask students to submit a related essay, with citations, that teachers read and assess with regard to its introduction, evidence, sequence, logic, transitions, and concluding statement.

Similar tasks can be assigned to assess other standards, such as those that assess the decoding rule via "running records," a "think aloud" problem-solving task performed during a student-teacher conference, or a teacher's observation of a student's science inquiry skills during the design and implementation of her own experiment. Through these evaluations, many teachers will discover the value of performance assessment as a useful pretesting tool.

Assessments may also be administered to the entire class, especially in the beginning of the year. Although these may involve more teacher effort, they provide opportunities for all students to demonstrate their strengths. In fact, involving everyone in the process can boost student confidence and create a stronger sense of community in the classroom. Equipped with a matrix of learning goals and standards, teachers can analyze test and assessment results and form small, flexible groups based on students' strengths and needs.

Mastery levels will fluctuate among students. Students with learning disabilities, visual or hearing impairments, or who speak English as a second language, must often be evaluated differently than their peers. Consider, for example, a student who demonstrates superior understanding of science concepts. If the goal of compacting is to develop the potential talents of all students, then shouldn't she, too, be allowed to take part in alternative learning activities even if her spelling and language arts skills are below grade level? There are, in fact, several ways to accomplish broader patterns of assessment, including the following strategies:

▶ Compact students' work in their most advanced content areas, even though performance may be below grade level in another content area. Students can spend classroom time, as well as free time during school and afterschool time, pursuing alternative activities.

▶ Students may be able to participate in enrichment activities during the language arts period, since language arts are incorporated into most other subjects. Although students may not be working with the same set of skills as those being taught, they would apply other language arts skills during research, problem-solving, and project-sharing exercises.

Implementing curriculum compacting for special needs students may be difficult for many teachers. But studies show that the rewards justify the hours spent. Engaging these students in the process can elevate self-esteem, foster positive attitudes toward learning, and, in the long-term, improve performance. Teachers can implement many different resources to help conduct preassessment, including:

▶ parent volunteers, aides, and tutors to help administer tests and other assessment techniques;

▶ reading, math, and other curriculum specialists to assist in identifying learning outcomes and student strengths;

▶ district consultants and enrichment and gifted education specialists to help with pretests and other aspects of compacting (This service is especially vital during the first few years, when teachers are trying to organize and implement the compacting program.); and

▶ new technologies to pretest and provide individual instruction to targeted students.

Step Four: Streamline Practice or Instructional Time for Students Who Show Mastery of Learning Goals and Standards, and Then Provide Small-Group or Individualized Instruction for Students Who Have Not Yet Mastered All the Goals, But Are Capable of Doing So More Quickly Than Their Classmates

Students who have a thorough grasp of the learning goals and standards should be allowed to participate in enrichment or acceleration activities. This provides an opportunity, during class time, for them to be exposed to material that is not only new and stimulating, but more closely aligned to their learning rates and abilities. For illustration purposes, let's say that a student has mastered three out of five standards in a given unit. That student should not take part in the classroom instruction for the three outcomes that they have already mastered. Depending upon the teacher, some students may be excused from specific class sessions (e.g., the Monday and Wednesday portions of vocabulary building), while others may be compacted out of certain chapters or pages in the text or specific sets of learning activities.

Teachers can provide differentiated opportunities to instruct high-potential students who qualify for compacting, but have not yet mastered all the outcomes. If this occurs, teachers can reduce the number of groups in their classrooms and provide help for students who have high potential, but have not mastered all of the same outcomes as their more academically advanced chronological peers. This may enable teachers to have fewer groups in their classrooms.

Concept compacting measures the previously mastered concepts in a course/unit and compresses the time that would normally be spent teaching these ideas. *Skills compacting*, on the other hand, eliminates specific skills that students have already acquired. Concept compacting is also designed for general knowledge subjects—social studies, science, and literature—whereas skills compacting is intended for mathematics, writing, reading, grammar, and language mechanics.

Skills compacting is easier to accomplish, because pretesting is simpler and mastery can be documented more efficiently. Concept compacting, on the other hand, is more flexible, as students can acquire the missing concepts through several alternative strategies. In concept compacting, assessment and evaluation is often less standardized: some teachers may require concept examples, while others use graphic organizers, or the Frayer model, which asks for definitions, synonyms, examples, and nonexamples of essential content.

Step Five: Offer Academic Alternatives for Students Whose Curriculum Has Been Compacted and Maintain Records of the Compacting Process and Instructional Options for Compacted Students

There are many alternatives and options for students whose curriculum has been compacted. For this reason, this step was often the most challenging and the most open-ended for teachers who participated in our study. The possibilities for replacement tasks are numerous and include:

- ▶ provide an accelerated curriculum based on advanced concepts and/or skills;
- ▶ offer more challenging content (alternative texts, fiction or nonfiction works);
- ▶ adapt classwork to individual curricular needs or learning styles;
- ▶ initiate individual or small-group projects using contracts or management plans;
- ▶ use interest or learning centers;
- ▶ use technology for self-selected or teacher-designed enrichment and independent work;
- ▶ provide opportunities for self-directed learning or decision making;
- ▶ offer mini-courses on research topics or other high interest areas;

▸ establish small seminar groups for advanced studies;

▸ use mentors to guide in learning advanced content or pursuing independent studies; and

▸ provide units or assignments that are self-directed, such as creative writing, game creation, and creative and critical thinking training.

Teachers, working collaboratively with their students, will have to decide which replacement activities to use. These decisions are usually based on factors such as time, space, resources, school policy, students readiness for independent work, and help from other faculty (such as an enrichment program teacher or a library media specialist). But while practical concerns should be considered, what should ultimately determine replacement activities are the degree of academic challenge *and* students' interests. If students understand that if they demonstrate proficiency, they will earn some time to pursue their own interests, they will often work to earn this opportunity. Our role as teachers is to escalate the challenge level of the material students are pursuing to be able to provide adequate academic challenges.

Any differentiated program requires added assessment and record keeping. Unlike a typical classroom where all students are on the same page or exercise at any given time, teachers who provide a compacted curriculum have students doing different assignments at different levels and different times. Keeping concise records, then, is essential, and can be time-consuming without proper planning. Teachers and administrators should collectively decide how the compacting process should be documented, and all written documentation should include these basics:

1. student strength areas, as verified by assessments, test scores, or performances;
2. the pretests used to determine mastery, and the learning outcomes that were eliminated; and
3. recommended enrichment and acceleration activities.

Examining Curricular Alternatives: The Most Challenging Task in Compacting

The most challenging part of compacting is deciding what students should do with time that they have earned by demonstrating mastery of content. In deciding which curriculum alternatives and enrichment materials to use, teachers should first consider all of the enrichment and acceleration activities available to them, which may be organized around several major clusters:

1. **Classroom Activities:** These include independent or small-group study, escalated coverage of the regular curriculum, mini-courses, special interest groups, clubs, interest development centers, technology enrichment, curriculum extension and enhancement, and special lessons for furthering cognitive and affective processes.
2. **Enrichment Program and Special Class Programs:** These include advanced or enriched activities, introduced in the enrichment program, and may be taught by enrichment teachers.
3. **Accelerated Studies:** These include grade-skipping, honors and Advanced Placement courses, college classes, summer or evening classes, early admission to kindergarten or first grade, cross-grade grouping, continuous progress curricula, and special seminars.
4. **Technology Enriched or Accelerated Opportunities:** Numerous and often times overwhelming, the advent of enriching opportunities has made replacement opportunities for compacting ubiquitous and the teachers' role much more complicated, but options exist for independent study, contests, critical and creative thinking, competition, and enrichment according to the Triad Model.
5. **Out-of-School Experiences:** These include internships, mentorships, work-study programs, and community programs, such as theater and symphonic groups, artists' workshops, and museum programs.
6. **District, School, or Departmental Programs:** Encompasses the options above, plus curriculum enhancement using several of the opportunities described in this book, as well as programs for independent study, special counseling, curriculum enrichment, and acceleration.

Enrichment Materials in the Classroom

Enrichment specialists or gifted education teachers, if they are available in your school, are often excellent sources for enrichment activities. The services they supply range from alternative teaching units or materials to mentoring student projects. For teachers who don't have access to these specialists, there are a host of commercially published materials available as well as hundreds of thousands of options available online. Other programs, curriculum enhancement opportunities, and units of challenge (see for example, the curriculum work of Kathy Gavin and her colleagues, Sandra Kaplan, and Joyce VanTassel-Baska and her colleagues) can also be purchased for individual or small groups of students of all ages.

Assessing Students' Interests

Student interests are key in choosing enrichment or acceleration options. When asked what they enjoy most about compacting, children consistently cite the freedom to select their own topics of study; conversely, their biggest objection to regular curriculum is the limited opportunity to pursue their favorite subjects.

We commonly assume that when a student excels in a given area, he or she has a special interest in it. This is not always true. Often, students do well in a course because they've been directed and rewarded by parents and teachers. Students may also lean toward one academic area simply because they've had little exposure to others.

Still, if a youngster is outstanding in math, for example, the teacher should try to promote further interest in the subject. A good way to do this is to suggest an accelerated math activity; if the student and parents agree to it, they should proceed. If, however, the student would rather work on a self-initiated project, then the teacher should try to accommodate those wishes while also considering how to provide an appropriate level of challenge.

Interest Assessment

The Interest-A-Lyzer (Renzulli, 1977; see Appendix B) is a family of questionnaires devised to help students examine and focus their interests. Basically, students are asked to imagine themselves in a series of real and hypothetical situations, and then relate how they would react. The purpose of this student survey is to stimulate thought and discussion. Students not only come to know themselves better, but have the opportunity to discuss and share their interests with both teachers and peers. Teachers play a dual role in fostering student interests. Once students have identified general categories of interest, they must refine and focus them, then provide students with creative and productive outlets for expressing them. A child who enjoys rock music, for instance, may want to become a musician. But there are other opportunities students can pursue as well, such as that of radio announcer or concert producer. Teachers must be aware of students' talents and inclinations within their fields of interest, and at the same time, encourage them to explore a range of options within those fields. We have included a series of Interest-A-Lyzers in Appendix B for your use.

The Interest-A-Lyzer has been used with students in grades 4–9, and it has also been adapted for use with students in primary and secondary grades. The items include a variety of real and hypothetical situations about which students can respond regarding the choices they would make (or have made) were they involved in these situations.

Our decades of using the Interest-A-Lyzer have demonstrated that it can serve as the basis for lively group discussions or in-depth conversations with individual students. It also is designed to facilitate discussion between students with similar interests who are attempting to identify areas in which they might like to pursue advanced-level studies. Field tests have also shown that the self-analysis of interests is an ongoing process that should not be rushed, and that steps should be taken to avoid peer pressure that may lead to group conformity or stereotyped responses. An attempt has been made to overcome some of these problems by asking teachers to give students maximum freedom in choosing how and with whom they would like to discuss their responses. A free and open discussion should lead students to the conclusion that the instrument is an attempt to help them both explore a wide variety of interests and subsequently focus on a particular topic.

Teachers may also want to suggest that students discuss their interest assessment with their parents, emphasizing that it is students' rather than parents' opinions that are being sought. It is also a good idea to suggest that students do not discuss their responses with other children until after they have completed it, when opportunities for group discussion and sharing will be provided.

Interpreting the Interest-A-Lyzer. The Interest-A-Lyzer is not the type of instrument that yields a numerical score, but rather is designed in a way that allows for *pattern analysis in major areas of interests, including the arts, sciences, writing, mathematical, historical, managerial, business, and technological fields.* Remember first that these areas represent *general* fields or families of interest and second that an individual's interest might be expressed in numerous ways. Identifying general patterns is only the first step in interest analysis. General interests must be refined and focused so that students will arrive at specific problems within a general field or a combination of fields. This is often more difficult than identifying general patterns, because in moving from general to specific, there is the danger of steering students to such an extent that a problem may be imposed on them rather than be determined by them. Steps are included in a later section for helping youngsters pursue topics that they may become interested in exploring in more depth.

In this chapter, we have discussed the steps used when teachers implement curriculum compacting, based on our years of working with teachers. We have also introduced some ideas about the most challenging and creative work related to compacting, that is, how teachers guide students to complete alternate work, based on deeper, richer learning experiences instead of doing regular curriculum work that has already been mastered. In the next chapter, we expand that discussion with many additional examples and ideas of how teachers can enrich, deepen, and accelerate content based on students' interests, strengths, and demonstrated and undiscovered talents.

3

Replacement Activities for Students to Pursue in Time Saved by Curriculum Compacting

In the previous chapter, we discussed the steps involved in compacting and the ways in which teachers can supplement numerous choices in the time saved by identifying students' curriculum strengths and competencies. In this chapter, we elaborate on some of the ways that replacement activities can be implemented by teachers whose efforts with compacting often focus on finding enough interesting content that both engages and challenges their students. For example, online activities, independent and small-group studies, contests and competitions, and more challenging accelerated work can all be used to replace previously mastered content.

A wide range of online activities can be used to excite and motivate students to pursue diverse interests. Students can, as long as there is a computer and Internet available to them, participate in activities related to a host of high-interest areas, from animals to the FBI, from Lewis and Clark to Andy Warhol, to the secret of the Mayan glyphs, to the Underground Railroad. Some online activities enable children who are interested in the arts to have outstanding artistic enrichment by exploring the history of art, art careers, and learning about art techniques by watching short video clips, for example. Perhaps some examples will be helpful. For students who are interested in nature, Environmental Education for Kids (http://www.dnr.state.wi.us/org/caer/ce/eek/nature/track.htm) provides opportunities for studying animal tracks and learning more about how to track certain types of species. An online activity such as this one presents a mystery where students are asked to solve where an animal was going and what it was doing when it was going there. Students are taught to carefully examine animal tracks to learn more about them.

How do you encourage students who have had their curriculum compacted to become involved in exciting and challenging online activities? Some sites can be visited briefly as some children will spend a few minutes reading about the site to find out whether they want to participate in an activity. They may then decide that they do not want to participate in the follow-up activities and move on to another site. Other children who visit a site will become extremely interested and spend much longer periods of time there. A third-grade student whose curriculum was compacted recently spent 2 hours on a site about animals and had to be reminded by her teacher that it was time to go to lunch.

It is appropriate to enable children to learn more about topics of interest by visiting exciting online sites. But when students have intense interests, they should be encouraged to carefully read the material offered at some of the sites and spend time learning some material in greater depth. That is, we do not want to encourage children to simply spend their compacted time surfing from site to site without ever carefully reading and analyzing information.

If children are interested in journalism, for example, they should be encouraged to spend time participating in activities such as the ones at The Write Site (http://www.writesite.org), where children can research and write their own news stories, follow enjoyable links to newspapers and news agencies around the world, and interact with other students also interested in journalism.

In the examples provided above, the breadth of some of online activities show how students can have their learning enhanced in compacted time. These represent just a few examples of the countless online activities available for students. Here are other enriching and interesting online activities:

- ▶ Students who may want to learn more about astronomy, outer space, deep space, space exploration, and civilian space travel may access the "How Big Is the Universe" activity at http://www.kidsastronomy.com.
- ▶ If students are interested in animals, they can follow the movements of animals like the white-sided dolphin, which was tagged in collaboration with the New England Aquarium and the Cape Cod Stranding Network, at http://whale.wheelock.edu/whalenet-stuff/stop_cover.html#tags.

Using Contests and Competitions to Motivate Students in Compacted Time

Contests and competitive activities can also help students learn important skills and life lessons. Renzulli Learning, now called GoQuest (https://compass learning.com/goquest), includes different contests that provide an exceptional way to match students with natural audiences for their interest-based activities. Contests also provide a safe place for students to aspire to higher levels of excellence as other audiences see their work.

Contests and competitions also help students enjoy their own creative processes and better understand their own creative potential. Contests can teach students important values, life skills, and rules, as well as organizational, time management, and self-regulation skills about meeting deadlines and fulfilling personal goals. Contests can also enable students to learn about personal safety issues, such as how and when to provide information about home addresses, e-mails, and phone numbers and whether or when parental supervision is necessary. Contests and competitions can also help students learn to meet deadlines, follow a specific set of instructions, and take safe risks by competing in different types of endeavors. For some students who don't like or excel in athletics, contests can offer an opportunity to learn to compete. Contests and competition can enable students to learn how to lose with courage and grace and to win with humility tempered by pride in one's accomplishments. As a competitive swimmer learns that one can take a risk, lose, and still continue swimming, contests help kids learn how to compete with honesty and continue striving, even when they lose. We often teach students the old adage of "Good, better, best. Never let it rest, until the good is better, and the better, best!" And contests can do this.

Some early exposure to competition is healthy, as students should have an opportunity to experience academic and social situations relating to how to compete with integrity. How can teachers help if a child wants to enter a contest or a competition?

First, determine whether the contest is a good match for the child's interests and abilities and whether support will be needed and can be given for participation. Second, teachers can help a child learn more about the specifics of the contest to determine if eligibility requirements can be met, based on age and background, and to understand deadlines and specifics of how to enter. Last, teachers can support students' entry into competitive ventures by helping them establish deadlines, encouraging them to do the very best work they can, helping them have a plan for completion, and helping them stay on target to finish the work. We have found many competitions that match most children's interest areas. A few competitions that we have used with talented students include:

▶ **PBS Kids Writers Contest** (http://pbskids.org/writerscontest): In recent years, more than 45,000 kids entered this yearly contest, which is held by local PBS stations for kids in grades K–3.

▶ **The Gloria Barron Prize for Young Heroes** (http://www.barronprize. org): The Gloria Barron Prize for Young Heroes awards recognize outstanding youth ages 8–18 who have shown courageous leadership in service to people and our planet. Each year, 10 national winners each receive $2,000 to support their service or educational goals.

Using Independent Studies and Self-Selected Projects

Compacting enables teachers to complete independent projects available in multiple areas of interest that were specially developed for students, as well as many that are available online. The projects that we have developed over the years are based on a research process that teachers have used to produce high-quality enrichment projects, based on multiple experiences in helping students develop these projects. We've devised a 12-step process for teaching students how to produce quality enrichment projects. This process, which has evolved over several decades and countless activities, can be applied in classroom and resource room settings. Two comments on the steps themselves: first, they don't have to be followed in the order given and second, some steps can be eliminated if students can accomplish these tasks in other ways.

The 12 steps can teach students how to produce high-quality products using the time saved in the compacting process. These steps have emerged from many years of working with above-average students in programs based on focusing student interests into manageable products.

Teachers or media specialists may also first instruct students in these steps. They can be modified for use with primary students or introduced in a written format for upper elementary or secondary students. In a heterogeneous classroom, the methodology of independent research can be taught to students whose curriculum has been compacted, or it can be introduced to the top reading group (usually above-average students) or even the entire classroom. When the latter approach is used, a student's positive response and desire to follow through is an excellent indication that this student is capable of independent work. Various degrees of response come from students of various ability levels. Our experience has shown that students identified as academically talented have the most potential for developing high-quality differentiated products, but that should not deter us from teaching the process to all students in a regular classroom setting.

Step 1: Assess, Find, or Create Student Interests

First, students should be encouraged to select a topic in which they have an intense interest. Too often, independent study is mistakenly confused with doing a research or term paper based on the subject area in which the paper is assigned. We cannot expect a student to become actively involved in a topic in which little or no interest is displayed. For example, a student who has a passionate interest in artificial intelligence and spends all of her free time devouring books on that topic probably will not expend high energy or commitment on a report or term paper on Shakespeare for an honors English class.

Students' interests may need to be sparked by exposure to new topics or disciplines of study or by extensions of the regular curriculum. An interesting observation about student interests is that they often decline as students get older. Primary-aged students have many interests they would like to pursue; middle and high school students indicate interest in fewer topics. In some cases, interests can be created by completing an open-ended instrument such as the Interest-A-Lyzer, scheduling high-interest speakers, or introducing high-interest topics into the regular curriculum. Casual interest may or may not be appropriate for an independent study. If a student's interest and questions about a topic can be addressed in a brief review of available references, it probably will not result in an extensive research project. Whether it is a casual or long-term interest can usually be determined by interviewing the student.

Step 2: Conduct An Interview to Determine the Strength of the Interest

Several important topics should be dealt with in a student interview. The teacher or a media specialist or librarian should try to assess how much interest is really present for further pursuit of the topics. Several questions may be asked that will lead the teacher to determine whether or not a true interest is being pursued. If the interest involved journalism, for example, and the student wanted to produce a monthly school newspaper, the following questions might be asked at an initial interview:

1. How long have you been interested in journalism?
2. What sources have you contacted to learn more about this subject?
3. Have you ever tried to publish a class or neighborhood newspaper? If not, why?
4. Have you ever tried to visit our local newspaper?
5. Do you know any other students or adults who are interested in this topic?
6. Have you looked at any books or talked with anyone who might help you get started on a monthly newspaper? If I can help you find some books or someone to talk to about this project, do you think this might give you some ideas?
7. How did you become interested in journalism?

Questions such as these will help to assess both interest and commitment. The last question is especially important because we want to be certain that the interest is, in fact, the student's. If the student responded that he had not contacted any sources or read any books or made any attempt in any way to learn more about journalism, one might question whether or not this would be an appropriate topic to pursue. Every attempt should be made to encourage the interest and assist the student in finding information about the interest. If, however, these attempts do not generate the type of follow-up that should be required to produce a high-quality product, it is unreasonable to expect that a student should or would want to continue in this endeavor. Questions such as these will help to determine if the student has really considered the amount of work involved in the actual completion of the independent study. If the student indicates that he has only an hour a month outside of school to spend on this project, suggestions should be provided for how more time might be spent pursuing this idea both at home and in school. Curriculum compacting frees up several hours a week for bright students in their classroom that might be spent producing a differentiated product. A student often will not know *how* to develop a newspaper that is different from other student efforts. This is the crucial step in producing a differentiated product; at this time, the methodology of how to produce something qualitatively better can be introduced.

Step 3: Help Students Find a Question (Questions) to Research

This step is also referred to as problem finding and focusing. Most educators have little difficulty recognizing general families of interest: scientific, historical, literary, mathematical, musical, athletic. However, problems arise when they attempt to capitalize on these general interests and use them as the starting point for (1) focusing in on a specific manifestation of general interests, and (2) structuring specific interests into researchable problems. How teachers deal with interests, both general and specific, is crucial. If handled improperly, it will undoubtedly get students off on the *wrong* track.

We know of one youngster, for example, who expressed an unusual interest in sharks. The teacher appreciated the child's enthusiasm and reacted in what he thought was an appropriate fashion: "I'm glad that you have such a great interest in sharks. Why don't you do a report about sharks?" Those words, "do a report . . ." led to an inevitable end result—yet another summary of facts and drawings based entirely on information copied from encyclopedias and "all-about" books. Although the student prepared a very neat, accurate report, her major investigative activity was looking up and summarizing already existing information. Although gathering background information is always an important starting point for any investigative endeavor, one of the goals of independent study is to help youngsters extend their work beyond the usual kinds of *reporting* that result when teachers and students view this process as merely looking up information. Some training in reporting is a necessary part of good education for all students.

Indeed, the pursuit of new knowledge should always begin with a review of what is already known about a topic. The end result of independent study for gifted students, however, should be a creative contribution that is beyond the already existing information typically found in encyclopedias and "all-about" books.

How can we help students learn to focus problems and become involved in more advanced types of creative and productive involvement? The first step is to help students ask the right kinds of questions: those routinely raised by those who do investigative research within particular fields of knowledge. At this point, however, we are faced with a practical problem. Because most teachers are not themselves well-versed in asking the right questions about all fields of study, they cannot be expected to generate appropriate questions in any field of study their students might want to investigate. Teachers, therefore, can assist students in obtaining the methodological books (or resource persons, if available) that routinely list these important questions. In other words, if a student wants to ask the right questions about focusing a problem in anthropology, then he or she must begin by looking at techniques used by anthropologists.

Every field of organized knowledge can be defined, in part, by its methodology. In every case, this methodology can be found in certain guidebooks or manuals. These "how-to" books are the keys to escalating students' research beyond the traditional report-writing approach. Unfortunately, some of these books are not ordinarily included in elementary or high school libraries because of their advanced nature, but that does not mean that able students cannot make appropriate use of at least selected parts of advanced materials.

How-to books can help a teacher to find appropriate research questions for students. Jason's teacher was aware of his special interest in anything and everything having to do with science. (Keep in mind that science is an area rather than a problem.) She provided him with several copies of *Popular Science* and asked him to pick out the articles he liked best. She could have also given him access to the Internet to let him explore the magazine's website. This is a good example of an exploratory activity because these magazines include many topics not ordinarily covered in the science curriculum. When the teacher asked Jason if he would like to follow-up on any articles by doing some research of his own, he selected hydroponic gardening. (The general area of science has now been narrowed somewhat, but hydroponic gardening is a topic rather than a problem.) The teacher obtained resources on hydroponic gardening from the media specialist, and Jason practically "devoured" these, as well as numerous websites on this topic.

Through discussion with his teacher, Jason came up with the idea of growing corn under varying conditions. His research question became: Will corn grow at different rates when certain macronutrients are varied while other conditions stay constant? He constructed several growing trays using paper milk cartons and obtained the necessary nutrients from his chemistry set, a high school chemistry teacher, and a university extension agent with whom he made contact through assistance from his teacher. By varying the amount of certain macronutrients (nitrogen, phosphorous, potassium) and keeping other conditions constant [good research procedures] he was able to observe different rates of growth. Meticulous records were kept and weekly measurements of growth rates and plant "health" [data] were recorded. He also photographed plants grown under varying conditions by placing a standard growth-grid chart behind each plant [visual data]. Graphics and statistical summaries were prepared [data summary and analysis] and a written report was developed [communication of results]. Jason also organized an audiovisual presentation of his work [another mode of communication].

Step 4: Develop a Written Plan

Once students have generated a question or a series of questions, they should be encouraged to develop a written plan. Some educators who have been successful in facilitating independent projects like to use a contract with students; others prefer the use of a student journal or log. The Management Plan for Individual and Small-Group Investigations (see Figure 6) has also been an effective way to help organize ideas and develop a timeline. The Management Plan is an educational device containing a format that is not very different from the procedures followed by the firsthand inquirer.

The adult inquirer intuitively engages in certain activities described on the Management Plan. For example, a sociologist working on an attitude survey may not actually list her intended audiences; however, she usually has a fairly good idea of the journals to which her results may be submitted and of the professional societies or organizations to whom such a research paper might be presented. After the student has identified a general area in which to do advanced-level work and has used appropriate problem-focusing techniques, the student can begin to fill in the material requested in the box entitled "Specific Area of Study." A great deal of careful thought should be given to completing this box because all subsequent activities will reflect the degree of clarity with which the problem is focused and stated. The teacher and student(s) should answer the two questions listed in the box by using a frame of reference that characterizes the actual thinking of a real investigator in this field. If such a frame of reference is not apparent to teacher or student, a community resource person who knows that field or a methodology book will help to start them on the right track.

The two boxes labeled "Intended Audiences" and "Intended Products and Outlets" are designed to help steer the student toward thinking about the final form that the investigation will take and about the audiences potentially inter-

Management Plan for Individual and Small-Group Investigations

Name: _____ Grade: _____ Estimated Beginning Date: _____ Ending Date: _____

Teacher: _____ School: _____ Progress Reports Due on Following Dates: _____

General Area(s) of Study (Check all that apply)

☐ Language Arts/   ☐ Science   ☐ Personal and Social
   Humanities   Development
☐ Social Studies   ☐ Music   ☐ Other (Specify) _____
☐ Mathematics   ☐ Art   ☐ Other (Specify) _____

Specify Area of Study

Write a brief description of the problem that you plan to investigate. What are the objectives of your investigation? What do you hope to find out?

Intended Audiences

Which individuals or groups would be most interested in the findings? List the organized groups (clubs, societies, teams) at the local, regional, state, and national levels. What are the names and addresses of contact persons in these groups? When and where do they meet?

1. _____
2. _____
3. _____
4. _____
5. _____

Intended Product(s) and Outlets

What form(s) will the final product take? How, when, and where will you communicate the results of your investigation to an appropriate audience(s)? What outlet vehicles (journals, conferences, art shows, etc.) are typically used by professionals in this field?

Methodological Resources and Activities

List the names and addresses of persons who might provide assistance in attacking this problem. List the how-to books that are available in this area of study. List other resources (films, collections, exhibits, etc.) and special equipment (e.g., camera, tape recorder, questionnaire, etc.). Keep continuous record of all activities that are part of this investigation.

Getting Started

What are the first steps you should take to begin this investigation? What types of information or data will be needed to solve the problem? If "raw data," how can it be gathered, classified, and presented? If you plan to use already categorized information or data, where is it located and how can you obtain what you need?

Figure 6. Management Plan for Individual and Small-Group Investigations.

ested in the results. The questions and information sought in these boxes are derived from the role and purpose of the firsthand inquirer discussed above.

The two larger boxes on the Management Plan (Getting Started and Methodological Resources and Activities) are intended to provide a running account of the procedures and resources that will be used during an investigative activity. Both of these boxes should be completed cooperatively by the teacher and student, and modification should be made as new activities are followed through and as a greater variety of resources are brought to the student's attention. A "mushrooming effect" often takes place as resources become more familiar and the greater variety of resources, in turn, advance the level of sophistication that is brought to bear on a particular problem.

The completion of the Getting Started and Methodological Resources and Activities boxes will often be dependent on the availability of appropriate resource guides. For example, if a youngster is studying the attitudes of other students about an issue such as dress code regulations, an interviewer's manual or guidebook for constructing attitude questionnaires will be a key resource. In many cases, these types of references provide the step-by-step procedures that will assist students in completing the Getting Started box and the activities section of the Methodological Resources and Activities box.

In certain respects, the two larger boxes on the Management Plan should parallel each other. In the Getting Started box, the student should list the early steps necessary for beginning an investigation and the types of information that will be needed to pursue the study, at least in the initial stages. Because early success is an important factor for continued motivation to complete the study, teachers must work very closely with youngsters in helping them to complete this box. The information in the box can serve as a checklist for determining whether the student is heading in the right direction. It can also assist in setting target dates for progress reports. In certain instances, a student may want to lay out the entire plan in the Getting Started box, and, in other cases, the plan may begin here and be continued in the Methodological Resources and Activities box. In view of the wide variety of topics that students may choose to pursue and the many variations in methodology that characterize various areas of study, a rigid prescription for completing these two boxes of the Management Plan is difficult to outline. In some instances, students may wish to use a flow chart and record their activities in a log or notebook. Whenever space does not permit the recording of necessary information, the reverse side of the Management Plan, additional pages, or even a separate notebook can be used.

Step 5: Help Students Locate Multiple Resources and Continue Working on the Topic

In addition to helping students focus their problem through the methods described earlier, how-to books should be located to help provide advanced content and methodological assistance. Students should also be directed to the numerous resources at their disposal and encouraged to delve deeply into these. These resources include but are not limited to textbooks, resources on the Internet, biographies and autobiographies, periodicals, films, letters, surveys, phone calls and personal interviews, almanacs, and atlases. Educators should encourage students to use many different types of resources and to carefully examine the resources that they find online. Librarians and media specialists are also able to help students with this.

Step 6: Provide Methodological Assistance

Methodological assistance means helping students acquire and make appropriate use of the specific data-gathering tools and investigative techniques that are the standard and necessary methods for authentic research in particular fields of study. If a problem is well-defined and focused, the correct guidance by teachers, media specialists, or librarians during this phase of a study can almost guarantee that students will be firsthand investigators rather than reporters. This step of the process involves shifting the emphasis from learning *about* topics to learning *how* one gathers, categorizes, analyzes, and evaluates information in particular fields. During this crucial time of independent research, we can almost guarantee that student products will be differentiated by the methodological assistance and instruction they receive.

Every field of knowledge is characterized in part by certain kinds of raw data. New contributions are made in a field when investigators apply well-defined methods to the process of synthesizing previously random bits and pieces of information. Although some investigations require levels of sophistication and equipment that are far beyond the reach of younger students, almost every field of knowledge has entry-level and junior-level data-gathering opportunities. At this stage of the independent study process, the teacher's role is to help students identify, locate, and obtain resource materials or persons who can provide assistance in the appropriate use of investigative techniques. In some cases, teachers may have to consult with librarians or professionals within a field for advice about where and how to find resource materials. Professional assistance also may be needed to translate complex concepts into ideas students can understand. Although methodological assistance is a major part of the teacher's responsibility, to expect teachers to have mastered a large number of investigative techniques is neither necessary nor realistic. That is one reason that a critical role can be played by media specialists and librarians. A good general background and orientation toward the overall nature of research is necessary, but the most important skills are the ability to know where and how to help a student obtain the right kind of material and the willingness to locate the necessary resources for students.

For elementary classroom and secondary subject area teachers, the first step in learning about methodologies involves identifying the disciplines within the subject being taught, the "-ologies" and "-ographies" of the field, such as:

▶ **Social Science:** History, geography, economics, sociology, political science, anthropology, psychology, theology, philosophy;

▶ **Sciences:** Biology, microbiology, botany, zoology, ornithology, herpetology, entomology, oceanography, ecology, biochemistry, chemistry, physics, astronomy, geology, meteorology;

▶ **Language Arts (Modes of Communication):** Fiction writing, journalism, play writing, literary criticism, poetry, cartooning, drawing, graphics, photography, cinematography, drama, oratory, debate, storytelling, mime, dance, song writing, music; and

▶ **Mathematics:** Number theory, statistics, probability, geometry, topology, logic, calculus, mathematical modeling.

Once the disciplines have been identified, teachers or students can be helped to focus on areas that are of interest to many students (based on information from an interest inventory). One example of a process skill that would prove useful in almost any independent project is research methodology, including aspects such as problem finding and focusing, research question and hypothesis generation, research design, data gathering and analysis, and dissemination of results.

Once an interest is chosen, the teacher should help the student to identify methodologies used within the particular discipline. This can be accomplished by obtaining "how-to" books that explain the methodologies of practicing professionals in terms that students and teachers can understand. A few are texts, but most are published as trade books, intended for a general audience.

Using "how-to" books or websites as a source of professional expertise for students is an excellent way of upgrading the quality of independent study products. Depending on the ability of the student and the readability of the book, the teacher may choose to have the student work with the book independently, teach the techniques, or work with the student using the book as a resource. The book might provide suggestions for research or real-world problems to be solved. The book should provide guidance and instruction in professional-level methodologies that the student can use to carry out the project after a problem has been brought into focus. Finally, the book might have information about appropriate audiences and formats for communicating findings.

Step 7: Help Students Decide Which Question(s) to Answer

Once students have learned about the disciplines, become more aware of their interests, and identified the methodology, they are then able to decide which question or area they want to research. Students often begin investigations when they see how particular methodologies make it possible for them to pursue an interest.

Step 8: Provide Managerial Assistance

Managerial assistance consists of helping students make arrangements for obtaining the data and resources necessary for independent investigations. Setting up an interview with a public official, arranging for the distribution of a questionnaire to students or parents, and providing transportation to a place where data will be gathered are all examples of managerial functions. Additional activities might include gaining access to laboratories or computer centers, arranging for the use of a college library, helping students gain access to conferencing programs such as Skype or equipment such as scanners and copiers, and driving to pick up some photographic materials or electronic parts. Our responsibilities concerning this are similar to the combined roles of research assistant, advocate, ombudsman, campaign strategist, and enthusiastic friend. At this stage of product development, the student should be the leader and emerging expert while the teacher or librarian assumes a supportive rather than authoritative posture. The teacher's typical comments should be: "What can I do to help you? Are you having any problems? Do you need to get a book from the university library? Would you like to bounce a few ideas off me? Are there some ways that we might explore raising the money for solar cells?"

The major purpose of the managerial role is to help the student stay on track and move toward each intermediate goal. A planned strategy for up-to-date progress reports between meetings such as a log, notebook, or annotated timeline will create a vehicle for fulfilling the managerial role. And of course, this procedure should involve a review and analysis of the Management Plan or any other written plan being kept by the student.

Step 9: Identify Final Products and Audiences

We believe that finding an audience is the key to improving the quality of products and developing effective ways of communicating results with interested others. A sense of audience is a primary contributor to task commitment and the concern for excellence and quality that we have witnessed in many high-quality products resulting from independent study projects.

Attention must be given to helping students find appropriate outlets and audiences for their most creative efforts. This concern is once again modeled after the *modus operandi* of creative and productive individuals. If we could sum up in as few words as possible the *raison d'être* of highly creative artists and scholars, it would certainly be *impact on audience*. Creativity is a source of personal satisfaction and self-expression, but most rewards come from bringing about desired changes to make the world a better place. The writer hopes to influence thoughts and emotions, the scientist carries out research to find better ways to contribute to the knowledge of their field, and artists create products to enrich the lives of those who view their works. Teachers can help young people to acquire this orientation by encouraging them to develop a sense of audience from the earliest stages of an independent investigation.

It is the teacher's role to help students take this one small but often neglected step in the overall process of product development: selecting an outlet and an audience. How people typically communicate results or products within a field should be considered. The final product should be decided by the student based on the student's interests. Students who are interested in media or film should not be forced to write an article. Once a type of product has been chosen, audiences should be explored. For teachers to have the names of all possible audiences and outlets at their fingertips is neither necessary nor practical; however, classroom teachers need to find out about the existence of audiences and outlets. What historical societies or conservation groups are in your community? Do they publish newsletters or have regularly scheduled meetings? Would they be receptive to including a student's article in their newsletter or perhaps having a student present the research results at one of their meetings? How-to books may also be used to provide guidance for identifying products and audiences.

Although school and local audiences are an obvious starting point, teachers should help students gain a perspective for more comprehensive outlet vehicles and audiences. Many organizations, for example, prepare newsletters and journals at the state and national levels. These organizations usually are receptive to high-quality contributions by young people. Similarly, state and national magazines often carry outstanding work by young people. Whenever a student product achieves an unusually high level of excellence, encourage the student to contact one of the publishing companies and magazines that specialize in or are receptive to the contributions of young writers, artists, and researchers. Just as gifted athletes extend their involvement into larger and larger fields of competition, so should young scholars and artists be encouraged to reach out beyond the local levels of success they have achieved. This involves an element of risktaking and the chances of not having one's work accepted in the wider arenas.

Step 10: Offer Encouragement, Praise, and Critical Assistance

Even the most experienced researchers, writers, and creative producers need feedback from persons who can reflect objectively on their work. For students beginning the often-frustrating task of firsthand inquiry, feedback must be given firmly but sensitively. The major idea underlying the feedback process is that almost everything can be improved through revision, rewriting, and attention to details, both large and small. This message must be conveyed to students without harsh criticism or discouraging comments. Each student must be made to feel that your most important concern is to help the aspiring artist or scholar reach the highest possible level of excellence. Just as a champion athlete or dancer knows that a rigorous coach has the performer's best interests at heart, so must students learn that critical feedback is a major service that good teachers must offer.

Bright students often are unaccustomed to any criticism of their work. Therefore, encouragement must be given throughout the process, and students must understand that all professionals regard feedback as a necessary, although sometimes unpleasant, way to improve their work.

Step 11: Escalate the Process

The teacher, media specialist, or librarian should view his or her role in the feedback process as that of a "resident escalator." Sensitive and specific recommendations about how particular aspects of the work can be improved will help the aspiring scholar to progress toward higher and higher levels of product excellence. Every effort should be made to pinpoint specific areas for suggested changes. This will help avoid student discouragement and reconfirm a belief in the overall value of their endeavors.

How many of us have encouraged students to do research only to have them return with a synthesis of magazine articles (at best) or website references? Even when we encouraged students to go one step further and do surveys, how often have we found that each polled the same 10 friends or classmates? Academically talented students should not be blamed for using simple or unimaginative methods when they are not taught more advanced or appropriate ones. If teachers want students to act like firsthand researchers, they must teach them how these professionals work. Media specialists and librarians can also help in this process. Students need to understand how to identify and phrase research questions and hypotheses, design research that will answer their research questions appropriately, gather and analyze data without bias, draw conclusions, and communicate their results effectively. Although the specifics change from discipline to discipline, all professionals use the research process in their work. Authors may state their premises less formally than scientists and may gather data through observations and introspection rather than experimentation, but the underlying processes are similar.

Step 12: Evaluate or Assess Your Project or Independent Study

An almost universal characteristic of students at all ages is a desire to know how they will be evaluated or "graded." We would like to begin by saying that we strongly discourage the formal grading of products resulting from independent study. No letter grade, number, or percent can accurately reflect the comprehensive types of knowledge, creativity, and task commitment developed within the context of independent study. At the same time, evaluation and feedback are important parts of the overall process of promoting growth through this type of enrichment experience and therefore students should be thoroughly oriented in the procedures that will be used to evaluate their work.

We believe students and teachers should both be involved in the evaluation process. Additionally, if an outside resource person or mentor has been involved in the development of the product, he or she should be asked to provide evaluation input. Numerous forms have been developed to help students evaluate their own work. An effective and simple questionnaire that has successfully been used in many enrichment programs includes these questions:

1. What were your feelings about working on your project?
2. What were some of the things you learned while working on your project?
3. Were you satisfied with your final product? In what ways?
4. What were some of the ways you were helped on your project?
5. Do you think you might like to work on another project in the future? What ideas do you have for this project?

Teachers can use the steps above to help students begin the process of completing a small-group or independent study project. If students need additional scaffolding, they can also work on independent study projects that are available online, such as the following:

▸ **Castle Builder (http://score.rims.k12.ca.us/activity/castle_builder):** This site asks students to take on the role of a medieval castle builder in Wales, having them work to create their own historically accurate castle.

▸ **Collapse: Why Do Civilizations Fall? (http://www.learner.org/exhibits/collapse):** At this interactive site, students find out more about what caused famous civilizations to fall apart. They examine the clues left at archaeological sites to learn more about four civilizations, record their findings in a journal, and check their progress along the way.

- **NOAA Ocean Service Education—For Fun (http://oceanservice. noaa.gov/education/games.html#6_up):** By downloading and following the instructions from this website, students can build a weather station, make a weather report, and even track a hurricane!
- **Make Puppets and Marionettes Crafts for Kids (http://www.art istshelpingchildren.org/puppetshandpuppetsfingerpuppetsarts craftsideaskids.html):** On this website, students will learn to make a puppet out of simple materials. Then they will write their story in script format, hide behind a pair of covered chairs, and perform!
- **Make Trading Cards (http://www.readwritethink.org/files/re sources/interactives/trading_cards_2):** Who are the MVPs of medical science, World War II, or a favorite book? Students can create printable trading cards for people, places, things, or even abstract concepts! They can create a set to exchange with friends.

Using Critical and Creative Thinking to Challenge and Engage Students

Another way to replace compacted content is to find appropriately challenging critical or creative thinking skills. Critical thinking is defined as the ability to critically analyze material for skills such as point of view, bias, logically supported conclusions, and sequential development of a point. Critical thinkers plan their actions, clarify, explain, and interpret information. They also carefully consider which information is accurate and use good judgments to make decisions. Critical thinking activities emphasize analysis, synthesis, classifying, patterning, sequencing, and reasoning. We have identified many materials, activities, and resources (both books and electronic) to improve children's critical thinking skills because we believe that helping students learn critical thinking skills and apply them to content areas or to real-life experiences is essential for success in life. Here are some examples of specific critical thinking activities that can be used during compacted time:

- **Forensics in the Classroom (http://forensics.rice.edu):** Do your students love *Law and Order* or *CSI*? Check out this great site where they can be detectives and learn how crime-solving happens. Students can help solve the mysteries of the canine caper, the burning star, and the bitter pill—all through forensics!
- **The Great Green Web Game (http://go.ucsusa.org/game):** This interactive game is fun and educational and helps children to begin think-

ing about the impact of an average American household on the environment. Students can work to make some changes in their households.

▶ **Art Detective (https://kids.tate.org.uk/games/art-detective):** Students can use clues to learn the secrets of a mysterious object that has arrived at Tate Britain's art gallery.

Using Virtual Field Trips to Excite and Motivate Students

We have also found virtual field trips to serve as exciting experiences to enrich learning and motivate students. In the Enrichment Triad Model, we advocate the use of Type I enrichment to engage and motivate students and to help them find and discover their interests. Although real field trips can be the reason that some students become interested in topics, we know that traveling to multiple locations across the globe is not feasible for most students. Few students, for example, can travel to Europe, Asia, or Africa to be exposed to new areas of interests, cultures, art, and sciences. We can, however, offer these options virtually and some of our favorite activities to be pursued in compacted time are virtual field trips. We have identified outstanding virtual field trips in a wide variety of content areas to enable students to experience exciting places they can "virtually" visit. Some students will glance at virtual field trips very briefly to find out whether they want to learn a little and then move on to another activity. Other students become extremely interested and may spend long periods of time on one virtual field trip, following links from that site to other sites that they want to pursue. Teachers may want to make sure that students take the time to read the material offered and spend some time learning material of interest in more depth. We have included below a few examples of some virtual field trips that represent the hundreds of opportunities available online for students. More are being created every day as the Internet explodes with enrichment activities.

▶ **100 Incredible & Educational Virtual Tours You Don't Want to Miss (http://www.onlineuniversities.com/blog/2010/01/100-inc redible-educational-virtual-tours-you-dont-want-to-miss):** This site's virtual tours enable students to explore cities, famous landmarks and buildings, museums, college campuses, and even outer space. Students can learn how things are made, explore the human body or the body of a life-sized whale, and take several amazing virtual tours that Google Earth has compiled.

▶ **Panama Canal (http://www.pancanal.com/eng/general/howit works/index.html):** Visit Central America to view one of the greatest engineering marvels of all time, the Panama Canal. To view how the canal works, click on "Transit" and "Operation" to watch the animated video. Also try viewing the link on the left of the homepage entitled "Photo Gallery" to see actual panoramic and historical photographs!

▶ **Hoover Dam (http://www.sunsetcities.com/hoover-dam.html):** One of the largest dams is located on the border of Nevada and Arizona. Consider having students read the historical background and view the photos on this site.

▶ **The White House–Tours and Events (http://www.whitehouse.gov/ history/whtour):** Take a virtual tour of the White House and explore all the different rooms to find out the importance of each one while learning about the history of the White House!

▶ **Virtual Egypt (http://www.virtual-egypt.com/newhtml/orienta tion/index.html):** Take this virtual tour of ancient Egypt and learn about the different stages in Egyptian history and what remains today.

▶ **The Virtual Body (https://www.innerbody.com):** Explore the human body by visiting the brain, the heart, and the skeleton to learn about our bodies.

▶ **Astronomy for Kids (http://www.frontiernet.net/~kidpower/ astronomy.html):** Explorations of the solar system, planets, sun, stars, asteroids, and galaxies are all available on this site.

▶ **The Aurora Page (http://www.geo.mtu.edu/weather/aurora):** What is the "aurora?" What causes it to happen? Information, links, and images of the Northern Lights can be found here.

The examples in Table 2 enable teachers to consider how virtual field trips can be used to help students be exposed to certain high-interest opportunities, the Type II training that accompanies that exposure, and the products that may emerge after the interest and training emerges. A Type II ½ is a project, study, or inquiry that is suggested, directed, and supervised by a teacher, while a Type III study is more student driven, with choice opportunities and most decisions led by a student.

Using the Internet to Provide Enrichment in Compacted Time

Below are some additional ideas for resources to differentiate instruction and facilitate independent student learning as you compact curriculum for some students in your classroom. Teachers may want to consider selecting some of these

TABLE 2

Example of How to Use Virtual Field Trips

Type I Experiences
• What Is Weather?—Introduction to topic forecasting
• Making a Weather Station—How-to site
• Weather Extreme: Tornado—Types of tornados
Type II Training
• Funology—Experiment
• Exploring the Environment: Modules & Activities—Reading satellite photos
• Extreme Weather—Use for note-taking lesson
Type II ½ Projects/Products
• Explore the Environment—Hurricane tracking simulation
• Interactive Weather Maker—Simulation of weather
• Kidstorm—Weather topics
• Earthwatch: Weather—Monitoring weather conditions
• El Niño: Hot Air Over Hot Water—Research
• Cloudy With a Chance of . . . Become a Weather Forecaster—Simulation and project
Type III Projects/Products
• Create a tornado in a bottle
• Build a weather station and track local weather conditions
• Create a newscast featuring a major weather event and forecasting
• Track cloud patterns over the region for one month using satellite imagery
• Build a model to demonstrate how landforms affect weather conditions
• Compare and contrast weather in two distinct areas of the United States using local weather data

ideas as they compact curriculum and subsequently scaffold instruction to enable their students to pursue independent, project-based learning.

1. Identify one of the virtual field trips that connect to a regular curriculum unit you are developing. Conduct mini-lessons with the whole class to teach students how to access the information on the website and suggestions for follow-up work to help them determine if the area is one that they want to explore more independently.

2. Spend time as a whole class going to specific sites and discussing the positive and negative features of the site. Developing skills to critically eval-

uate web-based resources is important for the students to be successful when using technology.

3. Ask your students to critique each website or resource they explore in a session, including the categories below. Teachers may want to discuss evaluation criteria with students in a whole class mini-lesson. The type of criteria that students may want to consider are:
   a. Can I read and understand this resource?
   b. Do the graphics (pictures, illustrations, print characteristics) grab my attention and make me want to explore the site more?
   c. Does this site have the type of information I thought it would?
   d. Does this resource have the kind of information that I am looking for?
   e. Is this resource something that will help me learn more about a topic or subject?
   f. Does this resource teach me something new or help me practice something I already know?
   g. Can I create a product (some type of work) on this site that I can share with others?
   h. What type of site is this?
      i. a game site
      ii. one with many facts
      iii. one that teaches me a new skill
      iv. a site that lets me create something on it

As an extension, the students can take turns presenting their critiques of virtual websites or tours to the rest of the class and students can analyze this in Figure 7.

After students have had the opportunity to explore several sites and online activities, they should be asked if they have developed an area of interest that the student will pursue in more depth during their compacted time. The student would then look for resources related to that interest and begin completing a Management Plan that is meant to be enhanced over time as the student learns more about the selected topic and develops the project/product. This project does not have to be large in scale. Teachers may want to require students to produce a smaller piece of work the first time they pursue an idea.

The teacher can require each student to identify one area of interest, along with 2–3 sites that will give him or her information about that interest. Then students will create some type of product that demonstrates their learning. The idea here is not to create a big independent project, but to do something smaller in scale. It could be a written report with information from the site, a visual display of new information learned, printouts from a site that help the student create

Resource Name:			
Description:			
What's Good About It	**What's Not Good About It**	**How It Connects to My Learning in School**	**New Thinking or Ideas It Gave Me**

Figure 7. Table for website analysis.

written work, demonstration of a critical thinking game a student learned, or a completed creativity training activity, etc.

The teacher can require each student to select one site to work on for an extended period of time during a session. The student would give the teacher a rationale for his or her use of the site (e.g., I want to learn more about horses and this site has a lot of information about horses; I want to get better at math so that I can learn about baseball stats; I found a site that teaches you how to think more creatively and it is helping me come up with new ideas).

The teacher can identify a site (or a few sites) for students to visit and define an activity to scaffold instruction on how students should be using the sites to enhance their learning. An example could be as follows:

> Students are going to learn about mammals. In order to create a booklet that has different types of mammals, including pictures of the adult and baby of the species, description of their habitat, the food they eat, and other facts, students will be required to locate and go to the sites listed below. The students could then be required to locate one online resource that has information about mammals and use information from that site as well.

The teacher can define a task, such as an online game, to help direct online student learning during compacted time. Suggestions include:

▶ Find a website that will help you in one of your subject areas in school (reading, writing, math, science, social studies). Locate five interesting findings that you think will be new information for your teacher or classmates, and share those at the end of class.

▶ Find a resource that you think would be the best one for your teacher to use with the whole class in a subject area (reading, writing, math, science, social studies). It has to connect with something you are doing in that class right now.

Interest Centers

Creating interest development centers is also an effective strategy that enhances compacting. Unlike traditional learning centers that focus on basic skills, interest centers invite students to investigate topics within a general theme, such as bicycling or the education of people with hearing impairments. Shelves, therefore, must be stocked with manipulative, activity-oriented tools. Films, pamphlets, magazine articles, library books, slides, display items—all are standard fare. Resources that introduce children to research skills, not just reference skills, are valuable, too. An interest center on bicycling, for example, could feature texts on how to make a bike path, seek city council permission to erect public bike racks, or plan a bike safety rodeo.

Interest centers can be created at the back or side of your classroom or even in connection with your library or media specialist. Catchy titles, appealing graphics, and colorful pictures may be added to foam core trifold boards to expose students to areas of interest, as can activities and research suggestions. Because each center can require hours to complete, only a few can be created in a school year, so some teachers share centers within schools or districts as part of a traveling lending library. That way, available centers in each classroom can be changed every 6–8 weeks.

As part of developing an interest center, teachers can display items, links, and electronic resources, as well as narrative information. In our experience, a quality interest development center works best when it includes the items listed in the following sections.

Narrative Information

Introductory books, magazines, professional journals, biographies, career pamphlets, videotapes of public television specials, movies, records, and film-strips are excellent ways to introduce students to interest areas. An interest development center on photography might contain old photographs, old issues of *Digital Photo* or *Popular Photography* magazines, and library books. Many teachers also use newspapers as a source of community talent or current events. Related news articles can be clipped and attached to the interest development center as they are found. Issues of *National Geographic*, *Discover*, or *Scientific American* work well for this.

Information, activities, photos, and exposure to big ideas are popular ways to have students begin to use interest centers that are often developed by teachers but can be jointly completed with students. Women's history, scientific topics such as solar energy and dinosaurs, nutrition, historical events, and big events in political science have been popular topics with elementary and secondary students. Teachers can introduce new centers with a lecture by a community speaker or a webinar. This approach can add interest and motivation for the center's suggested activities.

Suggestions for specific activities, experiments, or research should emerge from an interest center, for even if students are interested in a topic, they may not have sufficient expertise to devise their own exploration or research tasks. As students will have difficulty perceiving real-life problems or societal issues related to this topic, it is appropriate that the teacher recommend readings, investigations, experiments, or activities for further study. But the choice for a long-term investigation should be the student's and not the result of a class or individual assignment. Written suggestions about future study should focus on the topic and stress creative thinking, problem solving, career exploration, higher level thinking, moral dilemmas, imagination, or related academic concerns. Survey ideas, suggestions for sending e-mails, writing letters or making phone calls, gathering data, or developing a product are good possibilities for activity suggestions.

Perhaps an example will help: A center that allows elementary students to explore education of the hearing impaired or sign language might contain 20 or 30 suggestions that vary in complexity like these:

▶ Find out the difference between American Sign Language and signed English. How would you prefer to learn? Which do students who are deaf and teachers of the deaf prefer?

▶ Visit a class for the hearing impaired. What is similar and what is different from your classroom?

> ▸ What is our community doing or not doing to remove communication barriers for people who are deaf?
> ▸ Contact a rehabilitation center and arrange an interview with a client who is deaf.
> ▸ What are some of the problems faced as a result of being deaf? Can you do anything to alleviate one of these problems?
> ▸ Use the sign language dictionaries on this table to learn a few basic signs for the members of your family.

These suggestions are placed on index cards and mounted near the center's pictures or narrative information. Another center on bicycling might include suggestions such as these:

> ▸ Map an original bicycle trip across your state. Include historical stops along the journey.
> ▸ Plan a bicycle safety fundraiser for your community.
> ▸ Develop a bicycle safety talk to present to your class.
> ▸ Find a book, film, or manual that explains gear ratios for your 10-speed bike. Can you draw a chart or graph that explains this gear system?
> ▸ Try your hand at designing a bicycle storage unit for commuters.
> ▸ Compare the costs, features, use, etc., of bicycles on the market.
> ▸ Design safety clothing and gear to be worn on a bike trip.

The age of students and intensity of their interests will ultimately influence a teacher's choice of topics and suggestions for further study in an interest center, and the more ideas one proposes, the more likely it is that one suggestion will spark a student's interest.

Community Resources

Students frequently enjoy having a list of e-mails and phone numbers, names, or addresses of adults willing to let students visit their homes or places of business. Students might also communicate, with adult supervision, with a practicing professional or use the addresses to request brochures and documents about the topic. A weather center we created contains websites of the town's airport-based weather station, the contact information of a local principal who served as a meteorologist in the Armed Forces, and a suggestion to interview a local celebrity who had been accurately predicting our county's number of snowfalls for more than 40 winters. A professor of meteorology also volunteered to demonstrate weather forecasting equipment.

Display Items

A collection of slides, specimens, samples, photographs, tools, or raw materials housed in the center are often prime motivators for students. Good sources for these materials are other teachers, parents, community agencies or clubs, and the children themselves. Students who have completed projects in related areas are usually happy to loan their materials to other children. Poetry, artwork, records, or picture books that deal with the subject may also make useful display items. Once the center is dismantled, these items can be returned to the original owners or stored in an accompanying container.

The components described above comprise most of the necessary ingredients for stimulating the curiosity of students with interest centers. The most important stimulation is how the teacher presents this opportunity to students.

Using Centers in Your Classroom

Although the actual design and construction of the interest center usually takes the majority of the teacher's preparation time, one cannot minimize the importance of the relatively few minutes it takes to display and introduce the new center to students. Decisions about the location of the center, the number of students who will use it at a time, hours of use, and the kinds of students who will have access to it cannot be ignored.

It has been our experience that centers have the greatest effect when they are introduced to the class during a brief overview Type I session conducted by a teacher or speaker. During this time, the speaker can create enthusiasm for the center's topics and activities through the use of an introductory film, speaker, book, or controversial classroom discussion. Current newspaper or magazine articles about the topic are also ideal for this purpose. Directions for using the center's audio-visual equipment can be explained at this time, and demonstrations of some of the center's optional activities can be conducted.

Not all students whose curriculum has been compacted may be interested in exploring the topic of any center, and even fewer will have the necessary task commitment to become involved in long-term projects. This should not be construed as lack of motivation or independence, but more likely a lack of interest in, exposure to, or experience with self-initiated projects. With the introduction of several centers over the school year, we found that many students will become involved in at least one center's activities. In addition, the use of information from students' interest assessments should help focus future center design on topics of greatest interest to the majority of students.

Even more important is the teacher's attitude and behavior toward the use of the interest development center. If, on introducing the new center, the teacher is adamant that this may only be used by students who consistently finish all of their work, students will perceive that interest development centers depend upon basic skills completion. Students may conclude erroneously that activities involving interest exploration and creative production are not as valuable as time spent in textbook assignments and worksheet completion. On the other hand, the teacher who allocates some scheduled amount of time to interest exploration is conveying yet another nonverbal message, one that more closely parallels the philosophy behind strength-based, interest inspiring learning.

By praising and encouraging children to take risks and learn to independently gather information, the teacher can encourage behaviors that most likely will lead to a love of independent learning. The opportunity for students to explore interests and solve real-world problems, rather than to be merely involved in acquiring basic skills at a superior level, seems the most likely way to foster habits that will help all children actualize their potential for creativity and problem solving. Encouraging students to experience risk-taking and independent learning reinforces important behaviors that lead to an understanding of and the capacity to learn and work independently.

In summary, replacing the content when curriculum compacting requires creativity, time, and energy from both teachers and students. Yet, over the years, we've discovered that once a series of exciting and interesting replacement activities based on students' interests and teachers' desires and commitment to differentiate instruction is implemented, teachers (and their students) can actually save precious hours that they would have spent repeating content. Once they identify a broad set of replacement activities, most educators who compact effectively have told us that it takes no longer than their previous teaching practices. More importantly, they tell us that the benefits to their high-potential students, and often many other students, make the effort to differentiate content both important and worthwhile, as students flourish in the classroom and continue to learn new ideas and content that makes school appropriately challenging so that all children continue to make progress.

4
Enrichment, Acceleration, and Grouping Strategies That Enhance Curriculum Compacting

Previous chapters of this book have defined compacting, provided a rationale for its use, and explained how to implement the process. This chapter offers the reader an overview of several different enrichment and acceleration models, as well as grouping strategies, that can be employed to supplant the grade-level curriculum, or a specific curriculum unit, after compacting has been completed. Readers are most like to consider these options when they are selecting learning alternatives and noting them in the third column, "Change It," of the Compactor.

Who makes the decision about what should be done during compacted time? In some cases, the classroom teacher makes the choice; in other situations, the gifted education teacher selects the tasks. Variables such as the availability of resources, time limitations, prior experiences, opinions, school policy, and personal preferences may also have a bearing on these decisions.

The most meaningful alternatives usually involve a collaborative decision made by the student, the classroom teacher, and the gifted education specialist. Educators should consider students' interests, strengths, talents, and personal goals when selecting appropriate alternatives. A mutually acceptable choice is more likely to increase student effort and educator involvement and foster significant academic growth or talent development. Regardless of educators' personal preferences, it is likely that some students would rather explore a new topic than delve more deeply into the concepts or examples aligned with the grade-level curriculum. Still other students prefer acceleration, problem solving, creating, or inventing tasks. To the extent possible, a student's preferences should carry the most weight when making choices about tasks that will be completed during compacted time.

When educators place students' preferences at the forefront of the compacting process, the effectiveness of the process, especially with regard to replacement activities, increases. Such growth can be assessed by measuring changes in student engagement and effort, academic achievement, creativity, critical thinking, or problem solving. Such choices enhance educators' and students' rapport and mutual enjoyment of learning and challenge, but it all begins by keeping student needs, interests, goals, and perspective front and center.

The kinds of choices educators and students make for replacement tasks usually fall into two categories: enrichment or acceleration. Of course, the student and educators must also decide the kind of grouping strategy that best supports either the enrichment or acceleration work. Specialists in the field of gifted education spent decades developing and researching a variety of systems and models that can be used to address the needs, strengths, and learning characteristics of advanced learners and gifted students. These models generally fall into the three categories mentioned above: enrichment, acceleration, and grouping strategies.

Enrichment Models

Researchers who investigated enrichment strategies often focus their work in one of two ways. The first method emphasizes the development and implementation of enrichment experiences based on the interests and talents of children. The second strategy addresses the various ways in which the core academic curriculum could become more challenging, expansive, or intensive.

An in-depth discussion of all of the models that focus on these two kinds of enrichment services is beyond the scope of this book. For this reason, readers are directed to *Systems and Models in Gifted Education* (Renzulli, Gubbins, McMillen, Eckert, & Little, 2009), a text that provides a comprehensive overview of several different enrichment models. Instead, the next section of this chapter provides a brief overview of seven different enrichment models: three that focus on students' interests and talents and four that address techniques for enriching the breadth of the core curriculum. Readers can use these descriptions to help them identify the type of enrichment services that are the best fit for a given student with a compacted curriculum.

Three Enrichment Models That Address Student Interests

The Enrichment Triad Model

Joe Renzulli's research regarding the characteristics of gifted adults led to the development of his Enrichment Triad Model in 1977. Its broad implementation across the world and among all grade levels was made possible by educators who agreed to allow their classrooms to be used as research laboratories to investigate the characteristics of various enrichment services and the most effective strategies for implementation. Compacting was, of course, developed to be used within the Enrichment Triad Model, which is also the curriculum center of the Schoolwide Enrichment Model.

The Enrichment Triad Model includes three different kinds of enrichment activities that could be provided to students with a compacted curriculum. Type I activities offer opportunities to explore diverse topics that may spark student interest and engagement. They also provide experiences designed to deepen understanding about the essential content in a given field. Type II experiences provide technical training with skills, tools, and processes used in various professions and avocations. This training builds expertise and allows participating students to use the methodologies of the practicing professional. Type III investigations involve longer research, inquiry, design, or problem-solving opportunities within a field of strong interest to the student. Although all three of these types of enrichment experiences can be offered to students with a compacted curriculum, Type III investigations are the most frequently used option.

The Autonomous Learner Model

George Betts, a professor at the University of Northern Colorado, developed the Autonomous Learner Model (ALM). This model describes how to create or adapt curriculum components that also emphasize interest-based enrichment. Its goal is to develop students' sense of agency and personal responsibility for their independent learning. Betts's (1986; Betts & Kercher, 2009) research suggested that as students' cognitive, emotional, and social needs are met, they also become more self-directed. The ALM emphasizes self-esteem, social skills, student interests, and in-depth study, as well as interest-based content enrichment.

The ALM contains five different dimensions: Dimension One: Orientation; Dimension Two: Individual Development; Dimension Three: Enrichment; Dimension Four: Seminars; and Dimension Five: In-Depth Study. Across each of these dimensions, participating students investigate their own areas of interest, work closely with mentors, and become independent self-directed learners.

Students with a compacted curriculum may focus on one or all five of these dimensions. As with the Enrichment Triad Model, students usually require the support and services of a mentor, coach, or gifted education/enrichment specialist to facilitate and organize these opportunities.

Purdue Three-Stage Enrichment Model

John Feldhusen and Penny Britton Kolloff (1986) developed a third enrichment model that focuses on elementary students' interests. It is named the Purdue Three-Stage Model. The goal of this model is to create and implement curriculum that develops students' divergent and convergent thinking abilities as well as their creative problem solving abilities. Students who participate in the Three-Stage Model strengthen these skills by applying them to self-selected topics and problems as well as to creative pursuits. The Three-Stage Model can be used to support enrichment and the application of critical and creative thinking skills to the academic curriculum as well as within interest-based enrichment services.

Evaluating and Choosing an Enrichment Model

Educators who are deciding whether any of these three interest-based enrichment models can be used to accompany the compacting process as a replacement for compacted curriculum should first consider the purposes and components of each model. What are its goals? Which model components promote students' growth with each of these goals? Next, educators should identify their own reasons for creating or using replacement curriculum for a student. The chosen model should support these aims. The third consideration asks educators to consider yet another evaluation question. How well does this model, or one of its components, align with a given student's interests, needs, and strengths?

Last, educators need to consider the practical variables—training, resources, use for support personnel, time needed to write the replacement curriculum, time needed to implement the replacement curriculum—that are required to implement a given model. The use of these questions or variables, as part of the decision-making process, should allow users to select the enrichment model best suited to their needs, learner goals, and their teaching environment.

Which approach best fits a student's strength, needs, and interests is a prime consideration. Educators should also consider the time, training, and support necessary to implement the chosen model during compacted time. Will educators write replacement curriculum based on one of these models and use that replacement curriculum during compacted time? Would it be more beneficial to use only one of the components within a given model? Weigh these considerations in light of time demands, the needs for support personal, and most importantly, students' strengths, needs, and preferences.

Four Models That Enrich or Extend the Academic Curriculum

In addition to models that support the development of interest-based curriculum units and tasks, there are at least four other models that describe how to write replacement curriculum aligned to enrich the core academic content for a given grade level or course. Of course, one could also argue that the Enrichment Triad Model enriches the academic curriculum, as well. Under some circumstances, educators or students may find that replacement units or lessons based on these models are better aligned to a student's needs. The next section of this chapter briefly describes these models.

Talents Unlimited

Carol Schlichter used Calvin Taylor's Multiple Talent Approach to develop an academic enrichment model called Talents Unlimited (TU; see http://talentsunlimitedonline.com). This model provides a systematic and user-friendly process for teaching thinking skills in both regular education classrooms and gifted education programs. The Talents Unlimited model identifies five thinking talents. These include: productive thinking, decision making, planning, communication, and forecasting. Taylor identified these skills as common to most adult leaders, designers, and researchers. The Talents Unlimited model supports academic talent development by improving students' thinking skills and by making students aware of their own thinking processes.

Schlichter developed a comprehensive, step-by-step guide for the implementation of Talents Unlimited in the classroom that also defines each of the skills within the model and explains the cognitive steps necessary to implement and apply each of the five thinking skills. Teachers receive information about how and when to teach each of the five skills, and provide for their systematic instruction by including an introduction, explicit instruction, guided practice, reinforcement, and extension opportunities.

Students with a compacted curriculum would benefit from an opportunity to participate in Talents Unlimited lessons, as would all students in the general education classroom. These lessons and practice tasks could potentially be used as part of an independent study contract for a student with a compacted curriculum. In other cases, a student might use compacted time to meet with an enrichment or gifted education specialist to work on lessons designed to teach and apply these skills to academic content. Educators and students who decide that replacement activities that focus on thinking skills are the best enrichment choice for a given student with compacted time will often select Talents Unlimited as the model for developing those replacement lessons or curriculum units.

Kaplan's Depth and Complexity Model

Sandra Kaplan, a former president of the National Association for Gifted Children, and professor for the University of Southern California, developed a second academic enrichment model designed for use with advanced learners. Her model specifies the strategies and options educators can use to create units, lessons, and tasks with greater depth, breadth, and complexity. A curriculum or unit's content, learning processes, and/or products can become the focus for one or more of these three kinds of enrichment. Kaplan strongly recommends that educators begin by learning as much as possible about the unique characteristics of individuals with academic talent and then create curricula that align with these characteristics.

Kaplan specifies distinct components that should be included in the construction of differentiated curricula for the gifted. These elements include: the identification of the unit's essential elements, the format in which to present the curriculum, and an emphasis on the use of interdisciplinary themes as opposed to a focus on topics. Her accessible, practical system for organizing and expanding curriculum involves the organization of units of study that could easily become the foundation or backbone for replacement curriculum. Educators who plan to use Kaplan's model as the framework for replacement curriculum or tasks would benefit from training, readings, and a review of sample lessons and units. Students interested in learning academic content at greater levels of depth or complexity are the ideal audience for alternative tasks based on her model.

Integrated Curriculum Model

A third academic enrichment model was created by Joyce VanTassel-Baska, another former president of the National Association for Gifted Children, and a former professor from William & Mary. VanTassel-Baska designed the Integrated

Curriculum Model (ICM) for use with gifted learners. The model itself is based on Vygotsky's concept of Zone of Proximal Development, focusing on the importance of providing students with curriculum and learning tasks that support new and challenging learning, based on conceptual level and cognitive demand.

Three interrelated elements provide the foundation for the model, including components that support the teaching and learning of advanced content; attention to the overarching concepts, issues, and themes related to a given topic or academic discipline; and a process and product facet.

When educators use the Advanced Content Dimension, they engage students in pretesting to identify students' individual levels of proficiency within a specific subject area. Later, they identify and prescribe discipline-based content, concepts, and principles that align with individual students' Zone of Proximal Development. This content is learned and taught using strategies such as acceleration, compacting, and a focus on content that is typically addressed at higher grade levels.

The Process-Product Dimension of the models calls for student use of higher level thinking skills (process) to analyze and make sense of the advanced or complex content. It also supports the use of students' problem-solving and problem-finding skills as they apply the learned content to new endeavors, authentic issues, and unanswered inquiry questions. When working with the Overarching Concepts/Issues/Themes Dimension, students make connections between the advanced concepts and content they have learned and that content's overarching themes.

Educators and students who choose to use the Integrated Curriculum Model as a replacement for compacted lessons and units often do so when the desired goal is student exposure to more complex content and concepts. A number of educators have authored and published examples of Integrated Curriculum Model units, making preparation and implementation easier to achieve.

Multiple Menu Model

In addition to the Enrichment Triad Model, Renzulli also developed a second curriculum model, called the Multiple Menu Model. His framework for this model is the fourth of the curriculum designs described in this book that provide enrichment by altering various aspects of a student's academic curriculum.

The Multiple Menu Model (MMM) includes six planning guides that serve as menus during the curriculum development process. MMM's six planning components include the Knowledge Menu, the Instructional Objectives and Student Activities Menu, the Instructional Strategies Menu, the Instructional Sequences Menu, the Artistic Modification Menu, and the Instructional Products Menu, which is composed of two interrelated menus, Concrete Products and Abstract Products Menu.

The first menu, the Knowledge Menu, is the most elaborate and focuses on the essential concepts in the selected field of study (e.g., mythology, astronomy, choreography, geometry). The second through fifth menus deal with pedagogy or instructional techniques. The last menu, Instructional Products, is related to the types of products that may result from student interactions with knowledge about a domain or interdisciplinary concepts and how that knowledge is constructed by firsthand inquirers.

Although it was originally developed as a way of differentiating curriculum for high-ability students, the MMM curriculum development guide can easily be used by teachers who want to encourage firsthand inquiry and creativity among all students. It differs from traditional approaches to curriculum design by placing a greater emphasis on balancing authentic content and process, involving students as firsthand inquirers, and exploring the structure and interconnectedness of knowledge.

An analysis of these and other enrichment theories described in the *Systems and Models* book (referenced above) suggests that the following elements broadly describe enrichment theories that can accompany and extend the compacting process: they are interest-based; integrate advanced content, processes, and products; include broad interdisciplinary themes; foster effective independent and autonomous learning; provide compacted, individualized, and differentiated curriculum and instruction; develop creative problem solving abilities and creativity; and integrate the tools of the practicing professionals in the development of products.

Acceleration

In much the same way that a comprehensive description of the systems and models that can be used to provide curriculum enrichment is beyond the scope of this book, the same can be said for a comprehensive explanation of acceleration strategies. This segment of the chapter defines acceleration, describes its rationale, includes an explanation of two forms of acceleration, and provides examples. This section concludes with a description of an additional curriculum model that combines both enrichment and acceleration.

Acceleration is an academic intervention that enables advanced students to learn rigorous content and skills aligned to their prior knowledge, cognitive skills, and learning rate. Acceleration can also be used when educators want to allow some learners in a class to progress through the grade-level curriculum at a faster pace than provided through whole-group instruction. Acceleration reduces repetitive class work and eliminates practice tasks that are unnecessary for students who have already demonstrated mastery of specific standards, concepts, and skills.

There are two common forms of acceleration: (a) allowing students to attend classes or grade levels typically reserved for older students, and (b) pretesting students in a class and allowing some students to progress through the unit or curriculum at their own rate. Grade skipping, early entrance to kindergarten, and cross-grade-level instruction for one subject area are typical examples of the first type of acceleration. Online enrollment, computer adaptive learning, continuous progress, the Joplin plan, tiered assignments, and reading groups are examples of the second type of compacting.

Tiered Assignments

It is clear that the differentiation of instruction and content and curriculum compacting enables students to work at varied levels of content and task difficulty. The most common strategy usually suggested for advanced learners is to compact and accelerate their curriculum by providing them with content material that is beyond the grade-level expectations. One way to accomplish this goal is to provide all or some of the students in a class with tiered instruction and work.

Tiering involves the identification of all students' current knowledge and skill level with regard to a given curriculum standard or set of standards. Relevant and realistic progress goals for individuals or small groups stem from the analysis of this preassessment data. Students' current or prior knowledge is typically categorized in two or more levels, from basic understandings expected of students in lower grade levels, to grade-level expectations, to advanced or more complex learning goals.

Tiering occurs when an individual student's learning goals, teaching, and work is aligned with prior knowledge, cognitive skills, and level of engagement and effort. Progress goals become reachable by identifying the essential concepts and skills embedded in the standards statement, clarifying the time allocation for this content, and determining what is essential for each small group of students to learn, based on their current understandings. Each group learns, practices, and applies its tiered concepts and skills to tasks and applications that represent personal challenge, effort, and growth.

Tiered assignments and projects enable those students who have already mastered basic content to have the opportunity to discuss controversial issues, engage in more advanced independent work, and participate in less-structured teaching activities. Tiered teaching and tasks allow teachers to assign increasingly challenging content, critical and creative thinking skills practice, and enrichment activities. Examples of effective ways to combine tiering with curriculum compacting include:

- ▶ Use compacting to eliminate or streamline work that some students have already mastered and replace that work with appropriately challenging, tiered work.
- ▶ Accelerate the curriculum and provide tiered work to challenge students at different levels of proficiency.
- ▶ Use tiered technology and web-based assignments to provide challenging enrichment.
- ▶ Assign more complex independent or small-group writing assignments
- ▶ Provide enrichment centers in the classroom that offer tiered levels of challenge.
- ▶ Assign increasingly more complex creative or critical thinking tasks.
- ▶ Provide tiered independent or group study opportunities.
- ▶ Make changes in the way students are grouped (within class or across classes).
- ▶ Ask students to read books at different reading levels, but with similar themes. Use discussion groups to compare and contrast the ways in which the authors use literary elements to convey the theme.
- ▶ Ask tiered questions that vary with regard to the thinking skills that must be used to process the question's information.

The most comprehensive research available on the use of acceleration and curriculum enhancement demonstrates that its use results in higher achievement for gifted and talented learners (Colangelo et al., 2004). Educational researchers and practitioners working at the University of Iowa have produced materials and created a comprehensive website (http://accelerationinstitute.org) for teachers, parents, and policy makers that explains, clearly and succinctly, the definitions and benefits of acceleration.

Students with a compacted curriculum are likely candidates for acceleration services. Of course, prerequisites include the availability of appropriate resources and schedules, access to facilitators and monitors, student interest, and a willingness to work with rigorous content.

Combining Enrichment and Acceleration Services

Schoolwide Enrichment Model for Reading

Sally Reis and a team of reading and gifted education specialists developed and researched a hybrid curriculum model called the Schoolwide Enrichment Model in Reading (SEM-R). Its structure combines the benefits of content enrichment, interest-based enrichment, and acceleration with a focus on reading (Reis et al., 2007; Reis et al., 2008). SEM-R provides students with challenging, self-selected reading text, accompanied by instruction in high-level thinking and reading strategies. A third focus of the SEM-R is the differentiation of reading, phonics, and comprehension skills and strategies based on assessment evidence. Compacting and acceleration are natural byproducts of this type of differentiation. The SEM-R program challenges and prepares advanced readers to broaden their reading genre, to read more fluently, and to understand and analyze more complex informative text and literature. The program also encourages lifelong reading habits and fosters improved attitudes toward reading.

The goals of the SEM-R approach are to encourage children to begin to enjoy the reading process by giving them access to high-interest, self-selected books that they can read for extended periods of time at school and at home; to develop independence and self-regulation in reading through the selection of these books as well as the opportunity to have individualized reading instruction; and, finally, to enable all students to improve in reading fluency and comprehension through the use of reading comprehension strategies.

The SEM-R strategy for providing students with a challenging reading curriculum includes three phases. During Phase 1, the "exposure" phase, teachers provide short read-alouds using high-quality, engaging literature that introduce students to a wide variety of titles, genres, authors, and topics. Along with these read-alouds, teachers offer modeling and discussion, demonstrate reading strategies and self-regulation skills, and use higher order questions to guide text discussions.

Early in the SEM-R implementation, these Phase 1 activities last about 20 minutes per day; Phase 1 decreases in length over the course of the year when students are able to spend more time on Phase 2. The goal is to have all students read in Phase 2 for about 50–60 minutes each day.

Phase 2 of the SEM-R emphasizes the development of students' capacity to engage in supported independent reading (SIR) of self-selected, appropriately challenging text. Teachers provide instructional support during reading conferences. During Phase 2, students select books that are at least 1 to 1.5 grade levels above their current independent reading levels. Students use learned strategies to select appropriately challenging books that are also of high personal interest. This latter criterion promotes increased student engagement when students are working with challenging vocabulary, text structure, and content. Research studies regarding the implementation of SEM-R provide evidence that participating students increased their independent reading stamina from 5–15 minutes per session to almost an hour each day.

During this in-class independent reading time, students also participate in individual reading conferences with their teachers. On average, each student participates in one to two conferences per week, usually lasting about 5–7 minutes each. In these conferences, teachers and instructional aides assess reading fluency and comprehension and provide individual and personalized instruction in needed reading skills, including predicting, using inferences, and making connections. For more advanced readers, conferences focus less on specific reading strategies and more on higher order questions and genre and text criticism.

During Phase 3, teachers encourage students to move from teacher-directed learning opportunities to self-chosen activities. Activities include (but are not limited to) opportunities to explore new technology, discussion groups, practice with advanced questioning and thinking skills, creativity training in language arts, learning centers, interest-based projects, free reading, and book chats. These experiences provide time for students to pursue areas of personal interest through the use of interest development centers and the Internet. Students learn to read critically and to locate other reading materials, especially high-quality, challenging literature. Students also have options for independent study and Type III investigations (part of Renzulli's Enrichment Triad offerings). The length of Phase 3 varies and is based on the length of the other phases, with more or less time devoted to Phase 3 on particular days depending on individual student progress with independent reading and the need for independent project time.

During the research phase for the SEM-R model, all teachers who implement the program received approximately 350 high-interest books across several reading levels. Teachers augmented their collections as needed, choosing literature and informative texts based on students' interests and experiences. Teachers who did not have an extensive classroom library worked with the school or local librarian/media specialist to borrow needed books.

Teachers also used sets of specially developed bookmarks that listed higher order questions for use during reading conference. These are available free of charge at http://www.gifted.uconn.edu/semr. Each bookmark includes three to five questions that address a specific literary element, theme, skill, reading standard, or genre. Teachers use the bookmarks in both Phase 1 discussions and Phase 2 conferences to promote higher order thinking. Within the SEM-R framework, students also author weekly writing selections.

After almost a decade of research, the implementation of SEM-R has proven to be an effective model for increasing achievement in reading and encouraging talented readers to read more challenging material for longer periods of time. For students in need of a compacted reading curriculum, SEM-R can provide the direction for replacement and enrichment teaching and learning tasks in reading. The SEM-R has been found to be effective at increasing reading fluency and comprehension scores, as well as changing attitudes toward reading for elementary and middle students placed at risk of poor reading performance due to poverty, attendance at a low-performing school, or linguistic diversity (Reis & Boeve, 2009; Reis et al., 2007; Reis et al., 2008; Reis & Housand, 2009). In the SEM-R, students' strengths and interests are analyzed and reading instruction is delivered through the use of gifted education pedagogy, including curricular differentiation (both acceleration and enrichment), as well as instructional differentiation using Renzulli Learning/GoQuest. Research by Reis and colleagues (Reis & Boeve, 2010; Reis et al., 2007; Reis et al., 2008; Reis & Housand, 2009) suggested that students of various achievement levels have benefitted from the SEM-R approach. Gifted students as well other lower achieving students who participated in the enriched and accelerated SEM-R program had significantly higher scores in reading fluency and comprehension than students in the control group, who did not participate in the SEM-R. Results show achievement differences favoring the SEM-R treatment across all levels, including students who read well above, at, and below grade level (Reis et al., 2007; Reis et al., 2008; Reis et al., 2009).

Grouping Strategies for Academically Talented Students

The capacity to deftly negotiate large-group, small-group, partner, and individual instruction lies at the heart of effective compacting. For this reason, one of the most important choices a teacher makes during the compacting process pertains to decisions about how to group students for instruction and learning tasks. Flexible grouping practices makes compacting much less demanding, as it reduces the ranges of achievement in a group, and allows teachers to more readily address the needs of their students.

Note that flexible grouping is very different from tracking. Tracking is defined as the permanent placement of students into a homogeneous class or learning group based on a single criteria or test score. Flexible grouping, on the other hand, places students in either homogeneous or heterogeneous groups for a short period of time in order to address a temporary instructional need, or a single learning standard or task. Both tracking and flexible grouping can focus on remedial, intervention, accelerated, or enriched content and curriculum.

The results of several research studies (Gentry, 2014) suggested that cluster grouping gifted students together to provide differentiated curriculum and instruction increases their achievement. Talented students who were grouped together and received advanced enrichment or acceleration outperformed control group students, who were not grouped and did not receive enrichment or acceleration. Our colleague, Marcia Gentry, who studied cluster grouping with academically talented students, found that students at high, medium, and low levels all benefitted from cluster grouping when it was accompanied by differentiated instruction and content. In cluster grouping, high-achieving students are grouped in a cluster and then placed in a class with other students of heterogeneous achievement. High and low-achievement clusters are placed in separate classes to reduce the overall range of ability in each class. Students who were in cluster groups and who received advanced and enriched learning opportunities scored significantly higher than students who were not cluster grouped (Gentry, 2014). Other studies that researched flexible grouping strategies found similar benefits for students with average and below-average achievement levels (Gentry & Owen, 1999; Kulik, 1992; Rogers, 1991; Tieso, 2002). However, grouping alone, without curricular acceleration or enrichment produces few differences in student achievement.

Enrichment Clusters

Enrichment clusters (Renzulli, Gentry, & Reis, 2013), a component of the Schoolwide Enrichment Model, are flexible interest opportunities for nongraded groups of students who share common interests and who are grouped together during specially designated time blocks to work with an adult who shares their interests and who has some degree of advanced knowledge and expertise in the area. Although many schools offer enrichment clusters to all students, during a common time block in the school week, they may also be used as replacement learning opportunities for students with a compacted curriculum. In this situation, teachers in a grade level or subject area would agree on a common time for students with a compacted curriculum to meet in cross-class groupings to work on interest-based explorations and investigations. The implementation of enrichment clusters is an excellent way to identify and address student interests and to help teachers more effectively replace content eliminated during the compacting process.

A series of clusters can be planned and implemented for all students on a weekly basis in both the fall and spring. For example, in many SEM schools, clusters are held for 90 minutes each Friday afternoon from late September through

December as a way to introduce various enrichment topics and to provide authentic enrichment experiences for all students.

Students first complete an interest inventory developed to assess their interests (see Appendix B). An enrichment coordinator tallies all of the major families of interests and then recruits teachers and other professionals in the school to facilitate enrichment clusters based on these interests, often including areas such as drama, history, creative writing, drawing, music, archeology, science, and engineering.

Cluster facilitators participate in professional learning opportunities and parents receive a brochure with descriptions of the planned enrichment clusters. Students select their top three choices for the clusters and a coordinator places all children into one of the selected clusters. Like extracurricular activities and programs such as 4-H and Junior Achievement, the main rationale for participation in one or more clusters is that students and teachers want to be there. All teachers (including music, art, physical education, etc.) are involved in facilitating the clusters, and their involvement in any particular cluster is based on the same type of interest assessment that is used for students in selecting clusters of choice. Our research on clusters has also suggested that the use of enrichment clusters results in increased use of advanced thinking and research skills in gifted and in other students as well (Reis, Gentry, & Maxfield, 1998).

Renzulli Learning/GoQuest

Interest-based learning opportunities are extremely important for students who want to explore new topics, investigate issues and problems, and develop their personal talents and areas of expertise. However, scheduling and time constraints can often make it difficult for teachers to organize these interest-based events and sessions. When large- or small-group interest-based gatherings become prohibitive, many educators turn to online offerings to address students' strengths and talents.

One such example of technology-driven enrichment is a system formerly known as Renzulli Learning and now called GoQuest. In the past, schools that used the SEM administered paper-and-pencil student surveys and questionnaires about their interests, product preferences. In 2007, Renzulli developed software that supports both the administration of these instruments and their data analysis. Using desktop computers or mobile technology, each student completes a profile that describes his or her unique strengths and talents. Teachers can search for data patterns across the three types of instruments and use the data to plan personalized learning experiences.

Learning style categories include projects, independent study, teaching games, simulations, peer teaching, programmed instruction, lecture, drill and recitation, and discussion. Product style preferences include the kinds of products students like to complete, such as those that are written, oral, hands-on, artistic, displays, dramatization, service, and multimedia. Data regarding students' interests are combined with these two pieces of data and students are matched with specific online learning opportunities that reflect their interests, learning styles, and product preferences.

A search engine matches student strengths and interests to an enrichment database of more than 50,000 enrichment activities, materials, resources, and opportunities grouped into the following categories: virtual field trips, real field trips, creativity training, critical thinking, projects and independent study, contests and competitions, websites, fiction and nonfiction books, summer programs, online activities, research skills, and high-interest videos and DVDs. These resources are not merely intended to inform students about new information or to occupy time surfing around the web. Rather, they are used as vehicles to help students find and focus a problem or creative exploration of personal interest to pursue in greater depth. Many of the resources provide the methods of inquiry, advanced level thinking and creative problem solving skills, and investigative approaches of professionals in the discipline. Students are guided toward the application of knowledge to develop original research studies, creative projects, and action-oriented undertakings that put knowledge to work in personally meaningful areas of interest. Many resources also include suggestions of outlets and audiences for their creative products.

A project management tool guides students and teachers to use specifically selected resources for assigned curricular activities, independent or small-group investigative projects, and a wide variety of challenging enrichment experiences. The Wizard Project Maker helps students focus their web-based explorations and undertake original research, investigative projects, and the development of a wide variety of creative undertakings. Specifically, the Project Maker provides support for the metacognitive skills of defining a project and setting a goal; identifying and evaluating both the resources to which they have access and the resources they need (e.g. time, websites, teacher or mentor assistance); prioritizing and refining goals; balancing the resources needed to meet multiple goals; learning from past actions; projecting future outcomes; monitoring progress; and making necessary adjustments as a project unfolds.

Finally, Renzulli Learning/GoQuest enables the automatic compilation and storage of all student work and responses into an ongoing student record called the Total Talent Portfolio (TTP). This management tool allows students to evaluate each site visited and resource used. Students can complete a self-assessment, and if they choose, they can store favorite activities and resources in their portfolio.

This feature allows easy return access to ongoing work. The portfolio can be reviewed at any time by teachers and parents through the use of an access code that allows teachers to give feedback and guidance to individual students and provides parents with information about students' work and opportunities for parental involvement. The TTP can travel with students throughout their school years and serves as a reminder of previous activities and creative accomplishments that they might want to include in college applications. It is an ongoing record that can help students, teachers, guidance counselors, and parents make decisions about future educational and vocational plans. Teachers can also make use of the TTP within Renzulli Learning/GoQuest by placing differentiated, tiered, and compacted assignments directly into students' portfolios. Renzulli Learning/GoQuest enables students to access enrichment services anywhere and at any time they have Internet access.

Field (2009) studied the use of this innovative online enrichment program with students in both an urban and suburban school. In this 16-week experimental study, all students who participated in this enrichment program and used Renzulli Learning for 2–3 hours each week demonstrated significantly higher growth in reading comprehension than control group students who did not participate in the program. Students also demonstrated significantly higher growth in oral reading fluency and in social studies achievement than those students who did not participate (Field, 2009).

Conclusion

Educators enhance the effectiveness of curriculum compacting through the careful and purposive selection of appropriate replacement tasks. This chapter reviewed the various types of replacement and enhancement work, including subject area enrichment, interest-based enrichment, acceleration, and tiering. The text also described hybrid models that combine one or more types of enrichment with both compacting and acceleration. In addition, readers examined the tenets, components, and research findings about the various systems and models designed to provide these services. Flexible grouping supports the organization and management of teaching and learning tasks that replace the compacted curriculum. Technology and online resources provide alternatives for both enrichment tasks and content acceleration.

5

Compacting Challenges and Research-Based Strategies to Address These Issues

This chapter summarizes several of the challenges encountered by teachers who implement compacting. Also included is an explanation of some of our most important research on the effects of compacting (Reis & Purcell, 1993; Reis et al., 1993; Reis, Westberg et al., 1998). Finally, this chapter shares effective strategies that can be used to implement compacting.

Challenges Associated With Compacting

Teachers who are interested in providing a more appropriate content or skills curriculum for their above-average-ability students will undoubtedly encounter several challenges when they initiate the compacting process. Although none of these issues are insurmountable, they must be recognized and considered as concerns that need to be addressed if compacting is to be effective and successful. In this section of the chapter, we describe the seven most frequent challenges that can be anticipated when implementing a curriculum compacting initiative.

Challenge #1: Repetition Within the Grade-Level Curriculum

One problem that teachers frequently encounter is caused by the repetition of content and practice opportunities built into many commercial resources and curriculum units. A quick glance at the scope and sequence chart of a curriculum guide or the teachers' handbook within a textbook series often reveals the extent of curriculum repetition. Most publishers list the learning objectives for each of several grade levels in this kind of chart, and by examining the similarities and progressions between the grade levels, the extent of repetition can be measured or estimated.

The repetition of content, skills, and practice tasks is often necessary for novice learners who are trying to master challenging concepts or multistep skills and procedures. However, repetition becomes redundancy when one, some, or several students demonstrate mastery of the standards prior to instruction, or after a brief introduction to the content. Such mastery can be determined through student responses to formative assessment questions or tasks.

When advanced learners—who have already mastered the related standards, concepts, and skills—encounter such repetition, it often causes them to lose some of their motivation for learning. Lack of engagement can also result. At the very least, the mandatory, whole-class assignment of practice tasks and assignments that address previously mastered learning goals represents a loss of valuable learning time for advanced students.

Challenge #2: Prevalence of Whole-Class Instruction and Common Assignments

In order to deal with this problem, teachers must abandon the assumption that every student in the class needs to learn every one of the grade-level learning goals and standards. This assumption needs to be replaced with a premise that surmises that one or more students in any classroom may already have prior knowledge, familiarity, or mastery of one or more of the grade-level learning goals in a given subject area or curriculum unit.

When this theory of action supplants a whole-group instruction mindset, it also opens the door to standards-based preassessment, formative assessment, and the implementation of introductory learning activities that invite students to verbalize or demonstrate what they already know about the content within a new curriculum unit.

Rather than assuming that every objective in a textbook's scope and sequence chart represents new or relevant learning for every student, the teacher must determine which goals, standards, and learning objectives are most appropriate for academically talented students. In order to decide whether such repetition is appropriate, the teacher must determine the grade level at which the skill or content objective is first introduced, and what differences in complexity, if any, exist when the skill is reintroduced at a later grade. Students can then be preassessed on these objectives to determine to what extent they have already mastered them, keeping in mind that it is critical to eliminate repetition of mastered content.

Challenge #3: Poor Curriculum Articulation and Clarity

In some school districts, teachers who are willing to entertain the concept of curriculum compacting are often stymied by the absence of grade-level curriculum guides that contain measureable content and skills standards, goals, and objectives. In other cases, some teachers report that they do not understand the behavior that students must exhibit to demonstrate mastery of a given standard or learning goal.

The absence of district or state department learning standards and learning goals often causes teachers to question which content and skills students are expected to learn. The Common Core State Standards (for English language arts and math), the Next Generation Science Standards, the National Council of Social Studies, and the National Association for Gifted Children learning standards, mentioned earlier in this book, all can be used by a curriculum committee or teacher to create a well-sequenced and standards-based curriculum that becomes the basis for compacting. Without such a clear understanding of major curricular goals and objectives, curriculum compacting becomes extremely difficult.

Challenge #4: Lack of Support for Innovation and Change

Even though the arguments in favor of curriculum compacting are extremely compelling, the negative attitudes of colleagues can dampen the enthusiasm of teachers trying to use this practice. The reading supervisor who will not allow a classroom teacher to use out-of-level testing, the educator evaluation system that judges teachers negatively if all students are not working on the same learning target at the same time, or the fourth-grade teacher who objects when a third-grade teacher wants to accelerate bright students into grade 4 math can all create an adverse impact on a teacher who is trying to implement the curriculum compacting process.

Several school districts with whom we have worked report that one way to overcome the potential problems associated with negative attitudes toward compacting, enrichment, and acceleration is to convene a task force of parents, teachers, and curriculum specialists to study the practice of curriculum compacting and recommend related school and district policy. A district policy that describes both the definition of curriculum compacting and the necessary procedures for identifying appropriate student candidates as well as the implementation procedures not only sanctions, but promotes its use.

In addition to a formal policy adoption by the school board, efforts to increase parents' understanding of the compacting process often prompts participating parents to ask for or question the need for compacting during parent conferences and in home-school communication. Brief descriptions of curriculum compacting on the website for the school or district's gifted program and informational workshops by teachers, administrators, and gifted education specialists can also enhance stakeholders' appreciation for curriculum compacting within the school climate and create greater awareness of its usefulness and importance.

Challenge #5: Insufficient Enrichment Resources

Another challenge to compacting that must be confronted is the need for appropriate and engaging enrichment and acceleration materials or resources for the students whose curriculum has been compacted. It is of little benefit to compact 6 months of a child's math standards and tasks if the teacher has no enrichment or acceleration options to offer in place of the grade-level curriculum.

If a gifted education or enrichment specialist is available, this individual can certainly help the student pursue investigations or research during compacted time. Yet again, if there is little expertise about gifted education in the school or district, compacting can still be implemented if the appropriate supplemental resources are available.

As mentioned in previous chapters, many new opportunities exist to enrich and engage students with technology as well as a multitude of research-based strategies. The use of books on tape, eBooks, computer software, interest centers, classroom libraries, small-group instruction, mentors, and independent study can all provide enrichment and acceleration in the regular classroom. With Internet access, a nearly endless supply of enrichment, acceleration, and independent study becomes available for these students. In order to provide these options, a committee of classroom teachers or media specialists can work together to organize and share various enrichment and acceleration materials with classroom teachers who are implementing curriculum compacting.

Challenge #6: Weak Classroom and Time Management Procedures

Curriculum compacting can assure content mastery, alleviate curriculum repetition, and provide time for enrichment and acceleration, but the procedure can run into implementation problems if the necessary classroom management procedures are not yet in place. Students who are working with the grade-level curriculum can complain that it isn't fair that some students are working on enrichment projects while they are repeating basic instruction and practice. Students with a compacted curriculum can become concerned that they seem to be "teaching themselves" when they are asked to work on an accelerated or enrichment curriculum without the necessary teacher monitoring, feedback, or instruction.

Compacting becomes an accepted part of classroom expectations when students, as a result of their beginning-of-the-year orientation activities, come to understand why different learners may be working on different tasks at different points in time. When students understand that they will be spending time working alone, with different partners, in different small groups, and as a member of the whole class at other times, they learn to expect flexible grouping as a natural response to different student needs, strengths, and interests.

In addition to explaining differentiation, pretesting, and flexible grouping, all students, regardless of their academic proficiency, need to understand that they will be allowed to participate in interest-based options at appropriate times within the curriculum. This type of orientation and explanation alleviates students' concerns about "fairness." Students who are comfortable with differentiated instruction and assignments rarely become concerned when students with a compacted curriculum are working on tasks that are different from their own work.

Challenge #7: The Lack of Professional Learning Opportunities

The last, but possibly the most important issue that confounds the implementation of compacting is a lack of effective professional learning opportunities. Although differentiation is often mentioned in many undergraduate and graduate courses, with compacting being one of the related strategies discussed under its umbrella, these participating preservice and inservice educators usually spend most of their time reviewing the rationale and strategies for compacting or planning an example of compacting. For compelling reasons, far less time in these undergraduate and graduate classes is spent actually implementing compacting and addressing its inherent screening, pretesting, and management phases. Unfortunately, it is the coached practice of compacting under supervised conditions, with modeling and feedback, and not the conceptual awareness of its strategies and rationale, that lead to its successful implementation under actual classroom conditions.

This book provides most of what teachers need to know about the compacting process to get started. But before teachers become interested enough to take the time to read a book like this on compacting, professional development should be provided to introduce them to the concept.

If, as a result of the professional development, a teacher, enrichment specialist, or principal becomes committed to implementing curriculum compacting as a school or district policy, interested educators will then need to experiment with compacting and practice adopting and modifying the examples and techniques discussed in this book to meet their own style and classroom management strategies, as well as to engage and challenge their students.

What types of professional development are necessary for teachers to implement a new strategy like compacting? We have found, over many years, that introduction of the strategy, followed by time for trial and error, accompanied by support and time to reflect is critically important. Research on professional development has consistently suggested ways to best implement a new practice. The best professional development includes brief information about the theory and research underlying the strategy, a demonstration of how to accomplish the new strategy, initial practice using the strategy, and prompt feedback about the strategy and coaching to improve in its use.

Research Regarding the Impact of Compacting

We have conducted several studies (Reis et al., 1993; Reis & Purcell, 1993; Reis, Westberg et al., 1998) to learn more about how teachers implement curriculum compacting for high-achieving students. As a result of these studies, a great deal has been learned about effective compacting strategies. This section of Chapter 6 describes those studies and the conclusions drawn from the research we have conducted.

Teachers Have a Strong Interest in Learning about Curriculum Compacting

In our work, we have found that teachers want to understand the theory and guiding principles behind the practice of compacting. Many educators are also interested in the impact of compacting on student achievement. Many have reported that the assessment data and achievement gains that result from curriculum compacting have given them the confidence needed to initiate the process themselves.

Professional Development Is a Crucial Component That Predicts the Success of a Compacting Initiative

In our largest national study on compacting (Reis et al., 1993), teachers from 20 school districts throughout the country were randomly assigned by district to three treatment groups that provided increasing levels of staff development. After receiving staff development services, teachers implemented curriculum compacting for one or two students in their classroom who were identified on the basis of their advanced academic abilities.

Seven other school districts were randomly assigned to serve as the control group. The control group teachers identified one or two high-ability students and continued normal teaching practices without implementing curriculum compacting.

Teachers Can Successfully Assess, Enrich, and Accelerate the Curriculum for Their High-Achieving Students

A battery of achievement tests (out-of-level Iowa Tests of Basic Skills [ITBS]), content area preference scales, and a questionnaire regarding attitudes toward learning were given to identified students at the beginning and end of the school year. The most important findings from our curriculum compacting study are included below:

- ► Ninety-five percent of the participating teachers were able to identify high-ability students in their classes and document students' strengths.
- ► Approximately 50% of grade-level content and assignments in mathematics, language arts, science, and social studies could be eliminated or compacted for selected students.
- ► The most frequently compacted subject was mathematics, followed by language arts. Science and social studies were also compacted when students demonstrated very high achievement and ability in those areas.
- ► A majority of the teachers in all three treatment groups said they would compact curriculum again; additional teachers remarked that they would implement compacting again if they had additional information and assistance from a specialist.
- ► A significant difference was found among treatment groups with respect to the overall quality of curriculum compacting, as measured by teachers' documentation on the Compactor form. Those teachers who received the highest quality and greatest amount of professional development (e.g., watching a professional lecture on compacting, reading the book about compacting, and then receiving peer support and coaching) had significantly higher quality Compactor forms than teachers who had less professional support.
- ► Eighty percent of the teachers in the three experimental groups were able to document the curriculum that high-achieving students had yet to master. These teachers could also list appropriate instructional strategies for assessing students and measuring mastery. These teachers were also able to identify and adhere to an appropriate achievement level to indicate mastery.

- ▶ Replacement strategies consisted of three broad instructional activities: enrichment, acceleration, and "other" (peer tutoring, cooperative learning, correcting class papers).
- ▶ The majority (95%) of teachers used enrichment as a replacement strategy, while another 18% also used acceleration.
- ▶ Approximately 60% of the replacement strategies reflected students' interests, needs, and preferences.
- ▶ Three different types of requests were made by teachers as they compacted curriculum:
  - ▷ additional time for students to work with the gifted or enrichment specialist (if one was available);
  - ▷ assistance in locating additional appropriate enrichment and acceleration materials; and
  - ▷ assistance from a colleague, coach, or specialist to support teachers' decision making and planning during the compacting process.

- ▶ When teachers eliminated as much as 50% of the regular curriculum for gifted students, no differences in the out-of-level postachievement test (ITBS) results between treatment and control groups were found in math computation, social studies, spelling, or reading.
- ▶ In science, students with a compacted curriculum scored significantly higher on the out-of-level posttest (ITBS) than did the students in the control group whose curriculum was not compacted.
- ▶ Students whose curriculum was compacted in mathematics scored significantly higher on the math concepts posttest (ITBS) than those in the control group.

The findings from this study strongly suggested that classroom teachers can effectively implement curriculum compacting after being provided with just a few hours of professional development. These same teachers were also able to provide more appropriate, differentiated educational experiences for gifted and talented students.

Teachers Need Support to Implement Compacting on a Regular Basis

Additional professional development and peer coaching can increase teachers' use of the compacting strategy and improve the quality of the compacting process. It is especially important to allocate time and coaching to support teachers' ability to identify or develop appropriately challenging replacement content for students whose curriculum has been modified. Overwhelmingly, the teachers who were randomly selected to participate in one of the three levels of treatment within the curriculum compacting study found that compacting had a positive effect for their students.

Recommendations for Implementation

Over time, several recommendations for implementing curriculum compacting successfully have emerged from our research and field-testing. Attention to these findings provides guidance during the planning and implementation phases of a new compacting initiative. The consideration and application of these principles increases the likelihood of success and continued use of the compacting process.

Recommendation #1: Start Small

Begin the compacting process by targeting a small group of students for whom compacting seems especially appropriate. We have found that in the earliest stages of learning how to compact, it is better to try to implement the service for two or three students than it is to tackle a whole reading group or an entire classroom. Learning how to preassess, finding available pretests and other means of learning how much content students already know, identifying the students' interests or talent areas, modifying curriculum, and replacing regular curriculum with interesting and challenging alternatives takes time and effort. Therefore, starting with two or three students who obviously require the service makes the process easier.

Recommendation #2: Select One Content Area

Select a content area to start the compacting process in which: (a) the targeted student has demonstrated previous mastery or curriculum strengths, and (b) teachers have the most resources available to pretest for prior mastery and to enrich or accelerate the content. Research (Reis et al., 1993; Reis, Westberg et al., 1998) on the compacting process has demonstrated that the most frequently compacted content areas are mathematics, language arts, and spelling (which is often taught separately from language arts). The percentage of content eliminated in mathematics ranged from 39%–49%; in language arts, between 36%–54%. Teachers preferred compacting in mathematics and language arts because it is easier to compact basic skills than content. Most teachers beginning the compacting process (approximately 70%) only compacted in one content area at first.

Another 25% compacted in two content areas and the remaining 5% compacted in three or more.

Recommendation #3: Experiment With Pretesting

A third strategy that enhances the success and impact of compacting involves the use of pretesting. Teachers who become proficient with compacting usually begin their implementation experimenting with different resources and methods for preassessment. They tend to be flexible in their approach to compacting, and often ask for assistance from other faculty members, aides, or volunteers.

Many different types of assessments can be used for the students in the class who should be considered for curriculum compacting. A table can serve as a pretest center, and students can decide if they want to take the pretest. Reading or math consultants often help locate, prepare, or administer pretests, and other faculty members can be asked to help as well. Alternative assessment techniques (essays, portfolios, students' products) can also be used to demonstrate proficiency and content expertise.

Recommendation #4: Compact by Unit, Chapter, or Topic Rather Than by Time Block, Marking Period, or Quarter

Teachers who participated in various research studies about compacting differed with regard to the method by which they organized the curriculum compacting process and in the degree of specificity with which they described content material identified for compacting. A small number of teachers compacted by time, indicating either weeks or a marking quarter. The vast majority of teachers compacted by units or chapters of materials and documented that they would compact, for example, parts of speech, two science chapters on matter, or a unit in social studies.

This decision allowed them to more easily select the measureable learning goals for these units or chapters and locate the appropriate preassessments. These teachers' success with unit or chapter-bound compacting prompts this recommendation to do the same when implementing compacting under normal teaching conditions. Compacting by units, modules, or chapters creates definite boundaries for the use of the strategy, allows for easier access to the appropriate preassessments, and clarifies the time available for enrichment or acceleration should the pretesting verify mastery of the unit or chapter learning goals and standards.

In addition, many units and chapter written by commercial vendors often include related enrichment and acceleration suggestions and resources. Although these suggestions may not always match the interests and talents of the students who are receiving compacting, and choice should be an essential component for such decision making, these vendors' resources provide a starting point for content-based enrichment and acceleration.

Recommendation #5: Document the Process as Clearly as Possible

One of the findings in our research related to curriculum compacting was the ways with which the documentation of the compacting process and decisions varied across teachers and school sites. These differences included the specificity of the communication about the subject area, unit, goals, and standards being measured; the assessments used to measure mastery; the level of proficiency needed to declare mastery; and the use of a common document to record the various compacting decisions and plans. In most cases, these differences emerged as a result of staff consensus or district policy.

Either the Compactor or a locally designed alternative form can be used to document all phases and decisions within the compacting process. In the research described in this chapter, participating teachers varied in the degree of specificity with which they documented the material to be compacted.

A small percentage of teachers did not list the subject(s) to be compacted. Approximately 15% of teachers listed just the subject area in the first column of the compactor, with text such as "math" or "spelling." The majority of teachers listed specific units, such as the solar system, electricity and magnetism, plants, air and weather, and the human body. This latter approach, naming the unit or chapter, in addition to listing the specific standards addressed in the unit or text, provides the clearest communication to other educators and parents with regard to the decisions made during the compacting process. For these reasons, we recommend using the first column of the Compactor form to list the subject area, unit, and standards for greater clarity and accountability.

Teachers also used a variety of tools to measure the selected content and to decide on the necessary level of proficiency. The most frequently mentioned strategy for measuring proficiency across all treatment groups was the use of units, chapters, and review tests. Other strategies included asking students to complete content outlines, responses to reading comprehension questions, the successful completion of practice worksheets and weekly tests, constructed written responses to teacher-selected problems, teachers' notes and observations during group learning tasks with other high-potential students, and individual work at the board with the teacher. The majority of teachers (80%) identified a specific proficiency standard by which to evaluate whether students had mastered the regular curriculum, and that criteria for determining proficiency ranged from 80%–100%.

Of course, assessments with documented and established reliability and validity data represent the gold standard for selecting assessments to measure mastery of standards and subject area content. Given the unavailability of such assessments, the use of common assessments, standards-based assessments, and standards-based assessment criteria provide several aspects necessary to establish content validity.

Recommendation #6: Get Help and Support for the Compacting Process

The highest quality compactors that emerged in the research studies were prepared by classroom teachers who had worked with a peer coach and who had other consulting assistance available to them. This help was provided by teachers in the gifted or enrichment program or content-area specialists who provided materials or help with preassessment. In some cases, a librarian/media specialist also helped by working with targeted students on advanced research projects or study skills.

The importance of working with others when implementing compacting for the first time cannot be underestimated. Colleagues can provide information about a student's subject area strengths in previous grade levels, administrators can arrange for substitute teacher coverage so that teachers can meet with team members to plan, content-area specialists can help locate appropriate preassessments, and all of these groups can help to support teachers' communication with parents. Most importantly, these fellow educators can be of invaluable assistance when attempting to locate appropriate enrichment materials for students. Sharing dilemmas, brainstorming with each other, and celebrating successes are also important tasks that can be accomplished with a professional learning community.

Lastly, the opportunity to work with others increases the likelihood that compacting will be successful, effective, and an integral part of educators' instructional toolboxes. This collaborative planning and support usually requires additional funds for support, planning, and collaboration time. Without it, compacting is likely to have a very short life span.

Recommendation #7: Find a Broad Variety of Enrichment and Acceleration Alternatives

It is important to note that the most difficult task for teachers who participated in our compacting studies cited earlier was replacing compacted content with appropriately challenging content and interest-based options. Surprisingly, only 18% of teachers in the study used acceleration as a replacement strategy.

In most cases, this low number is indicative of school districts in which existing school board policy does not allow for subject-area acceleration. In these situations, the best that teachers could do was to allow students to progress through the grade-level curriculum at a more rapid pace without the opportunity to learn content in the next grade level. When this happens, students who are accelerated may simply cover material in October that they would not have done until May or June. This type of acceleration is often minimally challenging for very bright students and it often becomes necessary to locate other alternatives.

Exploratory and topical websites can be of great assistance when looking for appropriate replacement activities. Request help and use all available resources to create a wide range of high-interest and engagement opportunities and alternatives to replace content that has been eliminated through compacting.

Recommendation #8: Experiment, Keep Trying, Reflect on What Has Worked, and Field-Test New Ideas

The compacting process becomes easier as it evolves into more than just a series of testing and record-keeping exercises. When teachers use compacting for a while, it opens the door to a new way of thinking about learners, the content area's key skills and concepts, and the role of acceleration and talent development within the grade-level classroom. In this instance, compacting becomes a common and anticipated instructional strategy, and a normal part of differentiating the curriculum. To achieve this kind of success with compacting, professional growth, a tolerance for the initial frustration, and collegial collaboration are essential.

6

Successful Compacting
Case Studies

Teachers who implement compacting successfully in their classroom often use a variety of instructional strategies to accomplish their goals. Some teachers and students prefer to focus on acceleration, others lean toward content area enrichment, and still others emphasize interest-based enrichment and inquiry. Whatever route they take, educators quickly discover that there is no one best method or technique that adequately addresses all of the differences in students' learning characteristics, needs, and strengths.

The various options available with compacting can often seem daunting, especially when teachers are trying to make the best instructional decisions possible, not only for the high-achieving students in the class, but for all of their learners. In addition, teachers who choose to assume the responsibility for implementing compacting usually work alone to administer the preassessments, locate the needed resources, and serve as a coach and facilitator for the resulting individual and small-group tasks and projects. This independence can cause uncertainty, especially among educators who want to do the best they can to meet the needs of their students.

This chapter attempts to addresses the uncertainty that teachers often feel when making compacting decisions by sharing the compacting work of others. It includes a set of case studies and compactor forms used successfully in elementary, middle school, and high school situations. The authors of each case study were the actual teachers who either supported or implemented compacting in their classrooms and schools. They share their stories in their own words, and with chosen areas of emphasis. A brief introduction to each author is included at the beginning of each case study. We hope that reading and reflecting on these teachers' thoughts, plans, decisions, and actions may help each reader to envision his or her own decisions and actions in similar situations.

Case Study 1: Knight, a Grade 5 Math Student

Sara Tucker is the author of this case study. She is a graduate student at the University of Connecticut, who currently resides in Utah with her husband Gailon. She has been teaching for 15 years in both gifted programs and general classrooms.

When I first met Knight, he was enrolled as a third grader in our rural, predominantly middle-class community school. He was full of energy and sass and had an amazing smile. He came from a family that valued education highly. Knight was the oldest of four siblings, with a younger brother and two sisters. He was very quick-witted and always had a joke ready or was eager to make one up on the spot. He loved to make you laugh and got great joy from seeing others happy. Knight was very concerned with right and wrong, fairness, and equality. He was extremely bright, especially in math; was quick to point out the unfairness of a situation or to correct a math calculation; and was often in motion. He loved to collect things: pencils, erasers, scraps of paper, broken crayons, and random items that fit into his pencil box. He enjoyed science and had a wonderful curiosity about how things worked and why they worked the way they do. This was not the case with other curricular areas; in fact, Knight detested writing, spelling, and cursive practice.

As a third grader, Knight already had an Individualized Education Plan to serve his "other health impairments" needs, as he was categorized as a student on the autism spectrum who struggled with attention. His school-day modifications included numerous snack times and frequent breaks. This meant that on a typical day, Knight was only in the classroom for a portion of time, as he spent most of his time with either the school psychologist or her assistant playing educational games, chatting, or having a snack.

Knight's academic performance was inconsistent. As a third grader, he had mastered most of the grade-level math curriculum and enjoyed complex calculations and algebraic problems. As a result, he was easily frustrated when other students did not immediately grasp a lesson's concept or a simple calculation, and would typically blurt out the answer so that the class could move on. He did not like to take tests and would frequently rush through them just to have them completed. He did not always complete his homework, and when he did, he frequently forgot to give it to the teacher.

Much of grade 3 and 4 was spent trying to figure out what made Knight tick and how to reach him in a way that would keep him in the classroom longer so that he could increase his academic achievement. As classroom teachers and his enrichment specialist built a rapport with him, things went much more smoothly and there were fewer moments in which he needed to go to the office and take a break. By the end of fourth grade, he rarely left for a time out.

When Knight reached fifth grade, there was a class for high achievers. When class lists were being considered, teachers discussed who should be placed in this class, using standard measures to determine eligibility: test scores, classroom grades, and teacher recommendations. By these criteria, Knight did not qualify, but as the teacher of the class, I had input and was able to convince the school administrator to allow him into the high achievers class. Knight, his parents, and I sat down to discuss expectations and desired outcomes. These were noted on his Individualized Educational Plan, and the year began.

Knight was a bright young man, and he had become calmer and more in control of his impulses. He still did not like writing, spelling, or taking tests. His parents and I worked together to identify a better way for him to complete homework, allowing him to submit it electronically as needed. What helped him most was the opportunity to compact assignments, units, and even exams. We put together a set of actions that met his needs and interests while continuing to address the grade-level curriculum. This experience made an amazing difference to Knight by offering appropriate challenge that gave him the motivation to stay engaged in learning.

The Compacting Process in Action

Knight's strongest area was math, so that is where we began compacting. In order for him to compact out of a particular unit, he needed to demonstrate at least 85% proficiency. He also had to be willing to return to the class for lessons in areas where he did not yet show proficiency. He agreed with the plan, and we moved onto the next step: determining what to do with his compacted time.

Knight had indicated his desire to continue to pursue his learning in math, so we looked for acceleration opportunities for him. Assessment data showed that he would be appropriately challenged with grade 8 and 9 math curriculum, so the junior high math teacher was asked if she would be willing to allow him to attend one of her classes. She agreed to the proposition and we set up a schedule that worked with our math time and hers. Knight attended the eighth-grade class. He was expected to complete work, take exams with the class, and to keep pace with them. We tried this for the first quarter of the school year and it worked fairly well. Knight was able to accelerate his math curriculum, remain interested in the class, and return to the fifth-grade class for remediation in areas that represented a learning gap.

During the second quarter of the school year, Knight was given the grade 5 end-of-unit exam, and teachers discovered another set of gaps, so he stayed in the fifth-grade classroom to learn those standards. We had a discussion as to what we should have him do during the times when we were focusing on a set of standards that he had mastered, and he said he would like to use that time to work on tasks within the Khan Academy website. This website tests students on their mastery of Common Core math standards and identifies both their baseline and next steps. When I mentioned to Knight that he would have to take a test to see where he would be placed, he was fine with the notion, and he did well. He began to understand that his placement was based on his achievement and work ethic.

He was placed at the eighth-grade level, which was outstanding for him. The combination of class instruction and web-based instruction worked very well. We were able to focus his efforts and see him reach his goals. Third quarter began much the same way, with the administration of the grade 5 end-of-unit exam. It covered fractions, an area of math that many students find challenging. Fractions were also an issue for Knight. He did not score as well as he had hoped and as a result remained in the class setting for the entire unit. We found ways to continue to incorporate Khan Academy, but in general, he stayed with the class.

Fourth quarter was a different experience. Knight did well on the end-of-unit exam, as this quarter was all about measurement and geometry. Although his pre-assessment scores meant that he could have been accelerated to the eighth-grade class, worked on Khan Academy, or chosen a different route, he chose to stay with the class. I think one of the reasons for this is that the measurement unit was more hands-on and project oriented, and potentially, more fun.

When Knight acted out, he was reminded that he had other choices, and that reminder was all he needed to either focus on the classwork, move on to Khan Academy, complete math task cards, or research how he could apply math into his future goals and plans. Having the options available helped keep him on task because he knew that if he wanted to explore further, he could set up a contract that would allow him to do so.

Summary

Knight was an amazing young man and I felt privileged to work with him. Throughout this process, I was able to see the light come back into in his eyes and watch as he learned that his efforts caused positive difference in his learning options. Compacting enabled Knight to move beyond the grade-level curriculum, delve into areas of math that would normally not be discussed in a fifth-grade classroom, and stay engaged in the learning process. Throughout the fifth grade, Knight was able to work collaboratively with me to identify and access classroom resources that he needed to grow, enjoy learning, and remain academically engaged.

Individual Education Program Guide
The Compactor

Student Name(s): Knight M. **Grade:** 5 **School:** Jones **Participating Teachers:** Sara Tucker

Name it.	Prove it.	Change it.
Curriculum Area	**Assessment**	**Enrichment/Acceleration Plans**
Name the subject area, unit, chapter, or learning standards that are the focus for compacting.	List the assessment tools and related data that indicate student strengths and interests. List the preassessment data and the learning standards that have not yet been mastered.	Briefly describe the strategies used to ensure mastery of the learning standards that have not been mastered. Name the enrichment or acceleration tasks that will be substituted for the compacted curriculum.
Math Class		**Compacting Strategy**
Place Value and Decimal Fractions: Knight has completed the end-of-unit exam with 95% accuracy. The material included in this unit comprises place value to millions, exponents, fractions in decimal form, fractions in expanded form, rounding decimals, using all operations with decimals, and solving word problems with decimals.	Given the very few areas in which Knight did not show proficiency, he will be asked to work with his class and his peers to master those areas. During this time he will complete work and tests/exams with his peers. We will also use other preassessments to understand his level of achievement—Khan Academy will be also be used to help him understand his level of challenge. Knight currently tested at the eighth-grade level with the assessments given.	For the areas in which Knight did document proficiency, arrangements have been made for him to attend an eighth-grade class to further work on higher level math. **Acceleration and Enrichment Tasks** Knight will also create board games or task cards on decimals and fractions. He loves games and would like to use his knowledge and skills to help others.
Using a profile provided by his teacher, Knight discovered that his preferred learning style begins with using games. This information will be used to inform the ways in which he will express learning as well.	Knight will continue to show competency through work completed in the eighth-grade class.	

Case Study 2: Kelly Smith, Grade 7

Sue Peyton has been teaching for 15 years in both public and private schools in Connecticut. She currently works in a prekindergarten through eighth grade public school as an enrichment specialist and library media specialist. She is pursuing a degree in Educational Psychology from the University of Connecticut.

Kelly Smith was a seventh grader at Pomfret Community School. As a primary grade student, Kelly excelled in school, with strong reading and English language arts skills. She also demonstrated a strong understanding of social studies and science concepts and skills. She was an above-average student in math and performed well both in class and on her homework. Her scores on standardized tests had consistently been in the proficient range. In addition, her district and state-level test scores have always placed her in the top 10% of her grade. She was very verbal and demonstrated high creativity through her artwork and her writing. By the end of fourth grade, Kelly was identified as a gifted and talented student. However, at that time there was no program in place to serve identified students.

Kelly had difficulty relating to other students and preferred interacting with adults. When there were other students around, she tended to be rude and noncompliant with adults as well. In fourth grade, educators created a behavior plan; Kelly was to be rewarded with various activities when she demonstrated positive peer interactions with various activities. Her options included working in the library and reading to younger students. Because Kelly was an avid reader, these were appropriate rewards. Initially, the plan increased her positive behavior with peers, but soon, she began to brag about the things she was allowed to do and to make others feel badly. The plan was eventually discontinued.

By fifth grade, Kelly's academic performance began to decline. She stopped doing her homework regularly and the quality of her work decreased. She often did not complete assignments and scored poorly on tests and quizzes. In addition, Kelly's interactions with both peers and adults became even more problematic. She received frequent behavioral referrals and did not seem to have many friends. Lying became a consistent problem. In sixth grade, she was involved in several instances of socially inappropriate behavior that eventually caused her parents to remove her from school a week early. Kelly's academic performance continued to decline in sixth grade, and she received C's and D's in most subject areas.

In seventh grade, Kelly received counseling both in and out of school to address social issues. However, her academic needs were still an issue. Test data suggested Kelly had a good deal of potential, but that she was currently underachieving in school. Even in fifth and sixth grade, when her academic performance was poor, Kelly continued to score well on standardized testing.

When the school implemented a new program for students with high academic potential, former teachers suggested that Kelly might benefit from participation. Although not everyone was in agreement, Kelly was admitted to the program, as some of her teachers assumed that greater academic challenge, closer monitoring, and the additional adult attention in the enrichment classroom would improve her academic performance

The seventh-grade schedule included options for both intervention and enrichment services. Both services were scheduled at the same time. Although Kelly's grades did not make her eligible for the enrichment group, teachers decided to allow her to participate. However, her participation in the group would be dependent on her mastery of the skills taught during the intervention period. The enrichment teacher and Kelly's subject-area teachers worked together to create a success plan.

The areas of focus for the intervention period included math and language arts. Kelly's math teacher agreed to give Kelly a pretest on the skills that were to be taught and practiced during each intervention unit. She had to score 85% or higher in order to be excused from the intervention period and attend enrichment instead. Math was not Kelly's strength area, so teachers assumed that she would not pass the pretest for all of the intervention units and that she would be required to attend intervention classes at various points throughout the year. However, the math teacher was available during an afterschool study session twice a week, and was willing to work with Kelly to shore up her areas of weakness.

Kelly's language arts teacher agreed to consider allowing Kelly to attend enrichment classes during the language arts intervention time because Kelly had demonstrated strong writing, grammar, and vocabulary skills. She was an avid reader, and she had already read several of the books that were part of the grade-level resources.

The language arts teacher assessed Kelly on the grade-level language arts skills. She examined the results, and when the class was learning skills that Kelly has already mastered, she was allowed to work on her enrichment project. She was also encouraged to read class novels ahead of time and take comprehension tests so that she could be exempt from the class assignments related to these novels and work on enrichment activities instead.

The seventh-grade team alternated between language arts and math enrichment on a daily basis, so Kelly would be able to attend enrichment at least every other day and sometimes every day. She would be with an enrichment group of seventh- and eighth-grade students who would meet for one half hour per day. When Kelly first began working in the enrichment classroom, she completed an interest inventory to determine what topic she may want to investigate. Her responses indicated a strong interest in both reading and writing, particularly fiction. She also expressed additional interests in the arts.

The grade 7 and 8 enrichment class enrolled 12 students and the services included Type 1 and Type II Enrichment Triad activities. Staff anticipated that students would eventually conduct Type III activities. However, students first participated in an organized problem-based learning scenario, often involving a contest or competition. They were guided through the steps involved in solving a real-world problem and learned the basic skills needed to conduct their own research.

At the beginning of the year, students were given the opportunity to work in small groups on an interest-based activity. Kelly chose to participate in a Future Problem Solving competition along with four other students. They researched this program's annual topic, waste removal, as well as basic city planning. They also learned about engineering, and an engineer mentored the group. The students worked together on the computer to design a city, build a model of a section of their city, create a supply budget for their model, and to write a description.

Because Kelly could not attend the enrichment class every day, she worked with her teammates to select those activities that she could complete for her team. Because writing was one of her strength areas, they decided that she would be primarily responsible for their written submission. She also conducted research and brought valuable information back to the group.

Kelly and her teammates were responsible for completing much of the paperwork required for a Type III enrichment project. They developed their own management plan, which included all of their action steps and a list of the resources they would need. They updated this form as needed, and also completed a weekly status sheet that listed their accomplishments and outlined what they planned to do in the coming week. Kelly was actively involved with all of this paperwork.

The future city project was to be completed by January. After that time, students would be able to begin their own individual Type III projects. Because Kelly would be substituting her language arts class time for enrichment, her teacher wanted her to complete a reading enrichment project based on a book that was both challenging and of interest to her.

Kelly was an avid reader, with a strong interest in literature, so this plan was more than acceptable to her. Kelly worked primarily with the enrichment teacher on her ideas and project.

Compacting and enrichment proved to be a successful way to increase her engagement and motivation for learning challenging content.

Individual Education Program Guide
The Compactor

Student Name(s): Kelly Smith Grade: 7	School: Pomfret Community School	Participating Teachers: Archambault and Slingo
Name it.	**Prove it.**	**Change it.**
Curriculum Area	Assessment	Enrichment/Acceleration Plans
Name the subject area, unit, chapter, or learning standards that are the focus for compacting.	List the assessment tools and related data that indicate student strengths and interests. List the preassessment data and the learning standards that have not yet been mastered.	Briefly describe the strategies used to ensure mastery of the learning standards that have not been mastered. Name the enrichment or acceleration tasks that will be substituted for the compacted curriculum.
• Kelly has strong skills in ELA, including reading, vocabulary, and grammar. She independently reads above-grade-level books and demonstrates understanding. Through her writing, she demonstrates the ability to appropriately use rules of grammar and a strong vocabulary.	• Vocabulary pretest. • Grammar pretest. • Literature posttest and interview with teacher. • Pretest of material to be covered in math enrichment.	• Kelly will not have to attend ELA intervention. • She will have the opportunity to compact her ELA class. • Kelly will have the opportunity to compact her math intervention, but will continue to work with her classmates during her regular math period. • Kelly will attend the enrichment class at least halftime, depending on her math pretesting. Her first project will be working with a group of peers and will involve STEM skills as well as writing. • Kelly will participate in the Type I and II enrichment activities provided for students in the enrichment program. • Kelly will participate in a teacher-led, in-depth independent research project using above-grade-level reading material.

Case Study 3: Jose

Katy Field was a high school social studies teacher for 12 years before entering the doctoral program at the University of Connecticut to study giftedness, creativity, and talent development. She taught Advanced Placement U.S. history, world religions, world history, global issues, and civics. In 2008, she won the Teacher of the Year award at the Providence Day School in Charlotte, NC. While at the school, she developed and taught a curriculum about global citizenship that melded advanced information and communication technology skills, literacy skills, critical thinking skills, and collaboration and leadership skills within an alternative degree program. In 2010, she was chosen to participate in the North Carolina Association of Independent Schools 21st Century Master Teacher's Academy, and in 2011, she earned her master's in educational policy from the University of Illinois at Urbana-Champaign with a focus on global studies in education. Her current research interests are student engagement and developing curricula that promotes engagement, ICT literacy, and higher order thinking skills.

Jose was a talented, enthusiastic, and animated student in Ms. Smith's seventh-grade math class. In order to make informed decisions regarding compacting and differentiation, Ms. Smith spent the first week of school collecting and analyzing data and information she had collected about her students' strengths and interests. First, she developed a survey based on Renzulli's Interest-A-Lyzer and asked all of her students to complete it. The completed surveys provided Ms. Smith with information about the topics her students found interesting, their ideas for creative productivity, and their learning preferences. Among other things, Ms. Smith learned that Jose loved collecting and trading baseball cards, and that he had dabbled in making videos to entertain and inform his peers, something that he found to be an interesting activity he would like to explore more.

In addition to the student interest survey, Ms. Smith also collected and analyzed the results of students' end-of-year math tests from grades 4–6. Ms. Smith was able to identify Jose as a highly talented math student based on his 95th percentile scores over the past 3 years.

Given Jose's demonstrated abilities in math and his potential for creative productivity, Ms. Smith pretested Jose in math to decide if parts of the seventh-grade math curriculum could be compacted in order to provide time for his enrichment goals.

Identifying Learning Objectives and Assessing Ability

Recognizing that she could not assume that Jose had already mastered the seventh-grade math curriculum merely because he had demonstrated high achievement in math in the past, Ms. Smith also designed a series of short pre-tests consisting of two or three questions that addressed each of the six main standards in Unit 1. The first unit for her class focused on proportional relationships and percentages. Jose answered all of the questions correctly and was able to explain most of his thinking, with the exception of a couple of the questions that required drawing and interpreting proportional representations through graphs. Given Jose's demonstrated mastery in all but one content area in Unit 1, Ms. Smith decided to compact and modify Jose's learning experiences to better meet his needs.

Saving Time Through Pretesting

Accelerating the math curriculum was not an option for Jose because his school had a policy that did not allow students to work on learning standards that were beyond the grade-level curriculum. Because Jose was already enrolled in the highest level math class, Ms. Smith decided to eliminate the practice time that other students used to master their learning objectives. Jose was offered individual and independent practice opportunities to learn the graphing objective that he had not yet mastered. Once that was complete, Jose was given the chance to take the end-of-unit test early. When Jose scored 95% or better on the end-of-unit test, he was allowed to spend the remainder of his time on his enrichment project.

Differentiation and Enrichment

Jose demonstrated an interest in baseball and designing videos, so Ms. Smith worked with the school's audiovisual director, Mr. Jones, who also oversaw the student news club. Mr. Jones agreed to offer Jose some guidance in developing video and presentation skills. Jose spent some of his class time learning how to make entertaining and informational videos, and then he applied those skills and produced a weekly series that explained and compared the statistics on the back of baseball cards and offered predictions about which players would likely be invited to the upcoming MLB All-Star Game.

Despite not being able to accelerate his math curriculum, this option engaged and stretched his talents as a gifted math student. It provided a differentiated means of applying the learning objectives related to math proportions and offered Jose greater depth, complexity, and independence. The open-ended structure of this option increased the challenge level and enabled Jose to deepen his understanding while still studying the same concept as the rest of the students.

In addition to added complexity, Jose also pursued both Type II and Type III enrichment activities that helped him discover and cultivate his potential as a creatively productive contributor within his domain of interest and talent. By working with Mr. Jones, Jose learned skills that helped him translate his interests and abilities into a tangible product, and by developing a weekly series for the school's news show, Jose produced a real product for an authentic audience. Jose had autonomy in choosing the players he critiqued and the artistic way in which he presented his material. He experienced competence when interpreting the mathematical information on the baseball cards and he enhanced his interpersonal skills as he responded to the feedback he received from Mr. Jones. His sense of acceptance and belonging also improved when his peers gave him positive feedback about his videos.

Individual Education Program Guide
The Compactor

Student Name(s): Jose	Grade: 7	School: n/a	Participating Teachers: Katy Field
Name it.	**Prove it.**		**Change it.**
Curriculum Area	**Assessment**		**Enrichment/Acceleration Plans**
Name the subject area, unit, chapter, or learning standards that are the focus for compacting.	List the assessment tools and related data that indicate student strengths and interests. List the preassessment data and the learning standards that have not yet been mastered.		Briefly describe the strategies used to ensure mastery of the learning standards that have not been mastered. Name the enrichment or acceleration tasks that will be substituted for the compacted curriculum.
• Recognize and represent proportional relationships between quantities. • Decide whether two quantities are in a proportional relationship (e.g., by testing for equivalent ratios in a table or graphing on a coordinate plane and observing whether the graph is a straight line through the origin). • Identify the constant of proportionality (unit rate) in tables, graphs, equations, diagrams, and verbal descriptions of proportional relationships. • Represent proportional relationships with equations. • Explain what a point (x, y) on the graph of a proportional relationship means in terms of the situation, with special attention to the points $(0, 0)$ and $(1, r)$ where r is the unit rate. • Use proportional relationships to solve multistep ratio and percent problems. Examples: simple interest, tax, markups and markdowns, gratuities and commissions, fees, percent increase and decrease, percent error.	• 95th percentile end of year math scores in grades 4–6. • 575 on the math portion of sixth-grade PARCC, distinguished understanding category. • Pretest in ratios demonstrates mastery of all objectives except for ability to draw and interpret points on graphs for the purposes of comparing proportional relationships. • Jose demonstrated mastery of these standards through his quizzes, drawings, interpretations of proportional relationships, and the end-of-unit test.		• Jose will complete extra practice assignments on drawing and interpreting graphs that represent proportional relationships. • Student will complete a baseball card project that compares and contrasts players using graphs, equations, and written explanations that help the viewer interpret and understand their comparative strengths and weaknesses. • Jose will use his presentations to make predictions about who will be invited to the MLB All-Star Game in the summer of 2016 in a weekly sports news segment on the middle school's news show.

Case Study 4: Sid

Ashley Carpenter is a mother and wife, and she has been a middle school science teacher for almost 15 years. She has taught science in exceptional student education (ESE), drop-out prevention, and gifted programs. She currently teaches at one of three centers for gifted studies in Pinellas County, FL. She has a bachelor of science degree in marine science from Eckerd College, and a master of arts degree in science education from the University of South Florida. She is currently working on a doctoral degree in educational psychology from the University of Connecticut.

Sid was a 13-year-old, Asian female of Indian descent, who lived with her parents in an affluent area of Seminole, FL. Sid was enrolled as a grade 8 student at the Center for Gifted Studies in Florida. The center is a full-time gifted magnet school that serves identified students across the state of Florida. When Sid was a student at the center, almost 300 middle school students attended the program. Depending on a student's placement, both the math and language arts curriculum were usually accelerated by one or two grade levels. Science was compacted and accelerated, and teachers taught social studies using the grade-level standards. Students enrolled in Spanish in both grades 7 and 8. They also participated in electives that included academic competitions, an affective education curriculum, and independent projects based on student interests. All students participated in the four core classes, Spanish, physical education, chorus, band, art, and gifted electives. Before attending the Center for Gifted Studies in middle school, Sid had been enrolled in a gifted magnet elementary school that provided similar offerings.

By grade 8, Sid had a 4.0 grade point average. She had successfully completed two high school credit courses (Spanish and Algebra I) in grade 7. In grade 8, Sid was enrolled in four more high school courses: geometry, Spanish II, English I Honors, and Integrated Science I Honors. At the end of middle school, Sid would have earned six high school credits. She consistently scored in the top level on all standardized test, especially in math, science, and civics. Specific information about Sid's testing results are displayed in Figure 8.

Sid's interests included science, technology, and engineering. In grade 7, she and her friends competed in our schoolwide Future Cities competition and were almost positive they were going to be the winning team, but came in third place. This was a disappointment to Sid, as she had expected to compete at the regional and state levels. Sid would often remark that she believed that it was mandatory to get the highest test score of all her friends, and that it was more important to get the highest grade than to extend the most effort. I also heard her say on several occasions that she would often go home and search online for an assignment or test a teacher was going to give to see if she could find the answers or examples

Test Name and Date	Subject Area Results		
2014 Grade 5 End of Course Exams	Algebra: Pass	Civics Level 5: 99th percentile	
2014 Redi-Step	Critical Reading: 84th percentile	Math: 99th percentile	Writing: 86th percentile
2014 Florida Comprehensive Assessment Test (FCAT)	Reading Level 5: 75th percentile	Math Level 5: 90th percentile	
2013 FCAT	Reading Level 5: 79th percentile	Math Level 5: 90th percentile	Science Level 5: 100th percentile

Figure 8. Sid's test results.

of finished products. She also said that if you cheat and get away with it, then you are just working smart. Based on these statements and behaviors, I determined that, in addition to any compacting she might receive, I would need to attend to both her work ethic and her mindset regarding honesty and integrity.

Sid had a tendency to put minimal effort into classwork and projects in school, but if a topic interested her, she would dive into it deeply. Sid was also the type of person who liked to get involved in heated debates with her peers about social, political, and science issues.

Sid had a remarkable amount of knowledge about science and technology, but her knowledge was spotty. Sid's interest seemed to be more in line with physics and chemistry, not biology or geology. She appeared to have most of the background information required to compact the chemistry units in her science class. She had an understanding of subatomic particles, quarks, and the forces that hold them together, but she did not understand key concepts about the cell, organisms, or ecosystems. Sid sometimes understood a concept but not the key vocabulary related to that content. This meant that even if a unit was compacted for Sid, vocabulary still needed to be understood and practiced. It became apparent that we would need to assess Sid's specific and prior understanding of each of the science standards.

Sid was a student who reacted best when she was offered choices. In the past, when she already knew what the enrichment project was for a unit and did not like it, she would purposefully fail the pretest to make her life easier. If she was not interested in the alternate assignment, she would find a way not to do it (such as purposely failing the pretest), but still do enough work to maintain an A average.

As a grade 8 student, Sid was a member of the Science Olympiad Team, a competition that requires students to perform varied science tasks, labs, and challenges. Sid tended to prefer these kinds of events. Because Sid was so interested in Science Olympiad, we integrated these types of challenges so that she would have a viable choice if and when she passed the benchmark assessments.

In order to evaluate the need for compacting, some or all of the students would be given a science pretest at the beginning of each unit. The pretest would include at least five questions per standard, using the Next Generation Science Standards as the focus for the curriculum. Items included a mixture of low, medium, and high levels of cognitive difficulty. Three to five standards were usually assessed on each benchmark test. If a student scored 85% or higher on an entire benchmark assessment, the student was expected to complete the enrichment project in lieu of classwork and homework. The enrichment projects included a rubric, directions, and a timeline. These components provided enough support to allow for student independence with minimal guidance from teachers.

Individual Education Program Guide
The Compactor

Student Name(s): Sid	Grade: 7	School: Morgan Fitzgerald Middle School	Participating Teachers: A. Carpenter
Name it.		**Prove it.**	**Change it.**
Curriculum Area		**Assessment**	**Enrichment/Acceleration Plans**
Name the subject area, unit, chapter, or learning standards that are the focus for compacting.		List the assessment tools and related data that indicate student strengths and interests. List the preassessment data and the learning standards that have not yet been mastered.	Briefly describe the strategies used to ensure mastery of the learning standards that have not been mastered. Name the enrichment or acceleration tasks that will be substituted for the compacted curriculum.
Integrated Science I Honors— Unit 1a Benchmarks: • SC.912.P.8.3 Explore the scientific theory of atoms (also known as atomic theory) by describing changes in the atomic model over time and why those changes were necessitated by experimental evidence. • SC.912.P.8.4 Explore the scientific theory of atoms (also known as atomic theory) by describing the structure of atoms in terms of protons, neutrons, and electrons, and differentiate among these particles in terms of their mass, electrical charges, and locations within the atom. • SC.8.P.8.7 Explore the scientific theory of atoms (also known as atomic theory) by recognizing that atoms are the smallest unit of an element and are composed of subatomic particles (electrons surrounding a nucleus containing protons and neutrons).		• 2014 end of course exams. • 2014 Redi-Step. • Critical Reading: 84th percentile. • Reading: Level 5 75th percentile. • Student was given a pretest and scored above 85% proficiency. • There were some gaps in vocabulary. • Rubric used to assess student product.	• Sid will complete a vocabulary chart including the word, definition, and a graphic depicting meaning of the word. • Sid will take the vocabulary quiz. • Sid will complete Crime Busters (Science Olympiad). • She will create a chart that describes the physical and chemical characteristics of a mystery powder mixture and compound. • She will use the physical and chemical properties of metals to identify common metals. • She will identify seven different types of plastics based on their physical characteristics. • She will find five substances that have characteristics that do not align with the rules for the four phases of matter.

continued

continued

Name it.	Prove it.	Change it.
Integrated Science I Honors—Unit 2		• Sid will create a product that explains how to classify a phase of matter. The product will address the temperature ranges within each phase.
• SC.912.P.8.1 Differentiate among the four states of matter.		
• SC.8.P.8.1 Explore the scientific theory of atoms (also known as atomic theory) by using models to explain the motion of particles in solids, liquids, and gases.		
• SC.912.P.10.4 Describe heat as the energy transferred by convection, conduction, and radiation, and explain the connection of heat to change in temperature or states of matter.		
• SC.8.P.8.9 Distinguish among mixtures (including solutions) and pure substances.		
• SC.8.P.8.8 Identify basic examples of and compare and classify the properties of compounds, including acids, bases, and salts.		
Integrated Science I Honors—Unit 3		
• SC.912.P.8.2 Differentiate between physical and chemical properties and physical and chemical changes of matter.		

continued

Name it.	Prove it.	Change it.
• SC.8.P.8.4 Classify and compare substances on the basis of characteristic physical properties that can be demonstrated or measured (for example, density, thermal or electrical conductivity, solubility, magnetic properties, melting and boiling points), and know that these properties are independent of the amount of the sample. • SC.8.P.8.3 Explore and describe the densities of various materials through measurement of their masses and volumes. • SC.912.L.18.12 Discuss the special properties of water that contribute to Earth's suitability as an environment for life: cohesive behavior, ability to moderate temperature, expansion upon freezing, and versatility as a solvent. • SC.8.P.9.2 Differentiate between physical changes and chemical changes. • SC.8.P.9.1 Explore the Law of Conservation of Mass by demonstrating and concluding that mass is conserved when substances undergo physical and chemical changes. • SC.8.P.9.3 Investigate and describe how temperature influences chemical changes. • SC.912.P.10.7 Distinguish between endothermic and exothermic chemical processes.		

Compacting Case Study 5: Ian

Kari C. Morse, a graduate student at the University of Connecticut, resides on Cape Cod, MA, with her husband and two sons. She has taught for more than 20 years in the general classroom and in gifted programs. Kari is currently the director of the Gateway Program in the Barnstable Public Schools.

Ian attended kindergarten at an independent school when he was 3 years old, a year earlier than his peers. At the end of that school year, his mother requested a team meeting at the neighborhood public school to analyze his progress and reports and to recommend the correct placement for entering the public school. The team, including the principal, reading specialist, school psychologist, and a gifted and talented teacher, determined that the appropriate placement was in a first-grade classroom. The team noted concerns about Ian's social and emotional developmental due to his young age and recorded specific needs related to an acute allergy.

Ian was enrolled in the classroom of a grade 1 teacher who had trained as a gifted and talented specialist. Throughout grade 1, the team met with the classroom teacher to monitor his progress. Their primary goal was to support Ian's social development as he navigated his way among peers who were a year older and had already been acclimated to public school routines. The secondary goal was to support his academic growth and learning. The reading teacher offered additional support by providing reading texts aligned to his independent and instructional reading levels. The gifted and talented teacher consulted with Ian's classroom teacher regularly and offered rigorous work that required the application of grade-level reading standards.

Ian participated in assessments in September 2014 using local and standardized benchmarks. Test results placed Ian's achievement as well above average in reading, writing, and math. Ian's mother informed his teachers of Ian's special interest in geography and countries.

In October 2014, Ian completed an interest inventory, If I Ran the School, that was administered by the classroom teacher (see results in Figure 9). The data from Ian's interest inventory guided the selection of nonfiction resources, enrichment activities, and content-area and standards-based tasks in science and social studies. Throughout the year, Ian completed math pretests and teachers offered enrichment menus to supplant work with standards he had already mastered.

In grade 2, Ian was enrolled in an inclusion classroom that included students with several different kinds of learning characteristics. His teacher used a new assessment, STAR, to evaluate Ian's reading and math achievement. Ian scored at the 90th percentile when the grade 1 math standards were assessed. His reading Lexile Level was 543 (low grade 3 level).

Ian's Major Interest Areas				
Science	**Social Studies**	**Math**	**Language Arts**	**Fine Arts**
▶ Human body ▶ Volcanoes and earthquakes	▶ The United States ▶ Other countries ▶ Native Americans ▶ Asian Americans ▶ Hispanics ▶ African Americans	▶ Buying ▶ Money ▶ Calculators ▶ Computers	▶ Writing a book ▶ Comic and cartoon strips	▶ Painting

Figure 9. Ian's major interest areas.

The district's gifted and talented director met with Ian's mother to discuss her questions and concerns for grade 2. During the meeting, they discussed his grade 1 progress, home enrichment work, motivation, allergies, social growth, and areas for support. Ian's mother provided several examples of work that had been completed at home over the summer. Analysis of these work samples showed well-above-grade-level proficiency in sentence completion, research skills, spelling, penmanship, spatial awareness, and content knowledge of geography and countries.

His mother indicated that although his reading level was 2–3 years beyond his age, he still needed to work on his ability to make inferences and self-to-text connections. She explained that Ian had begun taking piano lessons and struggled with reading notes. He preferred to compose his own music and had started investigating how to create his own sheet music. Geography continued to be his passion, however. Ian researched all 50 states and created scaled maps that included land and water features (capital, rivers, cities, topography). His notes were lengthy, neat, and well organized.

A team meeting was held with Ian's mother, the school principal, the reading specialist, the gifted and talented teacher, the gifted and talented director, the grade 2 teacher, and the school psychologist. As a result of the meeting, the classroom teacher, reading specialist and gifted and talented teacher created a curriculum compacting plan to meet Ian's needs. The district's scope and sequence for grade 2 Common Core State Standards for ELA was used as a reference point. The gifted and talented teacher made plans to administer an interest inventory later in the year to update his list of interests.

Based on math preassessments for place value and addition/subtraction (see Table 3), many units and tasks areas were compacted. When the teacher gave the class lessons about expanded form, Ian would be required to participate with the class. During all other lessons within the place value unit, Ian would have a compacted curriculum and work independently on the interest-based assignments and tasks listed on the Compactor form.

Based on the preassessments from the STAR reading assessment, Ian would also have some opportunities for compacted work in ELA. During the weeks when the class was learning about the structure of a narrative story, Ian would participate in the whole-class reading and then apply his knowledge of those elements to an interest-based book at his independent reading level. He would ask and answer questions about character, setting, and plot.

Ian also created a written story using the story elements studied in class. During the weeks when the class was to be reading and reciting poetry, Ian would participate in the whole-class instruction, followed by the opportunity to read from his independent-level selections when he finished with poetry assignments.

After the poetry unit, Ian participated in the whole-class lessons about the elements of realistic fiction. The realistic fiction selections assigned to Ian were at his independent reading level. When students were placed into instructional groups, Ian participated in the above-level reading group. Ian also participated with the whole class when writing letters to the teacher. Expectations for sentence structure, word choice, and elaboration of details were aligned with his achievement level.

TABLE 3
Results of Ian's Math Preassessments

Code	CCSS Math Standard	Assessment Problems	Correct Items	Score
	Place Value			
2.NBT.1	Understand that the three digits of a three-digit number represents amounts of hundreds, tens, and ones.	1, 2, 3, 4	1, 2, 3, 4	100%
2.NBT. 2	Count within 1000; skip-count by 5s, 10s, and 100s.	5, 6, 7, 8	5, 6, 7, 8	100%
2.NBT.3	Read and write numbers to 1000 using base-ten numerals, number names, and expanded form.	9, 10, 11, 12	9, 10, 11	75%
2.NBT.4	Compare two three-digit numbers based on meanings of the hundreds, tens, and ones digits.	13, 14, 15, 16	13, 14, 15, 16	100%
2.NBT.7	Add and subtract within 1000, using concrete models or drawings and strategies based on place value, properties of operations, and/or the relationship between addition and subtraction.	17, 18, 19, 20, 21	17, 18, 19, 20, 21	100%

Individual Education Program Guide
The Compactor

Student Name(s): Ian	Grade: 2	School: n/a	Participating Teachers: Second-grade team
Name it.	**Prove it.**		**Change it.**
Curriculum Area	**Assessment**		**Enrichment/Acceleration Plans**
Name the subject area, unit, chapter, or learning standards that are the focus for compacting.	List the assessment tools and related data that indicate student strengths and interests. List the preassessment data and the learning standards that have not yet been mastered.		Briefly describe the strategies used to ensure mastery of the learning standards that have not been mastered. Name the enrichment or acceleration tasks that will be substituted for the compacted curriculum.

• STAR Math—90% Computation and Problem Solving
• Place Value Preassessment—Standards:
  • 2.NBT.1 100%
  • 2.NBT. 2 100%
  • 2.NBT.3 75% * expanded form to 1,000
  • 2.NBT.4 100%
  • 2.NBT.7 100%
	• 2.NBT.1, 2, 3, 4, 7—Measure growth using Bloom's taxonomy higher levels (analysis, evaluation, creating) and Multiple Intelligences (nature, linguistic, visual, kinesthetic, music).
	• 2.NBT.3—teach expanded form to 1,000.
			• Create portfolio for Math Enrichment Menu activities.
			• Create his own logical activity—see rubric.
			• Use enrichment for extended learning and practice online.

• STAR Reading—Lexile 539—well above grade level • Narrative Fiction—story elements (character, setting, plot) • Poetry—read, recite, elements and dialogue • Realistic Fiction—story elements, key ideas	• Measure growth using Bloom's taxonomy higher levels (analysis, evaluation, creating) and Multiple Intelligences (nature, linguistic, visual, kinesthetic, music)		• Create a portfolio for Reading Enrichment Menu activities. • Create his own activity—see rubric. • Create a book box and gather 10 selections including narrative fiction, poetry, and realistic fiction at independent reading level.
• Writing Samples—well above grade level	• Write a creative writing excerpt with correct grammar use and proper sentence use. • Sentences are longer than simple sentences including details and elaboration.		• Write a story with at least one character, setting, and plot. • Use enrichment opportunities to create a book in an area of interest.

Compacting Study 6: Kyan

Stacy Hayden is a talented and gifted teacher in Alexandria City, VA. In addition to teaching elementary students, she implements the Young Scholars model in her district. She holds a bachelor's degree in elementary education from Radford University, and a certificate in gifted education from William & Mary. She is working on a master's degree in educational psychology from the University of Connecticut.

Kyan was a grade 5 student at Thomas Jefferson Elementary School, an urban school in a district in which 90% of students receive free and reduced lunch. Kyan was double promoted at the end of grade 1 and continued to achieve significantly above grade level in math and reading. In grade 3, he received subject area acceleration and worked with the math class for students identified as gifted. His teacher was able to teach this very talented group of students both the fourth- and fifth-grade math standards in one school year.

During grade 5, he was ready to complete the grade 7 math curriculum. His grade 5 teacher was concerned about him and wanted him to be challenged in class, because his previous teachers noted that he acted out when he wasn't engaged. She decided to review his previous grade levels' summative test scores and administer preassessments for the current grade level's math standards to determine when and if curriculum compacting would be appropriate for Kyan.

Compacting in Math

Kyan was the only student in his grade 5 class who was working on the grade 7 math standards. Nevertheless, his teacher predicted that he had already mastered many of its standards. A review of his records unearthed a note from his grade 4 teacher with consistent A grades for all standards. The records of his grade 3 and 4 state tests contained perfect scores. Even though Kyan was receiving excellent grades, he was also complaining about being bored frequently.

His teacher's predictions about the math course and its lack of challenge were confirmed when Kyan took the seventh-grade math preassessment and scored 77% mastery. His teacher decided that compacting his math curriculum would ensure that he wasn't working on assignments and standards that he had already mastered. Curriculum compacting would also enable him to spend time on his other interests as determined by the results on his Interest-A-Lyzer inventory.

Kyan's teacher analyzed his math preassessment to try to identify any patterns or trends in both the questions and responses. His teacher observed that Kyan had correctly answered 13 out of 14 (93%) of the questions in the strand that focused on patterns, functions, and statistics. As she continued with her item analysis, she found other standards that Kyan had mastered. Kyan's teacher decided that he would be exempt from all direct instruction and practice of skills with standards that he had already mastered. During the time he would normally be participating in large-group instruction and practice tasks, he would complete an interest-based project.

Kyan would still be required to take the end-of-unit assessments with his peers. When Kyan's answers were incorrect, the teacher checked for patterns and provided individualized instruction to ensure his mastery of the related concepts. The number of class lessons in which Kyan participated depended on the unit being taught and his previous performance. In general, he participated in approximately one to two lessons a week, for approximately 30%–40% of the instructional time.

During the time that he was not participating in whole-class math instruction, Kyan was able to spend time on an independent study Type III project. After reviewing his Interest-A-Lyzer, Kyan's teacher noticed that he was very interested in computers and learning to code. She knew that he didn't have the opportunity to work on this outside of school because he spent his evenings in childcare at the local recreation center. His teacher decided that she would offer Kyan the opportunity to spend his compacted class time learning to code.

The plan was easy to implement, as Kyan could go to work in the resource room during any time that he did not need to spend on math work. In the resource room, he would use an online coding program, Tynker, to learn to code, with the ultimate goal of creating a game that could help other students practice the skills required for one of the units in the patterns, functions, and algebra standards.

Kyan was required to keep a daily log of his accomplishments and meet with his math teacher weekly for a quick update. In addition to his time spent working with Tynker, she arranged a mentorship with a software designer from a local business, under the supervision of Kyan's parents. This mentor was able to help and encourage Kyan with his coding skills and also served as an excellent role model.

Compacting saved Kyan up to 6 hours of math work each week. He did join the class when new information was presented that he had not previously mastered. Kyan's Compactor covered the first two quarters of the school year and his teacher updated it in January with an extension to his enrichment topic. Kyan and his mentor continued to enjoy their time together so much that they decided to pursue additional topics in coding and he worked on developing an application for tablets.

Compacting in Reading

Reading was also one of Kyan's strengths; he was reading at a ninth-grade level and showed mastery of the beginning of the year grade 5 reading standards.

He received a 95% on the related preassessment in September, so it was easy to see that he needed additional challenge in this area. When examining past performance, his teacher noted that during the previous 2 years he had received a perfect score on the end-of-year state test.

Although the math curriculum was quite repetitive and easy to compact, his literacy class was different. Classes were grouped by reading level and his teacher used Junior Great Books and Literature Circles to differentiate for the class. Kyan was engaged and appropriately challenged for most of the year.

However, at the end of the year, the whole school was required to work for 2 months on test-taking strategies. Kyan's teacher knew that he did not need repetitive test preparation on material that was below his achievement level. This lack of challenge sometimes caused him to act out and distract his peers.

A review of his Interest-A-Lyzer and reading survey revealed an interest in reading and writing dystopian novels. Kyan enjoyed reading *The Giver, Among the Hidden*, and *The City of Ember*. His teacher decided that Kyan would read additional dystopian novels, analyze their themes, create his own dystopian world, and write a story based on it. Kyan eventually wrote his own short story that he published and donated to the school library.

Kyan's teacher and parents were very pleased when he began to enjoy school. He was much happier not having to sit through repetitive material that he already knew. Having him engaged with an enrichment task made his teacher's life easier too. Compacting was a process that seemed difficult at first but ended up being an excellent tool for differentiation, and Kyan's teacher plans to keep using it in the future.

Individual Education Program Guide

The Compactor

Student Name(s): Kyan	Grade: 5	School: Thomas Jefferson	Participating Teachers: n/a
Name it.		**Prove it.**	**Change it.**
Curriculum Area		**Assessment**	**Enrichment/Acceleration Plans**
Name the subject area, unit, chapter, or learning standards that are the focus for compacting.		List the assessment tools and related data that indicate student strengths and interests. List the preassessment data and the learning standards that have not yet been mastered.	Briefly describe the strategies used to ensure mastery of the learning standards that have not been mastered. Name the enrichment or acceleration tasks that will be substituted for the compacted curriculum.
Math • Virginia SOLs. • Number Sense: 7.1, 7.2. • Computation: 7.3, 7.4. • Geometry: 7.7, 7.8. • Patterns, Functions, and Algebra: 7.13, 7.14, 7.15.		• Course preassessment. • Six-week test practice unit. • Fifth-grade reading SOL pretest. • Student will participate in biweekly skill tests.	• Kyan will participate in end-of-unit tests and lessons for any work that has not been mastered except for any repetitious work. Time gained will go to his independent study of coding and time with his mentor. • **Technology enrichment:** To use the website Tynker to work through coding lessons and eventually create a game to help other students practice a unit from the patterns, functions, and algebra strand. He will then present this with his peers at the end of the project. • **Dystopian societies:** Kyan will read a selection of novels on dystopian societies. After reading, Kyan will write his own dystopian story.

Case Study 7: William

Maureen Zwiebel Danovsky has been a public school teacher in Hillsborough Township, NJ, for almost 30 years. She has taught second, third, and sixth grades, and is currently the gifted and talented specialist for her school. She has a certificate in gifted education from Rutgers University and is working on a master's degree in educational psychology from the University of Connecticut.

William, at 8 years old, was a new third-grade student in a heterogeneous classroom of 27 students. Over the summer, William's mother e-mailed the principal and his new teacher. She explained that although William had enjoyed second grade, he was bored, and she hoped he would have more "challenge" during his third-grade year. She also explained that that William and his twin sister, Katherine, were early readers, and had been privately tested before kindergarten due to their early advanced abilities. Their pediatric developmentalist initially suggested acceleration, but the parents and the school district were both firmly against this practice. Another suggestion was that Katherine and William be placed into different homerooms, in order to help both twins strengthen their social skills and interactions with others.

Early in September, the reading specialist assessed William's reading ability using a variety of measures. His Developmental Reading Assessment (DRA) and Running Records scores indicated that he read fluently and with expression. The Independent Reading Level Assessment Framework (IRLA) revealed that William had a vocabulary at least three levels above others in his class, and was the only student who qualified for the "purple section" (grade 6 level). His DIBELS benchmark scores indicated high decoding abilities. The only area of slight weakness was comprehension with inference. Due to time constraints, the reading specialist discontinued further testing, as he surpassed grade-level expectations.

William's grade 3 teacher spoke with his grade 2 teacher about his reading progress. She learned that William had been allowed to read independently in class whenever he wanted because he was so far ahead of the other students. He usually selected nonfiction books about science or history topics. When he was directed to choose fiction, he often chose humorous books, such as *Captain Underpants*, that were enjoyable but not challenging. He often reacted to these texts by laughing quite loudly and physically reenacting the story, often disturbing other children.

William's grade 2 teacher noted that he had difficulty maintaining eye contact when she worked with him in a reading group, and that he often seemed to "tune-out" when other students were sharing their thoughts or ideas. William frequently forgot to submit his worksheets or literature circle papers and would get off-task when he was expected to be completing seatwork.

William's mother indicated that he had a strong and consistent interest in science and math. When his teacher asked William about his favorite part of the school day, he said it was science time; which was only every other day for 40 minutes. His second-grade teacher noted that during science lessons, William enjoyed sharing his science knowledge and frequently volunteered during class discussions. However, he often called out, and would easily engage in tangents with talk of other science-related topics. William's above-level knowledge in science was assessed by his grade 3 teacher using teacher-created tests and unit posttests. William demonstrated above-level knowledge about Earth science in geology and space, two of the four units taught in third grade.

The school's math specialist assessed William's math abilities using the summative Everyday Math end-of-year grade 3 test. His mother also supplied the results of the MAP test he took over the summer that placed his math abilities at the grade 9 level. His responses to the Everyday Math open-ended questions demonstrated his firm understanding of the grade 3 math standards, and his scores suggested that compacting was in order.

The school's math specialist volunteered to draft the math portion part of the Compactor form. William's teacher decided that he was also an ideal candidate for content compacting. She met with the school's reading specialist and gifted and talented teacher to complete additional compacting options for reading and science.

Because William read fluently and had an advanced vocabulary, he attended his class reading group only for inference work. During the other days, he used reading time to meet with the gifted education teacher and a cluster group of other students with similar abilities. On one of the five days, the gifted education teacher conducted Junior Great Books discussions based on a piece of high-quality fictional literature. On other days, William chose reading selections from the Raz-Kids program based on his interest areas. He completed the corresponding comprehension quizzes online. Because William's Interest-A-Lyzer indicated that his preferred instructional styles included learning games and simulations, on the other days William chose to work on an independent activity using the Renzulli Learning System/GoQuest or he read self-selected nonfiction books and created a game or simulation to teach other students about the reading topic.

William's grade 2 teacher explained that William became disruptive during science class and often called out, played with items in his desk, or appeared to "dig" loudly on his chair between his legs. Because of this keen interest in science and his self-control issues, William's teacher sought a mentor to work with him during the geology and astronomy units. A middle school science teacher on sabbatical agreed to help. His teacher also asked William to complete a contract stating that when he worked independently, or while the teacher was instructing others, he needed to work quietly.

His teachers made arrangements for William and his mentor to meet twice a month in the gifted education room during William's lunch and recess time. During their first meeting, William and his mentor discussed his interests and reviewed his Interest-A-Lyzer. They decided to study the history of catapults, and finish the year by designing and building their own original catapults. William's mentor integrated math concepts into the design and construction of the catapults and a comparison of their performance with small objects.

William appeared to appreciate this one-on-one time with a strong male role model, and he became more aware of the importance of eye contact when speaking with others. William so enjoyed this time with his mentor that his teacher very rarely had to remind him of his contract obligation not to disturb his classmates. William's teacher worked collaboratively with the gifted specialist as well as the school's reading and math specialists. William's Compactor was updated during the second semester to enable him to construct a display of various catapults, and to create a computerized and annotated timeline of their history. He presented his work to grade 2 students at the end of their unit on castles. William's teacher was commended for being proactive in developing the Compactor at the earliest possible time in September, which helped William establish a strong work ethic and a habit for engaging in challenging work.

Individual Education Program Guide
The Compactor

Student Name(s): William S.	Grade: 3	School: Hillsborough	Participating Teachers: Pearson/McConnell
Name it.		**Prove it.**	**Change it.**
Curriculum Area		**Assessment**	**Enrichment/Acceleration Plans**
Name the subject area, unit, chapter, or learning standards that are the focus for compacting.		List the assessment tools and related data that indicate student strengths and interests. List the preassessment data and the learning standards that have not yet been mastered.	Briefly describe the strategies used to ensure mastery of the learning standards that have not been mastered. Name the enrichment or acceleration tasks that will be substituted for the compacted curriculum.

Reading

- Third-grade objectives.

Math

- Third-grade objectives.

Science

- Scott Foresman units.

Assessment

Reading

- DIBELS/DORF: Advanced third-grade levels for fluency, decoding; proficient for inferring.
- DRA: Level 50–fifth-grade level (teacher did not test any higher).
- Running Record: Reading A–Z level S (teacher did not test any higher).
- IRLA: Purple level (teacher did not test any higher); Vocabulary 3 levels above grade level.

Math

- End-of-year math test—scored 99%.
- Everyday Math open-ended questions: 12/12.
- MAP test—ninth-grade level (submitted by parent).

continued

Enrichment/Acceleration Plans

Reading

- William will attend regular reading/class group for days when lesson is on inferring/comprehension practice.
- William will attend GT room for Junior Great Books discussions.
- He will attend GT room to work on Raz Kids and complete comprehension quizzes online.
- William will work on independent project via Renzulli Learning/GoQuest.
- William will have choice to read nonfiction and create game or simulation to teach other third graders about the topic.

continued

Name it.	Prove it.	Change it.
	Science	**Math**
	• Scott Foresman unit posttests—97% or above: independent project with mentor.	• William will create and trade enrichment math boxes for other high-level students in other classes.
	• Teacher-made tests: 99% geology and space units, 95% average on other units.	• He will write open-ended questions for trading purposes.
		• He will complete Renzulli Learning/GoQuest math.
		• William will work on Khan Academy sites bookmarked by the math specialist.
		• He'll use hands-on manipulatives: pentominoes, tangrams, logic games, puzzles, word problems.
		Science
		• William will work with his mentor in the GT room twice a month during lunch and recess.
		• He will communicate with his mentor through Google Docs.
		• He will skip the geology and space units.
		• He will take virtual field trips using Renzulli Learning/GoQuest.
		• William will take on an independent project to work toward end-of-year project.
		• He will create his own rock/mineral display.
		• He will conduct research on his self-selected topic: black holes.

Case Study 8: Matt

Karin Barone is a National Board Certified Teacher who has been teaching in Orange, CA, for the past 15 years. She taught fourth grade and, for the last 10 years, has been teaching gifted students in grades 4–6. Karin earned her master's degree in education from Pepperdine University, earned a gifted and talented certificate from the University of Southern California, and is working on a master's degree in educational psychology from the University of Connecticut.

Matt was a grade 4 student in a class of 30 youngsters. His school was located in a middle income neighborhood in a suburban school district, with a significant number of English language learners who attended the school and received specialized literacy instruction daily through the services of Title I pullout program staff. The school had three gifted and talented classrooms on the campus for students in grades 4–6. Students qualified for admission to these classes based on their scores on the CogAT cognitive abilities test, in addition to other criteria.

Matt did not initially qualify for admission for the gifted program based on his CogAT scores, but he displayed very strong skills in math, reading, and spelling. He read at least two grade levels above his classroom peers. He also had strong interests in science. The gifted and talented teacher offered to help with curriculum compacting and enrichment as needed throughout the school year.

In an effort to provide enrichment experiences for all students in Matt's classroom, including those who were achieving below, at, and above grade level, his teacher asked all students to complete Interest-A-Lyzer surveys and the Renzulli Expression Style Inventory. Using data from these instruments, Matt's classroom teacher learned that he had many different academic interests. Three of his interests—architecture, building things, and art—served as the basis for Matt's acceleration and enrichment opportunities when he received a compacted geometry curriculum.

Compacting in Spelling

Matt earned a score of 100% after taking a pretest from the portion of the Houghton Mifflin spelling program that covered 4 weeks of spelling words. His curriculum was compacted, so he did not have to complete the regular spelling list each week or spelling practice from the language arts workbook. Instead, Matt was asked to spell eight teacher-selected bonus words each week and to choose eight of his own bonus words, either from the social studies or science textbook or from his Type III research. He was given a test on these words at the end of every week.

For spelling enrichment, Matt had the option of choosing two enrichment activities to complete each week from a list created by his teacher (see Figure 10). By choosing more difficult words and allowing Matt to have personal choice with some of his words, the spelling list was differentiated for his personal needs. This provided challenge in work that would otherwise be too easy for him. He worked with complex words when he was with the teacher, words that had just enough of a challenge so that he continued to learn without the frustration of it being too difficult. The use of challenging spelling words also helped to increase vocabulary, a skill that transferred into his reading and writing.

More enrichment choices were added as the year progressed, and Matt had the option of creating some of those choices. The chart listed below illustrates some of these enrichment options. Yearlong compacting in spelling remained a possibility based on each month's pretest scores. Matt's spelling work and related enrichment tasks were assessed using a general rubric scored with the following criteria: content learned, critical thinking, and creative thinking.

Compacting in Math

Matt's teacher administered the Pearson Envision chapter pretest for geometry, and Matt earned a score of 90%. As a result, he was excused from lessons and assignments in this chapter and completed a Type III investigation instead. In order to ensure that he learned the single math concept in which he did not demonstrate mastery on the pretest, he also completed the related classwork and homework for that lesson.

To extend his understanding of the geometry content, Matt completed challenge pages in his math textbook and worked with Marcy Cook math learning centers that focused on geometry and critical and creative thinking. Khan Academy and other web-based enrichment sites were also used as needed. As the year progressed, Matt's teacher was able to compact several more math chapters. Compacting provided considerably more time for Matt to work on his independent research project. Because Matt was given more free time to work in areas of interest to him, his organization, attention, and planning skills improved in all subject areas.

Matt's Type III product

Matt's Interest-A-Lyzer and classroom work indicated that he had strong interests in architecture, art, and building. His Expression Inventory demonstrated his preference for hands-on activities and presentations, tasks well-aligned to his interest in building and art.

Spelling Enrichment Activities

1. Create a crossword or acrostic puzzle.
2. Learn the pronunciation and spelling of the words on your list using a language other than English. Teach these words to the class.
3. Create riddles with the words.
4. Create limericks using the words.
5. Use all of the words in an original story.
6. Create alliterative sentences or tongue twisters.
7. Find synonyms for the words and create interesting sentences using those synonyms.
8. Use the words to create similes or metaphors.
9. Create your own spelling enrichment activities.

Figure 10. Matt's possible spelling enrichment activities.

After talking with Matt about possible projects, Matt and his teachers worked together to plan and implement his Type III investigation. First, Matt learned new content about architecture and building design. He also conferred with a guest architect who visited with him periodically during his exploration phase. Next, he learned about the connection between math, art, architecture, and building. Matt used this knowledge to construct a building using geometric shapes. He calculated the area and perimeter of the building and the rooms inside, measured their spatial dimensions, and explained what the building's purpose. He used recycled and inexpensive household items to construct his building, turning the model into a true work of art. Matt worked with the guest architect as he drew, designed, and constructed his building.

Upon completion of the building, Matt prepared a presentation for his class and others. He shared what he learned throughout the entire project and displayed his construction in the school library. Matt's oral presentation was videotaped and uploaded to the class website for parents, the school board, and administrators to view. His Type III product was assessed using a Student Product Assessment Form (SPAF). Matt, his classroom teacher, and the gifted education teacher held a conference at the culmination of the compacted unit to review the evaluation results with him, provide feedback, and share areas for improvement for his next Type III enrichment project.

Behavioral Strengths

Matt's behavioral strengths included his ability to work independently and his motivation to delve deeper into content. He completed class assignments quickly and with relative accuracy. His one area of weakness was that he did not spend sufficient time organizing and planning complex tasks. He usually wanted to get started and finish tasks quickly so he could start on the next task. This behavior caused problems when his final product did not meet his own expectations. His teachers used organizational templates and note-taking organizers to help him collect research data, plan the building process, and create his presentation. Although the entire class learned the related research skills, math compacting provided additional time for Matt to participate in several conferences to plan with the gifted education teacher. He also completed a brief questionnaire that served as a self-assessment of his work and product. Survey questions included the following:

- What new information have you learned?
- How did you complete your research?
- Did you make any changes to your project? If so, what were they? If not, why not?
- What questions do you have after working today?
- How could you find some of these answers? What took up a majority of your time today?
- Was this a success or do you need to rethink your idea?
- What do you need to do/get before your next project time?
- What do you need from your classroom or gifted and talented teacher to support your project?

Completing the reflection questions helped Matt become better organized, develop his self-regulation, and focus on his end goal: completing a high-quality product. The reflection questions also helped the classroom and gifted education teachers assess Matt's needs throughout the unit.

Continued Services

Matt's compacting process took place over the course of the geometry chapter, and he continued to be assessed for other compacting opportunities in math. His Type III project was fairly involved and he continued to work on the project after the geometry chapter was finished. Completion required 2 months of work. In order to continue to offer differentiated services to Matt, the gifted education teacher gave the classroom teacher several copies of the Action Information Message lightbulb. This communication memo allowed both Matt and his classroom teacher to share ideas for future projects, research, and investigation. Matt's classroom teacher enjoyed the compacting process and realized that Matt was able to learn more, be engaged, and provide Type I activities to the rest of the class. She also noted positive differences in his ability to slow down and organize his work and final products. She has decided to try to identify additional students who could benefit from math compacting as well as compacting in other subject areas.

Individual Education Program Guide
The Compactor

Student Name(s): Matt   Grade: 3   School: LaVeta   Participating Teachers: Barone (G/T) and Beutler (Classroom)

Name it.	Prove it.	Change it.
Curriculum Area	**Assessment**	**Enrichment/Acceleration Plans**
Name the subject area, unit, chapter, or learning standards that are the focus for compacting.	List the assessment tools and related data that indicate student strengths and interests. List the preassessment data and the learning standards that have not yet been mastered.	Briefly describe the strategies used to ensure mastery of the learning standards that have not been mastered. Name the enrichment or acceleration tasks that will be substituted for the compacted curriculum.
Spelling	**Spelling**	**Spelling**
• Four week unit of spelling words.	• Outstanding scores and grades; received 100% on pretest of all words for 4 week unit of spelling words.	• No reinforcement of words needed. • Matt will not need to complete review spelling pages from workbook. • Eight bonus words a week will be given by teacher; with eight student selected bonus words from the science or social studies text. • Matt will choose two two from a list of five enrichment spelling activities to complete a week.
Math	**Math**	**Math**
• Geometry chapter.	• Scored 90% on math pretest for Pearson Envision geometry chapter. He typically earns high grades on math chapter pretests and district periodic math assessments. • Matt will be given a pretest for every math chapter and every spelling unit. Depending on his pretest scores, he will have the ability to compact out of further chapters and units.	• Matt will join the class lessons for skills that were not mastered on the pretest. • Matt will complete Envision enrichment and or supplemental pages as needed.
Behavioral Strengths		
• Matt is self-motivated, working through class material quickly and with relative accuracy; sometimes needs assistance in the planning of complex tasks rather than rushing through them. • Matt is interested in architecture, building things, and art.		

continued

continued

Name it.	Prove it.	Change it.
	• Depending on how Matt scores on advanced spelling words and after conferencing with him, he may have the opportunity to compact out of advanced spelling words as well. If he is working on independent study during a unit that he has compacted out of, then his enrichment spelling time could be spent on his independent project instead.	• Matt will work on Marcy Cook logic and critical thinking math centers. • Additional math enrichment will be provided as needed. • Khan Academy and other web-based enrichment will be provided. • Matt will learn about math and its connection to art and building structures Type I and II. • Matt will complete an architecture/art Type III activity or a Type III from the interest centers. • Interact simulation work will be provided as needed or wanted. • His independent study project will incorporate math, art, and architecture. He will research math and art and their connection to architecture. Matt will use this knowledge to construct a building of his own that uses geometric shapes from recycled material.

Case Study 9: Nick

Pam Peters is the parent of two gifted children and very involved with their schooling. She is a member of the National Association for Gifted Children as well as the California Association for the Gifted. She has an undergraduate degree in psychology and is pursuing a doctorate in educational psychology from the University of Connecticut with a focus on gifted education, creativity, and talent development.

During the 2013–2014 school year, Nick was 8 years old and enrolled in a class with 33 other grade 4 students. His school was designated as a Title I center and it housed two other grade 4 classrooms. Nick entered kindergarten at 5 years of age. At the start of the year, his teacher found that he could read a few words and loved solving math problems. His mother reported that her favorite car game was to "solve adds." As an example, she relayed a story about when Nick was 4 years old and kept asking for harder problems. In response, she gave Nick the following: "You are going to the beach to play with two of your friends. You have seven sand toys. How many do you each get?"

His response: "Chloe and Hailey each get two and I get three."

Nick enjoyed kindergarten, progressed in all academic areas, and by the end of the year was reading chapter books such as The Magic Tree House and the Junie B. Jones series. Nick also excelled in grade 1 and 2. His first-grade teacher was able to differentiate the curriculum a great deal, but Nick started to complain that he "hated school math" even as he continued to enjoy working with numbers at home. In grade 2, it became clear that he was progressing much more rapidly than his peers, and Nick's teacher encouraged his parents to consider grade-level acceleration. Nick was beginning to show signs of disengagement: arguing with teachers and sitting through lessons with his head on his desk. During an intervention planning meeting with his parents, the school principal, and the school psychologist, his teacher cited a small-group discussion in which Nick was explaining to his group the differences between urban, suburban, and rural areas. According to his report, Nick was explaining everything very clearly and was correct in his interpretation, but "none of the other students were able to follow his line of reasoning." She felt very strongly that Nick needed to be with students who were older and had more intellectual maturity. Everyone present agreed to grade acceleration.

In June of his grade 2 year, Nick was double promoted to grade 4 at the suggestion of his classroom teacher. He was also selected to participate in the Gifted and Talented Education (GATE) program, which began in grade 4. His school district offered afterschool enrichment but no gifted education services were available during the school day.

As part of his transition to grade 4, school educators administered the summative grade 3 assessment; Nick scored well, and was found to be reading at the 10th-grade level. He read accurately and fluently with a high level of comprehension. Nick's grade 4 teacher knew that he would need several curriculum modifications, but his school did not offer subject-area acceleration, so his teacher implemented curriculum compacting. The three grade 4 teachers used flexible grouping for math, but it was clear that Nick would also need compacting and differentiation in math and possibly science and social studies as well.

To get a clearer picture of Nick's math achievement level, his teacher administered the summative grade 4 math assessment. Nick scored 90%, despite having received no math instruction beyond the second-grade curriculum. This assessment provided strong evidence in support of math compacting, but also revealed a few areas in which he would benefit from math instruction with the class.

Each Monday, the students in Nick's fourth-grade class were given a pretest on their 20 spelling words for the week. When students scored 90% or better, they were allowed to create their own list of 15 words to learn for the week, with the caveat that any words they missed must be included on their own list. Nick was able to create his own "challenge list" more than 70% of the time, and he expressed his appreciation for this system on numerous occasions. His personal spelling lists included words that were far more difficult than any on the regular list, and were a wonderful glimpse into his interests as well as the books he was reading. While reading Harry Potter, for instance, Nick's list included words such as *alchemy*, *transfiguration*, and *horcrux*.

Flexible grouping for reading also enabled Nick to work with other high-level readers on a regular basis. Nick's reading assessment placed him at a grade 10 level at the beginning of fourth grade. His reading group included 27 students with reading levels ranging from grades 6–10. The group was smaller than his regular classroom group because his school used Title I funds to hire a reading resource teacher who led a group of struggling readers.

Nick's reading teacher, who was also his classroom teacher, used small groups to challenge and engage each student. Students chose from a selection of novels and worked in literature circles with the other students who had read the same book. Literature circles encouraged him to discuss the books with his classmates and to think analytically about plot, character development, and other literary elements.

Because Nick loved to read, he was content to read some easier material during school and filled his reading time at home with more challenging work such as *Around the World in Eighty Days* and other classics. His teacher challenged him to take the Accelerated Reader comprehension tests to ensure that he had an understanding of the more difficult books he read at home.

Five additional students in Nick's class were identified as academically advanced in mathematics. As the class began each unit, those students were given a pretest, which was the end-of-chapter assessment provided in the textbook. Each of these students, including Nick, was allowed to work on other projects during math time if their pretest demonstrated a proficiency level of 85% or higher.

Nick's teacher anticipated that he would be able to compact a great deal of his math instruction. She met with him early in September to discuss what he might do during his compacted time. Together, they identified an interest that Nick had in starting a school newspaper. She found a parent who was willing to work with him on a volunteer basis to guide him in this process. An added benefit of this project was that he needed to recruit and work with other students, facilitating his connection with students in his new grade.

As expected, Nick passed the vast majority of the math pretests, resulting in a significant amount of time to work on his newspaper project. He was able to research student newspapers in the area, recruit other students to help, learn how to write editorials, visit other classrooms to investigate their activities, and learn about interviewing.

As a group, the student journalists published five editions of the *Lion's Roar*. One of Nick's least favorite academic activities had always been writing, but through his work on the newspaper he became more enthusiastic about it, and was able to focus on editing and revision skills, which he had previously tended to ignore.

Nick wanted to create a presentation about how he started the newspaper and present it at the Student to Student Conference sponsored by the California Association for the Gifted in his region. He was unable to secure a presentation spot, but he attended the conference and presented on another topic the following year. Because he was unable to secure a spot at the conference, his teacher arranged for him to give a presentation to students from another elementary school in the district interested in starting its own newspaper.

As a new fourth grader, Nick decided to run for student council vice president, an office that must be held by a fourth grader at his school. Part of his platform was his goal to start a school newspaper. Other students were excited about this idea and he won the election. He was able to maintain friendships with his former peers, who were currently in third grade, while making new friends in fourth grade.

Nick had a successful grade 4 year, ending at or above grade level in all academic areas. The disruptive behaviors he had begun to exhibit during grade 2 did not reappear, and he ended the year happy and well adjusted. Everyone involved agreed that the grade acceleration, combined with the compacting, was a huge success. As a 10-year-old grade 6 student, Nick adjusted well to middle school, and enjoyed the responsibility of keeping track of his classes and assignments. His parents shared his scores from the Smarter Balance test taken in fifth grade, with a perfect math score of 2700/2700 and a language arts score of 2693/2701. As a grade 6 student he received grades of A in each subject area, with a 4.0 average.

Individual Education Program Guide
The Compactor

Student Name(s): Nick Grade: 4	School: San Jose Elementary School	Participating Teachers: n/a
Name it.	**Prove it.**	**Change it.**
Curriculum Area	**Assessment**	**Enrichment/Acceleration Plans**
Name the subject area, unit, chapter, or learning standards that are the focus for compacting.	List the assessment tools and related data that indicate student strengths and interests. List the preassessment data and the learning standards that have not yet been mastered.	Briefly describe the strategies used to ensure mastery of the learning standards that have not been mastered. Name the enrichment or acceleration tasks that will be substituted for the compacted curriculum.
Mathematics • Nick was a second grader in 2012–2013. He skipped third grade, but tested extremely high on the end-of-third-grade math benchmark at the end of his second grade year. **Reading** • Nick's testing shows comprehension at a high school level. He also reads very accurately and fluently. **Spelling** • All students are given the opportunity to compact spelling on a weekly basis.	**Math** • In August of this year, he was given the end-of-fourth-grade district benchmark and scored 90%. • Nick will take a pretest (end-of-unit test in the book) for each unit covered this year. If he shows mastery (85% +), then we will compact that unit. If he shows less than 85% on any unit or topic within a unit, then he will work with the class on that specific area. As he will likely compact most units, pretests will be given during the final testing period for the previous unit. Separate times can be arranged as necessary. *continued*	**Math** • Subject matter acceleration is not an option in this school, so it is likely he will need the math curriculum compacted. • Nick has expressed interested in working on a Type III project that culminates in a presentation at the annual Student to Student conference in April. Our school does not have a resource teacher/GATE teacher, but a parent volunteer and I will guide him through this project. He will be given time to work on this during time saved by compacting. *continued*

Name it.	Prove it.	Change it.
	Reading	**Reading**
	• He will be asked to complete comprehension tests using the Accelerated Reader program to ensure understanding of the material. Observation of group discussions and collection of literature circle material will also show proficiency in this area.	• Students are ability grouped for reading instruction. Within these groups, they work in small groups to complete many of the instructional activities. Nick will be grouped with other advanced readers and given higher level books to read and discuss. The advanced readers will tackle more difficult books. They will discuss and complete literature circle packets that include higher level thinking topics and questions. Students in the group will get to choose their books from a given group, with each student having input.
	Spelling	**Spelling**
	• Each Monday, students are given a pretest on the weekly spelling list. Any student who scores 80%–100% correct is given the opportunity to compact. These pretests measure proficiency with the basic spelling lists.	• Students who score 80%–100% on the pretest will be given the chance to create their own spelling list for the week. The lists must have 15 words and must include any words that they missed on the original list. Students with "challenge lists" pair up and test each other during spelling test time.

Case Study 10: Max

Deborah Trethewey has been both a public and private school teacher for almost 11 years in Connecticut and New York City. Most recently, she has served as a second-grade teacher in Redmond, WA. She has taught at both the elementary and middle school levels. She has a master's degree in sociology and education from Teacher's College, Columbia University, has an administrative certificate from Sacred Heart University, and is working on a master's degree in educational psychology from the University of Connecticut.

Max was an 11-year-old boy who had recently completed grade 5. He attended an independent school in New York City and had been a strong math student since kindergarten. His former teachers had differentiated his grade-level curriculum. No formal gifted education program or identification process existed at the school and prior to grade 6; he had never had an opportunity to use an accelerated curriculum.

In general, school was very easy for Max, and math was his best subject area. Max achieved on or slightly above grade level in all of the other core subject areas. He had a good relationship with his English and social studies teacher, but he was disruptive in math, music, and art. He repeatedly said that "math is boring." He sometimes displayed impatience and inappropriate, disruptive behaviors.

Max often tried to dominate his class to gain his teachers' attention. When working alone, he would request a conversation with the teacher or interrupt other children and make his presence and opinions known. He often discussed age-inappropriate topics with peers and frequently used inappropriate language in the classroom. At times, Max exhibited bullying behaviors, such as calling other students fat, ugly, and stupid. He frequently blurted out comments in class and often did not follow directions. His teachers believed there was a social-emotional component to Max's behaviors. His needs were often discussed at grade-level meetings and various strategies were implemented to modify his behavior. As far as his teachers knew, there had been no diagnostic testing recommended for him.

Max enjoyed soccer, computers, and social media. He was also very interested in the Illuminati and conspiracy theories and would eagerly share information he had read or seen on YouTube. Max often left the Illuminati symbol around the school. He was one of the most popular boys in the classroom and his poor behavior influenced the other boys in the class. He was very competitive and enjoyed being challenged.

Max learned new concepts very quickly. His mother reported that he had been able to perform "advanced" math since about age 3. He solved most of his math problems mentally and often resisted recording his thinking process. If he was asked how he solved a problem, he could accurately articulate his process. Max liked to be given choice in the assignments he was to complete and would avoid doing any work that did not interest him.

Max could become very impatient and vocal when lessons seemed to be moving too slowly or when he already knew and understood the lesson before instruction began. This behavior, along with teasing other students who solved math problems more slowly than he did, could cause a classroom disruption. He would often call out and interrupt another student if he felt he or she was taking too long to explain or give an answer. His mother had visited the school numerous times throughout the year and she believed that boredom was the root of his disruptive and defiant behaviors.

In the past, the school support team had met to discuss Max's needs, but the math department chair spoke against allowing him to progress at his own rate and level. Instead, he was allowed to start his practice work during the large-group lesson and complete math puzzles, use the Khan Academy website, or play games on the computer after he had finished his work. At times, Max would incidentally learn a new mathematical property or algorithm, but there was no curriculum or scope and sequence in place to support an acceleration plan. The school had no formal process for identifying gifted students and no gifted services. In order to address Max's needs, the school created a gifted education team that included administrators and teachers. One of their tasks was to determine how to assess Max's math achievement.

Classroom observations suggested that Max had mastered many of the math standards taught at higher grade levels. Analyzing report card data provided some insight, because the school used a standards-based grading system along with achievement levels that included indicators for exceeding the standard. However, the math department administrators told teachers not to give too many "exceeding" grades. They told teachers that "meeting" expectations encompassed a huge range: "It's a lot like throwing darts, most kids should fall in the meets expectations category." Teachers frowned on that directive, but it may have led to inaccurate grades on Max's report card. In the end, Max's work samples along with observations and interviews provided the best information.

Curriculum Areas to Be Considered for Compacting

As stated previously, Max mastered mathematical concepts very quickly. During his grade 6 school year, teachers recommended that the sixth-grade math curriculum be compacted so that he could be accelerated and work with the seventh-grade curriculum and on an interest-based Type III investigation.

At the end of the school year, most grade 6 students take five Math Olympiad assessments and a summative test to determine if they should be enrolled in a regular or an honors-level grade 7 math class. Max took these assessments at the beginning of grade 6 so that his teachers could identify the math standards in grade 6 he had already mastered and those that he still needed to learn. Work samples, Max's scores on the math section of the grade 5 summative assessment from the previous school year, and information from his grade 5 teacher helped in determining which math skills to compact. Max also completed an Interest-A-Lyzer to identify his interest areas for a Type III investigation.

Procedures for Compacting Basic Material

Based on the results of the assessments and input from Max, his teachers developed a compacting plan. In areas where Max had not shown proficiency, he would participate in the regular grade-level math lessons. In addition, the teachers created a flexible small-group cluster of high-achieving math students so that they could work together on their accelerated math curriculum while the teacher worked with the rest of the class. The cluster met three times each week. Max met with this group to learn grade 7 math standards when he had demonstrated mastery of the content the rest of the class was learning. The goal would be for the cluster to meet at least three times per week. Members of this group pursued their accelerated math curriculum by using the Khan Academy website, attending the grade 7 math classes, or by working with the grade 6 teacher on an independent learning activity.

Acceleration and Enrichment Activities

Max was able to work on his Type III Enrichment project at least twice a week using time he earned though math compacting. He worked with his teacher to decide on his product and how he would present his learning. The teacher team also agreed to provide more Type II and Type III activities for more students in the future.

Individual Education Program Guide

The Compactor

Student Name(s): Max	Grade: 6	School: Columbia Grammar	Participating Teachers: Boyle and Trethewey
Name it.		**Prove it.**	**Change it.**
Curriculum Area		**Assessment**	**Enrichment/Acceleration Plans**
Name the subject area, unit, chapter, or learning standards that are the focus for compacting.		List the assessment tools and related data that indicate student strengths and interests. List the preassessment data and the learning standards that have not yet been mastered.	Briefly describe the strategies used to ensure mastery of the learning standards that have not been mastered. Name the enrichment or acceleration tasks that will be substituted for the compacted curriculum.
Math		**Math**	**Math**
• Grade 6 and grade 7 math standards.		• Achievement data from grade 5 math shows ERB scores by standard. • End-of-fifth-grade report card (teacher narrative and marks) shows that Max exceeded expectations on grade-level standards. • Discussions with prior-year teachers. • Max will take the end-of-unit math test as a pretest at the beginning of the unit. • The classroom teacher gathered work that demonstrated Max's understanding of grade-level content and beyond. This is done on a unit-by-unit basis. • Complete Interest-A-Lyzer to determine areas of interest.	• Max will work on the grade 6 math skills that he has not yet mastered. This will be done by limiting the number of skill sheets and workbook problems he is asked to complete. • In areas where Max has shown proficiency, he will complete advanced coursework using grade 7 units of study. • Max will use Khan Academy resources to support his math acceleration work. • Max will meet with the homogenous math cluster three times per week. • Max can work on his Type III Enrichment project. He is studying secret societies such as the Illuminati and their impact on history.

Case Study 11: James

Jana Sanchez-Terry is in her sixth year as the registrar for the Greenwich Education Group. She earned her bachelor of arts degree in communication studies from Indiana University and is pursuing her master's degree in educational psychology with an emphasis in gifted education from the University of Connecticut.

James was a rising grade 9 student in a small independent school where the average class size was quite small and students were grouped by achievement levels rather than by age. James achieved two grade levels above his peers. During the previous 3 years, his English grades had been outstanding and he sought additional challenge in reading. In grade 6, teachers placed him in the highest level of English class where he received a grade of B+. In a narrative report, his English teacher stated:

> I am always curious to see what James will pull from his bright, clever, witty mind when a writing assignment is given. If he is able to put a spin on an assignment, it often produces a product that in no way fits the parameters given, but is arguably better. If James does not come up with an "alternate route" for his writing assignment, the product is often a bare bones version of the assignment. Many times, James will turn in something well below the standards set for the assignment or opt to skip it all together, claiming that he would rather take a zero than complete a writing assignment.

In grade 7, James was placed in a grade 9 English class. James really soared in this setting and he earned an A- for the year. Giving James more challenging material ignited his passion for the subject. His grade 7 teacher commended him on his ability to turn class discussions into in-depth conversations that focused on details from the novel that other students overlooked. She also commented on his passion for reading and how it helped him with his comprehension.

This trend continued in grade 8 where James earned an A as his final grade in an Honors English 10 class. His teacher noticed his ability to support his class discussions with literary evidence, adding that James had the ability to recognize his subject area strengths and strove to challenge himself and the others in class. In grade 8, James scored in the 99th percentile on the Comprehensive Testing Program (CTP) in the areas of verbal reasoning, vocabulary, and quantitative reasoning. His highest scores were on his writing assessment, but he also did very well with argumentation and organization. James was an avid reader and often spent his free time reading various literary genres.

He also had a passion for computers and philosophy. During the previous three summers, James was enrolled in summer enrichment programs in which he participated in numerous philosophy courses, which were organized as discussion and debate classes moderated by the teacher. James's strengths lay in his ever-growing vocabulary and his class discussions. His innate ability to think deeply and well beyond others of his age allowed him to form opinions that he could substantiate with evidence. He also participated in various computer-programming classes in which he proved himself to be self-motivated and at times extremely committed.

Based on this history, it was clear that James would benefit from having his curriculum compacted and could use the time saved to participate in enrichment activities. In grade 8, he had proposed an independent project to his technology teacher: He wanted to build a computer from scratch. As a grade 9 student, he would be able to work with a faculty advisor to develop a Type II or Type III activity. He also volunteered to organize the debate club. Having compacted time made it possible for James to focus on his true passions: philosophy, debate, and computer science. We created a plan to implement curriculum compacting using the following bolded steps.

Identify the objectives. The objectives of James's English class were to strengthen students' reading, analytic thinking, grammar, and writing skills. These skills were practiced and enhanced through reading and analyzing novels and short stories, completing vocabulary exercises and quizzes, working in the *Writer's Choice Grammar Practice Workbook*, and completing exercises in *Writing Skills Book 3*. James developed his editing skills through self- and peer edits.

Find appropriate preassessments and identify students who should take the pretests. James loved reading and he had already read a few of the books on his English syllabus. Because of this, James would be allowed to demonstrate his level of mastery prior to the end of these units. He completed two types of assessments: objective-referenced and performance-based. First, James took a pretest on the unit vocabulary. If James earned a score of 80% or better on the vocabulary quiz, he was excused from the class time devoted to vocabulary.

James's teacher also gave him writing prompts to assess the writing and grammar skills addressed in the unit. James participated in a performance-based assessment to demonstrate his analytical and comprehension skills; he had a conference with the teacher and they discussed the themes and literary concepts of the unit. The teacher used a rubric to assess James's work. If James successfully demonstrated mastery of the unit's objectives, he was allowed to meet with his faculty advisor instead of attending class.

Because James's school and classes were small, teachers would often work with the same students every year, allowing them to design curriculum tailored to each student's strengths. Students who had attended enrichment programs in the summer often returned with new knowledge that compelled related compacting.

If a new student registered, teachers administered several assessments to ensure the student was enrolled in the proper classes. Once students were placed in a class, they had the option to demonstrate mastery, receive a compacted curriculum, and work on an enrichment project with a faculty advisor.

Pretest students to determine mastery levels and eliminate instructional times for students who show mastery of these objectives. Teachers administered the appropriate pretests, and if James demonstrated full or partial mastery of the unit's learning objectives, he was excused from the classes in which these standards and objectives were taught. Of course, he participated with his class when they worked on objectives that he had not mastered.

James was allowed to work with either his faculty advisor or the technology teacher during the times that he was excused from class. If other students met the same criteria, they were also assigned to a faculty advisor who would help with their enrichment work as well.

Provide small group or individualized instruction for students who have not yet mastered all the objectives, but are capable of doing so more quickly that their classmates. Because James was an avid reader, he was able to complete the work for the standards he hadn't mastered at his own pace, which was usually faster than the whole-class pacing. James was able to read novels in advance of his class and he chose to read in the library on the days the class read; however, James stayed in class to participate in class discussion because this was one of his strength areas.

Offer academic alternatives for students whose curriculum has been compacted. With the time made available through compacting, James participated in enrichment activities guided by a faculty advisor. He had strong interests in the areas of philosophy, computers, and debate. James met with his advisor during his English block. He and his advisor identified a topic for James to research, and they completed a Management Plan for Individual and Small-Group Investigations. This document helped James's advisor monitor and support his Type III investigation.

James also worked with his advisor to organize the debate club. He was responsible for promoting the club and researching debate topics. James also met with the technology teacher to complete the independent projects he proposed at the end of grade 8; he designed cyphers that could be used to crack codes in books, TV shows, and video games. He also built a computer from scratch.

Keep records of the compacting process. James's teacher maintained records of any pretests and written or oral assessments she administered to James. She also documented the scores and uploaded them into the school's student information system. She continuously updated his curriculum compacting form and recorded changes as soon as they occurred. When James was exempted from a unit of study, his faculty advisor completed a management plan that provided details about his investigation and research. By following these steps, James's teacher was able to successfully compact his English curriculum, leaving time for more satisfying enrichment activities.

James's teachers' use of compacting in English inspired other teachers to do the same with students in their own classes. Our school mission is to "provide an inspirational learning environment . . . and empower (students) with the love of learning, tools for ongoing success, and the courage to find their own light." By compacting the curriculum, we are providing our students the opportunities they need in order to find their own light. Working with faculty advisors on their enrichment activities, students truly empower themselves by taking control of their own learning.

Conclusion

Although no panacea exists for adjusting or modifying the regular curriculum for high-ability students, these case studies about the use of curriculum compacting provide both direction and specific examples as to what can be accomplished with some dedicated time and effort. Our field tests, case studies, and research indicate that compacting can be implemented by teachers who take the time and effort to implement this process.

Deciding which replacement activities to use is often the most challenging part of this process for teachers, and, as we have stated, some basic concerns should guide these decisions: (a) the appropriate level of challenge for the students; (b) the individual content strengths, interests and learning styles of the student; (c) the engagement and enthusiasm of the students toward the replacement work; and (d) the availability of advanced content and other enrichment and/or acceleration alternatives.

Many classroom teachers have not been exposed to the strategies needed to differentiate curriculum for high-ability and high-potential students in the regular classroom setting. For this reason, as much assistance and support as possible should be provided. As demonstrated in these case studies, there is more than one way to compact curriculum. The goal is effective, appropriate instruction for all students, and many methods, materials, and strategies can be employed to reach this goal. By tapping into the creativity of many teachers, such as those showcased in this chapter, the individual styles, strengths, and needs of both teachers and students can be addressed.

Individual Education Program Guide
The Compactor

Student Name(s): James H.	Grade: 9	School: The Beacon School	Participating Teachers: Andrea Caserta
Name it.	**Prove it.**		**Change it.**
Curriculum Area	**Assessment**		**Enrichment/Acceleration Plans**
Name the subject area, unit, chapter, or learning standards that are the focus for compacting.	List the assessment tools and related data that indicate student strengths and interests. List the preassessment data and the learning standards that have not yet been mastered.		Briefly describe the strategies used to ensure mastery of the learning standards that have not been mastered. Name the enrichment or acceleration tasks that will be substituted for the compacted curriculum.
• Vocabulary. • Analytical skills. • Writing skills.	• James is currently 2 years above grade level. He scored in the 99th percentile in verbal reasoning, vocabulary, and quantitative reasoning. • His grades over the last 2 years have increased with more challenging English levels. • James has already read a lot of the books covered in his English class. • Pretests will be given to James to show his level of mastery with vocabulary and grammar skills. • An oral unit assessment will be given to James to determine if he understands the themes of the novels he has already read. Ms. Caserta will assess him on his analytical skills as well as his comprehension on the novel. • James will be given writing prompts to assess his ability to write using proper grammar, literary concepts, analysis, and thesis development.		• James will be excused for the class periods that address content he has already mastered. He will remain with the class when he needs to learn a given standard. • When James has mastered the material from each unit, he will be excused from class and report to his faculty advisor or the technology teacher for his enrichment/independent projects. • James has strong interests in both philosophy and computers. James will decide which areas he would like to purse for a Type II and/or III Enrichment activity. His faculty advisor will help him with this decision. • James will work with the technology teacher on an independent project that was proposed last year: designing cyphers to crack codes in books, TV shows, and video games. James will also build a computer from scratch. • James will be in charge of the debate club. He will organize the meets and research topics to debate.

7 Assessment Strategies for Measuring Content Mastery and Students' Interests

Introduction

Previous chapters of this book have defined compacting, explained its rationale and process, reviewed its research, and provided examples of compacting forms and student tasks. This chapter is different. It builds on the concepts and processes explained in previous chapters, yet focuses on the importance of gathering and reviewing evidence that will support or refute a decision to provide compacting to a specific student or group of students.

This chapter asks and answers these questions: What is assessment, and what are its formats? What is the purpose of assessment, and what kinds of questions does it answer? What is the process for using assessment and analyzing its data within a compacting plan? What assessment resources and tools support compacting decisions and plans? What are some examples of Column Two in the compacting form? It is evident from these questions that this chapter's content is most closely aligned to the pretesting process and to the second column of the Compactor form, the one that is labeled "Prove it!"

> Recently, an instructional coach in charge of differentiation was working with a middle school principal who has a wonderful, but wry, sense of humor. The specialist asked the principal for his thoughts about how the educators in his school might best identify students who needed either math support or math acceleration. The principal glanced at her, slowly held up his index finger, placed it in his mouth, removed it, and waved his finger in the air, pantomiming the action for weather forecasting based on wind

direction. "Mike," said the coach in mock dismay, "I think we can do better than that!"

Let's hope this chapter provides the answers to her question.

A Rose by Any Other Name: Defining Assessment

Back in the day, it was called testing. Then, we ushered in the era of No Child Left Behind, with its federal mandate to test every student in grades 3–8 and once in high school. Testing became "high stakes," as state departments and journalists began to sort and rank schools and districts based on achievement levels. Both educators and researchers rightly complained of an overuse of restricted response test items (e.g., multiple choice, matching, and true/false), common on most state department and vendor-produced tests, that required only remembering, recounting, and paraphrasing—cognitive skills usually aligned with low-level thinking.

All of those bubble sheet assessments came into question when educators attempted to measure standards and learning goals that required more than recalling and paraphrasing. The concept of testing fell into disfavor.

Enter the alternative terminology: *assessment*. It gradually replaced the term *testing* as researchers and practitioners envisioned, and later developed, a comprehensive suite of measurement tools that included both restricted and constructed response items. Data tables, video clips, performance tasks, and cold and warm writing prompts (complete with related text evidence and data) became the preferred ways to measure standards that demanded analysis, application to unfamiliar content, problem solving, argumentation, synthesis, and communication.

These new item formats are indeed better aligned to the concepts and cognitive behaviors they attempt to measure. The original definition of both testing and assessment, however, remains the same. Regardless of the item format, both assessment and testing tools are vehicles that enable educators to measure and better understand the level of student learning, achievement, and the level of proficiency attained.

Educational achievement assessments are usually aligned with the grade-level learning standards, and these instruments provide evidence for related evaluations, judgments, decisions, and plans that impact curriculum, differentiation, grading, promotion, and program enrollment. With those ends in mind, assessment and testing can be considered both evaluative and diagnostic. An evaluative assessment uses test data to make a judgment about mastery that usually leads to a decision about a grade, promotion, retention, or program participation. On the other hand, the goal of diagnostic assessment is to identify the cause of a learning difficulty or the nature and specific learning problems a student is encountering.

As a general rule, the components within our continually evolving educational assessment system can be organized into at least three groups: summative, interim, and formative. Interim assessment is often further categorized as benchmark or progress monitoring assessment. Together, these categories represent the content being assessed, the time in the instructional cycle when that type of assessment is usually administered, the purpose for the assessment, and the type of question that can be answered with that type of assessment and its resulting data.

Summative Assessments

Summative assessments are typically administered at the end of the school year, marking period, or unit of instruction. Their data are used to synopsize the learning and mastery that has occurred during the given time frame. The purpose of summative assessment is largely evaluative; summative assessment data are used to make judgments about grades, promotion, teaching effectiveness, and the learned mastery of essential concepts and skills. Summative assessments are designed to answer the question: To what extent did students master the learning standards and content introduced and taught during this time period? Educators often use summative assessment data from previous grade levels, courses, or units of instruction to identify students who are potential candidates for compacting. Teachers also use the summative assessment instruments themselves to design duplicate preassessments for administration at the beginning of a unit of instruction. A teacher who uses summative assessments during the compacting process usually does so to identify potential candidates for compacting, to create a parallel pretest, or to measure the impact of compacting on overall student achievement. Summative assessments and their data ask and answer the question: What did students learn over the course of their enrollment in this class?

Interim Assessments

Interim assessments, also called benchmark assessments, are similar, but not identical, to summative assessments. They are administered approximately two, three, or four times during a school year or unit of instruction. Some interim assessments measure the same learning standards as those measured by a summative assessment. Students take these assessments repeatedly during the school year to measure growth and identify learning gaps and needs. A math fluency assessment that measures addition and subtraction skills with single digits is an example of an interim assessment that might be administered often during the same school year. The term *benchmark* arises from the purpose for this type of interim assessment, to measure growth and progress during the school year, with time available for either compacting or intervention.

Interim assessments can also measure a segment of the content or standards taught and learned at a given time of the year. These types of tests are sometimes referred to as unit tests or block assessments because they do not measure the expected learning goals for the entire school year, just the learning expected for a given section of time or block of content.

 To this end, educators and test constructors divide a grade-level course into units based on a few constructs or learning standards. These units of study and block assessments either correspond to the time frame during which that content is taught and learned by students or to the construct they are measuring, or both. For example, a social studies interim assessment for a grade 8 U.S. history class might measure student understanding of the U.S. Constitution while the entire grade 8 social studies curriculum addresses the time period between the Revolutionary War and Westward Expansion. In a similar manner, a language arts teacher might administer an interim block assessment that measures only one of the elements of this curriculum—that which addresses reading comprehension with informative text.

Although some interim assessments are used for the purpose of grading and reporting progress, most are used diagnostically to identify those students who may have learning gaps that can be corrected using small-group instruction and support. In many cases, interim assessments answer the question: How well are students progressing with current expectations and learning goals? A teacher who uses curriculum compacting as an instructional strategy may also use interim assessments to compact portions of a school year's subject-area curriculum.

Formative Assessments

Formative assessments comprise the third category or assessment component. These types of assessments measure student understanding of the daily lesson's content and learning goal. They can occur at the beginning, in the middle, or at the end of a lesson and they can be as simple as a private question posed to an individual student, a large-group assignment, an exit ticket, or individual student digital answers to teacher-designed questions using the Socrative or Kahoot! technology-based response system.

The important distinction between formative assessment and summative and interim assessment is that its data are used to modify instruction and provide immediate corrective feedback or to form temporary intervention groups immediately after the assessments are administered. Students who appear to be having difficulty understanding a concept or applying a skill are provided with supportive instruction. As such, formative assessment's purpose is diagnostic in nature. It aims to identify students who have not mastered the daily lesson goal and remedy the cause of the misunderstanding. Formative assessments and their data ask the question: How well do students understand the content and goal of today's lesson? Despite the significant, numerous, and beneficial outcomes for the consistent use of formative assessment, it is rarely used to decide for which students and what content should be compacted. However, it is a useful strategy when supporting enrichment or acceleration for students with a compacted curriculum.

The Purpose of Assessment Within the Compacting Process

The role of assessment within the curriculum compacting process can best be categorized as both evaluative and diagnostic. It is evaluative when educators make decisions about who is a potential candidate for curriculum compacting and when deciding which content can be eliminated from instruction and practice. It is diagnostic when assessments are used to identify the essential and authentic learning needs of individual students as they relate to the grade-level curriculum.

For example, consider a middle school life science teacher who constructs a pretest about cell organelles that parallels the summative assessment for the same unit of instruction. The pretest is aligned closely to the five essential standards within the unit, and there are multiple assessment items with varied formats, both restricted and constructed response, that measure each of those standards at the appropriate cognitive level. The teacher administers the pretest to students approximately 2 weeks prior to the beginning of the unit in order to have enough time to plan for differentiation and compacting prior to the unit's onset. When the teacher analyzes the pretest data, she examines it using a spreadsheet that is organized with the students' names listed in the first column followed by their standards-based mastery score levels in the next five columns.

This standards-based spreadsheet format allows her to identify individual student strengths and needs with ease. She uses her school's standards-based grading codes (the numbers 1–4) to note each student's proficiency level with each of the five standards. A score of 3 represents grade-level proficiency and standards mastery. The teacher then offers compacting to students who have mastered at least three of the five unit standards with the provision that they also complete either large-group or independent study work to learn the standards they had not yet mastered. This example illustrates the use of assessment, and its data, as both a diagnostic and a decision-making or evaluation tool.

For the purposes of curriculum compacting, the assessment process and the data that emerges from it can be used in at least four different ways. First, data from previously administered subject-area and grade-level assessments can be sorted and ranked to locate students who might be potential candidates for curriculum compacting. This often involves the use of summative assessment from the last grade level.

Second, a pretest or preassessment can be constructed to measure students' mastery of some or all of the subject area's, grade level's, or unit's learning standards at the beginning of the unit or school year, prior to large-group instruction. Alternately, a different version or form of the postassessment for the same unit or class can be administered as a pretest.

A third use for assessment during the compacting process involves sorting and analyzing the preassessment data by standards/learning goals and proficiency level. Standards-based compacting is provided to any students who demonstrate mastery with a given standard or set of standards.

The fourth use for assessment is to use the same pretest data to identify those standards that have not yet been mastered by a student who is or will be receiving a compacted curriculum and alternative enrichment or acceleration. It is just as important to find those learning gaps and resolve them as it is to provide both compacting and alternative enrichment and acceleration. This sort of assessment data analysis usually results in a student participating in enrichment or acceleration alternatives during the time when other students are working on the standards he or she already mastered. Conversely, the students with a compacted curriculum must either return to class or use an alternative method to learn the standards not yet mastered.

For a moment, consider assessment as a compass or road map. Assessment, and its subsequent data, doesn't give us step-by-step directions for data analysis, decision making, instruction, or pacing—let alone compacting. Assessments and their data don't tell educators what to do about compacting, but they do give teachers the evidence they need to make logical and data-based decisions. Instead of viewing assessment as a distasteful process that must be endured, as it often is when teachers administer the state and federally mandated high-stakes summative tests, the kinds of assessments used to support compacting are usually viewed as road maps that point the way to viable alternatives for students with advanced subject-area knowledge and skills.

The second column of the Compactor form is often labeled, "Prove it!" This nickname stems from the fact that the purpose of the second column is to document the process, tools, and data used to measure students' knowledge about concepts and skills that are about to be taught. The implementation of pretesting, as a common practice across all subject areas and grade levels, lies at the heart of the compacting rationale.

Describing the Assessment Process

Assessment data informs the compacting process, and many educators find it useful to include more than one type of assessment when making these decisions. Screening assessment data can be reviewed to locate students who are potential candidates for compacting. The data from preassessments that measure the learning goals and standards for a given grade level, subject area, or unit of study help teachers identify the specific learning standards, content, and skill instruction that can be eliminated for certain students based on evidence of prior mastery. Preassessment data can also be used to identify learning needs that are contraindicators for compacting—at least for the explicit standards not yet mastered by a student with overall advanced achievement. Fourth, interest and preference data helps instructors and students determine whether to offer content or interest enrichment or subject-area acceleration. Finally, measuring the summative achievement of students who received a compacted curriculum and reviewing students' end-of-year reflections about their compacting experience helps to evaluate the impact of the service on achievement and engagement.

These same five assessment findings should be documented in the second column of the compactor form. First, teachers should document the screening instrument and resulting data that indicated the student or students are viable candidates for curriculum compacting. Next, the teacher names the test or assessment strategies that were used as a preassessment to document student achievement for a given subject area or unit of study, listing the pertinent data. The second column of the compactor form should also identify the standards that were deemed not mastered on the preassessment instrument. Last, but not least, educators summarize information gleaned from individual student conferences, inventories, or questionnaires that describe interests, learning questions, and preferences for content-based enrichment, interest-based enrichment, or subject-area acceleration.

First Things First

Experience suggests that when a teacher decides to offer compacting to some of the students in a class, it is best to begin not by testing, but rather by making students aware of the compacting process and its impact on the grouping patterns and learning tasks provided to some students. Some teachers find that it is best to use the early weeks of the school year for this purpose. They can provide students with an overview about compacting, its purpose, and strategies, and this overview should be offered to all students in the class. Despite prior assessment evidence to the contrary, a few students who may seem to be unlikely candidates for curriculum compacting will rise to the surface once they know that the "reward" for mastery involves student choice of substituted, different work, often based on students' interests. Teachers report that is it also advisable to inform parents as well, so that they are aware of the potential teaching, learning, and assignment differences that can result from curriculum compacting.

If all students in the class will not participate in unit-based or subject-area preassessment, we suggest that teachers contact parents and receive permission for individual preassessment administration. Most states have laws and policies that allow teachers to administer curriculum-based assessments at will to all students in the class. However, these same laws usually prohibit educators from administering assessments or providing services to individual students or a select group of students without parental permission. And this is how it should be. Parents have the right to accept or refuse participation in assessments and services that are not provided to the entire class or student population. Accordingly, parents should be informed of plans to conduct preassessment with some, or even all students in a class before it happens. School or teacher websites, parent-teacher conferences, and large-group parent meetings are all viable options for sharing and explaining how assessment of this type works.

Screening

Compacting sometimes occurs when a student, parent, or teacher initiates a request for more challenging schoolwork. This is certainly one viable way to begin the process. There is also much to be said for a proactive approach that seeks out the likely candidates for compacting before they encounter too much coursework that they have already mastered. The squeaky wheel shouldn't be the only student who participates in compacting. Educators sometimes refer to this proactive search for compacting as a screening process.

Screening uses assessment data to identify students who are likely candidates for curriculum compacting. Similar to the universal screening common in Response to Intervention (RtI) initiatives, screening for compacting participants occurs prior to replacing grade-level units, tasks, and lessons with enrichment and acceleration alternatives. It is important to remember that the goal of screening is not to select the students who will receive compacting, but to identify those students who are likely to be good candidates for compacting.

For this reason, the use of existing assessment data can sometimes be more efficient than relying solely on teacher, parent, and student nominations. It is often more valid as well, as long as the assessment data comes from trustworthy sources, a test or assessment that measures the essential standards for that subject area or grade level. End-of-year state summative assessments offer one option for finding these students. Of course, using two sources of data provides even more assurance that the students selected during the screening process will in fact be the students who receive the eventual compacting service.

Some teachers substitute report card and assignment grades as evidence to support compacting decisions. These can be viable alternatives as long as the report card and assignment grade are linked to specific and named course or unit learning standards.

Teachers can also access their state department of education's online test reporting system. Download the data to a spreadsheet, including variables such as name, present teacher, subtest scale scores, overall scale scores, and proficiency level. These data can usually be sorted according to both the overall scale score and the overall achievement level. For example, if a state department sorts its student achievement level into four proficiency levels, and Level 4 represents above-grade-level expectations, the students in this top level have demonstrated that they are viable candidates for compacting. It is important to remember that this screening process does not identify the students who have mastered the present school year or grade-level curriculum, but rather helps identify those students who are likely to possess the most proficiency with the previous grade level's standards in that subject area.

Preassessment

Once a teacher has identified the students in his or her classroom who are candidates for compacting, the next step involves preassessing those students to measure their mastery of the standards and learning goals linked to upcoming curriculum units. A parallel version of the summative assessment for an upcoming curriculum unit might be a useful tool for this purpose. Some teachers prefer to select only those assessment items from the summative assessment that best measure essential concepts and skills. Still others use performance tasks, conferences (with standards-based questions culled from the unit), and rubrics to measure preinstruction mastery. Again, the name or format of the preassessment and the standards it measures should be documented in Column Two. The related preassessment data is also recorded. If the analysis of preassessment data identifies any subsequent learning goals or standards that have not been mastered, these too should be documented in Column Two.

Interest and Preference Assessment

Assuming that a student will receive full or partial curriculum compacting in one or more of the upcoming curriculum units, other assessment evidence needs to be gathered and documented related to the students and parents' partiality for a specific enrichment topic, investigation question, or acceleration option. Interest inventories, conferences, interviews, and conversations are all viable tools for unearthing these specifics. Again, the data from these sources should be documented in Column Two.

What Not to Do

At this stage, it is not necessary to plan for or document enrichment, acceleration, or individual instruction and practice for standards not yet mastered in Column Two. Educators are only concerned with providing the evidence of compacting candidacy, preassessment mastery, unit-based or subject-area-based learning needs, and students' interests and preferences for alternative learning tasks if compacting is implemented for some or all unit standards. There is time for these decisions and plans if and when the student is actually interested in having his or her curriculum compacted. Of course, explaining in detail the student's responsibilities within compacting is a crucial bridge that must be crossed prior to the onset of enrichment or acceleration services.

Sample Test and Assessment Resources

Assessments and resources used for compacting screening and preassessment generally fall into two categories: teacher-created assessments and vendor-published tests. Both can be useful, depending on the specific assessment's alignment to instructional standards and the worthiness of the assessment items. Although it's good to be able to purchase and use assessments with a track record of established reliability and validity, developed by a team of expert psychometricians who also have a deep understanding of the test content and the stages of child development, this isn't always possible.

Assessments created by teachers, subject-area departments, and curriculum central office administrators can be just as valuable, assuming they are well-aligned to the learning goals and standards they seek to measure. The items and item formats (e.g., constructed response, restricted response, etc.) on these educator-created assessments should also align to the cognitive demand inherent in the learning standard or objective.

Regardless of the format used, the assessment must have undergone some measure of content or expert judge validity, and reliability should be supported with common and standardized expectations for the inclusion of accommodations, time allocations, directions, and scoring procedures. This means that the tests, tasks, and rubrics educators create to measure student learning and make decisions about future differentiation actions need to measure what they are supposed to measure, and they must do so in a consistent fashion. Irrespective of the location, time, and person scoring the assessment, these tests must also be reliable—they must produce similar results, data, and levels regardless of the individual who is scoring the assessment.

Teacher-Developed Assessments

Educators have a wide variety of assessment tools at their disposal. Class assignments, conferences, and questions and student work samples can all be used as potential indicators that a student may have mastered some or all of the content that will be studied in upcoming curriculum units. A standards-based rubric is recommended as the scoring device for this type of constructed response preassessment evidence.

Other teachers use performance tasks and rubrics as preassessment tools, and two examples of performance task rubrics are included in Figures 11 and 12. When a learning standard calls for application to a new task or content, performance tasks are often the best means to measure learning and prior knowledge.

Sometimes, the unit assessments available in a textbook are well-aligned to unit standards and learning goals. When they are, teachers can consider using them as pretests. We suggest that teachers consider this type of preassessment information in a new light—that is, as an indicator of the need for curriculum compacting. Rather than focusing all of our attention on students who struggle with the grade-level curriculum, teachers can create and use pretests to find those students who already understand the content.

Standardized and Published Assessments

In addition to those assessments created by individual teachers, program administrators, or at the school district level, a number of commercial vendors publish assessments that can be used to measure many of the states' math, reading, and writing standards. Before readers get too excited about the thought of

---

**Smarter Balanced Rubric for Grade 6 Math
Performance Task for Statistics and Probability**

RANGE ALD
Target J: Investigate patterns of association in bivariate data.
Level 1
Students should be able to investigate a scatter plot for clustering between two quantities and construct a scatter plot from given data. They should be able to construct a two-way frequency table of given categorical data.
Level 2
Students should be able to investigate a scatter plot for positive, negative, and linear association and informally fit a line to data for a given scatter plot that suggests a linear association. They should be able to calculate frequencies from categorical data in a two-way frequency table.
Level 3
Students should be able to investigate a scatter plot for patterns such as outliers and nonlinear association. They should be able to write an equation for the trend line or line of best fit for a given scatter plot with a linear association. They should also be able to interpret and use relative frequencies from a two-way table to describe possible association between two variables.
Level 4
Students should be able to use scatter plots, trend lines, and associations between variables in two-way frequency tables to make predictions in real-world situations.

Figure 11. Sample rubric 1.

---

accessing and using third-party, standards-based, standardized assessments with established reliability and validity, the truth must be told and it comes with some bad news.

Vendors and commercial companies publish many more language arts and math assessments than those developed for science and social studies. By far, there are more reading assessments than those developed for any other subject area. Commercial assessments in art, music, and physical education are almost nonexistent, but there are some world language assessments that measure conversational fluency. When available, these published assessments tend to be

Grade 2 Common Core Writing Rubric for Student Research

Traits	4	3	2	1
Statement of Purpose or Focus	All of Column 3 and the inclusion of a segment of the text that specifically explains the purpose or focus for the writing.	The text focuses on the description and communication of a topic.	The text focus is implied, but requires revision for clarity and specificity.	The text focus is missing or unclear.
Organization	All of Column 3 and the inclusion of an identifiable text body aligned to the introduction and conclusion.	• Introduces the topic. • Develops the topic. • Provides a concluding statement or section.	The writing demonstrates at least two elements listed in Column 3.	The writing demonstrates less than one of the elements listed in Column 3.
Elaboration of Evidence	Supplies multiple and relevant facts, details, examples, and definitions to develop the topic.	Supplies sufficient facts and definitions to develop the topic.	Supplies some facts and definitions to develop the topic.	Supplies sparse facts and definitions that help to develop the topic.
Language and Vocabulary	All of Column 3 and the inclusion of appropriate academic and domain-specific vocabulary.	• Uses words and phrases acquired through conversations, reading and being read to, and responding to *continued*	The writing demonstrates at least two of the language expectations listed in Column 3.	The writing demonstrates less than two of the language expectations listed in Column 3.

Figure 12. Sample rubric 2.

Traits	4	3	2	1
Language and Vocabulary, *continued*		texts, including using adjectives and adverbs to describe. • Demonstrates understanding of word relationships and nuances in word meanings. • Distinguishes shades of meaning among closely related verbs and closely related adjectives.		
Conventions	All of Column 3 with minimal or no need for teacher feedback and support.	• Uses collective nouns properly. • Forms and uses frequently occurring irregular plural nouns. • Uses reflexive pronouns properly. • Forms and uses the past tense of frequently occurring irregular verbs. *continued*	The writing demonstrated at least eight of the 12 conventions expectations listed in Column 3.	The writing demonstrated less than eight of the conventions expectations listed in Column 3.

Figure 12. Continued.

Traits	4	3	2	1
Conventions, *continued*		<ul><li>Uses adjectives and adverbs, and chooses between them depending on what is to be modified.</li><li>Produces, expands, and rearranges complete simple and compound sentences.</li><li>Demonstrates command of the conventions of standard English capitalization, punctuation, and spelling when writing.</li><li>Capitalizes holidays, product names, and geographic names.</li><li>Uses commas in greetings and closings of letters.</li><li>Uses an apostrophe to form contractions and frequently occurring possessives.</li><li>Generalizes learned spelling patterns when writing words.</li><li>Consults reference materials, including beginning dictionaries, as needed to check and correct spellings.</li></ul>		

Figure 12. Continued.

summative in nature. The possibility of using end-of-the-year tests as preassessments depends on educators' evaluation of worthiness for each specific test reviewed.

Some state departments of education have commissioned social studies and science tests and created work sample and portfolio rubrics for art and music. Sometimes they are willing to share these assessments with educators in other states, sometimes not. Whether or not these content-area state assessments are aligned to the standards students are expected to master in other states depends on the state.

Publishers and state departments of education also provide more K–8 assessments than they do for use in high schools. As more and more high schools begin to be involved in more teaching and learning initiatives that address standards-based teaching and learning, differentiation, personalized learning, and a "move on when ready" approach to lesson pacing and seat time, assessment vendors may respond by developing and selling more content-based and high school assessments. In the meantime, K–12 science, social studies, art, music, and world language teachers and language arts and math teachers in grades 9–12 will continue to develop and refine their own district, department, or teacher-made unit pretests when they want to implement curriculum compacting.

Now for the good news. An increasing number of vendors provide web-based assessment platforms aligned to K–12 reading, writing, and math standards. The list in Figure 13 provides examples of some of these assessments and vendors. A more thorough Internet search will yield even more possibilities. All of the resources listed in Figure 13 can be configured as pretests for the purposes of compacting. Many of these vendors also allow educators to access the practice tasks and/or assessments by selecting only specific standards and choosing the proficiency levels and out-of-grade-level options, testing accommodations, and reading levels.

Examples of Column Two Documentation

For a moment, consider only the second column of the compactor form and the type of evidence and proof an educator might record to substantiate a decision to compact or not to compact a specific student's grade-level, subject-area, or unit curriculum. The directions in this section of the form ask the educator to: "List the assessment tools and related data that indicate student strengths and interests. List the preassesment data and the learning standards that have not

Vendor	Assessment Content	Grade Levels	Web Address
Smarter Balanced Assessment Consortium	Reading, writing listening, speaking, math concepts and procedures, data analysis modeling, and problem solving; math communication aligned to Common Core standards	3–8 and grade 11	http://www.smarterbalanced.org
PARCC	Reading, writing listening, speaking, math concepts and procedures, data analysis modeling, and problem solving; math communication aligned to Common Core standards	3–8 and grade 11	http://parcc.pearson.com
NWEA	Reading, math, and language usage	K–8	https://www.nwea.org
Houghton Mifflin Reading Inventory (formerly the Scholastic Reading Inventory	Reading level assessment based on literal and inferential comprehension; reported in Lexile units that correspond to Common Core expectations	K–12	http://www.hmhco.com/products/assessment-solutions/literacy/sri-index.htm
Math Reasoning Inventory	Diagnostic math assessment	K–5	https://mathreasoninginventory.com
IXL	Math, language arts, science, and social studies aligned to Common Core standards	K–12	https://www.ixl.com
ReadWorks	Reading comprehension aligned to Common Core standards	K–12	http://www.readworks.org

Figure 13. Vendor-created assessment options.

Vendor	Assessment Content	Grade Levels	Web Address
Ten Marks	Math practice tasks aligned to Common Core standards	K–12	https://www.tenmarks.com
Moby Max	Math, language arts, science, and social studies aligned to Common Core standards	K–8	http://www.mobymax.com
PEG Write	Automatic or teacher configured writing assessments with cold or warm prompts aligned to Common Core genre and long-write rubrics	3–12	http://www.pegwriting.com
Learn Zillion	Language arts and math assessment, instruction, and practice aligned to Common Core standards	K–12	https://learnzillion.com
Khan Academy	Math assessment, instruction, and practice aligned to Common Core standards	3–16	http://www.khanacademy.org
Aimsweb	Language arts and math assessment partially aligned to Common Core standards	K–3	http://www.aimsweb.com

Figure 13. Continued.

yet been mastered." This means that in order to be thorough with their decision making, planning, and record-keeping, teachers must include information about:

1. the name of the assessment(s) administered or reviewed;
2. the assessment data related to these instruments that demonstrate standards-based proficiency, or partial mastery prior to instruction;
3. the results of the student interest assessment that can be used to personalize the chosen enrichment or acceleration options; and
4. the learning standards for the specified course of study or curriculum unit that have not yet been mastered.

Several purposes exist for assessment documentation in Column Two. It is certainly a record-keeping tool that can be stored digitally or within a student's cumulative file as evidence of advanced academic achievement and differentiation. Written appropriately, without an excess of educational jargon, it also promotes school and home communication and planning with parents and students. In the learning team environment, its review often invites a continuation of the compacting process in other classrooms and grade levels. And, as a professional learning tool, it also provides evidence for rich, small-group collegial conversations about how best to gather and examine evidence prior to planning for differentiation and compacting.

Teachers can examine the samples provided below to evaluate the extent to which they include and describe all four of the elements expected for inclusion in Column Two. What needs to be revised, added, or deleted to ensure clarity, approval, and agreement from a colleague, administrator, or parent? What is the quality and trustworthiness of the assessments? What other assessment information is needed? How would the reader's colleagues react to this information? What, if anything, should be planned for alternative enrichment or acceleration? What standards, if any, need differentiated instruction, practice, or application?

Sample 1: Zoe (Grade 2 Reading)

- Zoe scored a 650 Lexile on her end-of-year grade 1 Scholastic Reading Inventory assessment. This score is aligned to a mid-grade 3 reading level.
- In September of grade 2, Zoe participated in the Developmental Reading Assessment (DRA) informal reading inventory and scored a 38, 1 year and 8 months above grade-level expectations. Miscues were minimal and oral reading fluency was well-above grade-level expectations. Literal comprehension was accurate; she erred on one out of three inferential comprehension questions.
- Zoe's interest inventory and student-teacher conference notes indicate that she is an avid reader who prefers chapter books and literature. She

has not yet read a great deal of informative text. Zoe enjoys spending time with her friends, traveling, gymnastics, and visits to museums.

▶ Conversations with her parents indicate that in addition to the daily 30 minutes of interest-based independent reading in the classroom, Zoe also reads for 30–45 minutes at home on most evenings. She spent a great deal of time reading over the summer.

Sample 2: Marcus (Grade 6 Science)

▶ Marcus told his grade 6 teacher, friends, and classmates how much he loves science. He wishes the science curriculum provided for more lab time. He participates in both the science and robotics clubs after school. During a recent robotics club meeting, Marcus remarked to the club leader that he wished he could be part of the gifted program's architecture project. The club's parent leader brought this request to the district's gifted education teacher.

▶ His grade 5 standards-based report card consistently shows scores of 3 (meets grade-level expectations) or 4 (exceeds grade-level expectations) for both the science concepts strand and the science inquiry and practices strand. His science strand scores for the first marking period of grade 6 are also 4s.

▶ Marcus's class participated in a standards-based pretest at the beginning of each of the last two grade 6 science units (life science and Earth and space science). Marcus demonstrated mastery of 50% of the science standards addressed in the first unit and 75% of the science standards within the second unit prior to instruction, reading assignments, and guided lab tasks.

▶ In the current unit of study (Earth and space science), he has not yet mastered NGSS performance indicator MS-ESS1-4: Construct a scientific explanation based on evidence from rock strata for how the geologic time scale is used to organize Earth's 4.6-billion-year-old history. Pretest data shows that he has mastered the other three standards in the same unit: MS-ESS1-1, MS-ESS1-2, and MS-ESS1-3.

Sample 3: Chao (Grade 3 Math)

▶ Chao's father e-mailed his teacher to suggest math acceleration. He indicated that he is a mathematician who works closely with his children on math games, puzzles, and exercises. The grade 3 classroom teacher confirmed his son's math expertise. No summative grade 2 assessment data are recorded in the district's achievement database system.

▶ With the classroom teacher's consent, Nancy Naleway, the school's instructional specialist, administered both the grade 3 and the grade 4 standards-based summative assessment using the Moby Max online subscription tool. Chao scored 80% or higher on test items that measured the five math strands, with the exception of geometry.

Sample: Marissa (Grade 8 Writing)

▶ In December of grade 8, during a writing conference, Marissa expressed a strong desire for an interest-based writing option. She would like to learn more about journalism and poetry writing.

▶ Marissa scored in Level 4 (the highest proficiency level) on the writing strand of the spring, grade 7 Smarter Balanced (SBA) state writing assessment.

▶ Her grade 7 standards-based report card consistently shows scores of 4 (exceeds grade-level expectations) for English language arts. Her writing strand scores (argument, informative, research, and narrative writing) for grade 7 and the first marking period of grade 8 are also 4s.

▶ Grade 8 teacher feedback to Marissa regarding her writing indicates strengths in organization, vocabulary, and transitions. In some written pieces, her sentence fluency and elaboration needs attention.

▶ Marissa's grade 8 writing teacher administered the SBA interim assessment writing block to her in January of grade 8. She scored a 3 (exceeds expectations).

These examples from the second column of the compacting form provide the reader with models that can be analyzed, evaluated, and discussed during department meetings and professional learning sessions. They offer evidence in support of the important role that assessment and corresponding data play in making appropriate decisions and plans about compacting. They also give readers an opportunity to grapple with judgments, using authentic data, about which learning goals should be compacted and what kinds of enrichment or acceleration options substituted. Working alone or with a coach, facilitator, or partner, educators can use these models as a scaffold and a confirmation as they create their own assessment indicators to document curriculum compacting outcomes.

Conclusion

The names at the top of the three columns of the compactor form also designate the steps in its process. The first step, as explained in previous chapters of this text, is sometimes referred to as the Name It! component. During this phase of the compacting process, the teacher selects, clarifies, and identifies the goals, standards, or learning objectives that are focus of the compacting process, decisions, and plans. The last step in the compacting process aligns with the third column of the compactor form (Change It!) and focuses on the type of enrichment or acceleration that is used to replace the compacted curriculum. The second step, Prove It! asks the teacher to assess and measure a student's proficiency with the selected learning goal(s) prior to offering alternative curriculum. This second step was the focus for this chapter.

In Chapter 7, we reviewed the definition of testing and assessment, as well as the evolving item formats that could be used to measure learning standards with varying levels of cognitive demand. There are at least three distinct categories of assessments: summative, interim, and formative. Assessments in each of these categories have specific purposes, administration calendars, and links to the compacting process. These purposes also align well with the type of evaluation question and the data analysis process teachers use to identify candidates for compacting, measure their proficiency with grade-level or unit content, and make plans for related compacting of that curriculum, as well as acceleration or enrichment options that supplant the compacted curriculum.

Sample assessment instruments useful for verifying the relevance of compacting for a given student include both vendor-produced and teacher-created options that should be aligned with unit and subject-area standards and reflect established validity and reliability norms. Illustrations of Column Two documentation enable readers to envision the assessment component of the compacting process.

8

Frequently Asked Questions and Answers About Compacting

During the last few decades, the authors have conducted hundreds of staff development sessions that have included both introductory and follow-up training about curriculum compacting. The questions and answers contained in this chapter represent those that are often raised in both the preliminary and advanced professional learning sessions. These questions have been divided into their relevant categories: prerequisites for successful curriculum compacting; consultation with school administration; district and school policy; student, teacher, and parent orientation and collaboration and communication; getting started with compacting; compacting in specific content or skill areas; grouping and classroom management strategies; assessment, mastery, and grading; and compacting for nonidentified students. Questions are set off in italicized text, with their answers following immediately after.

There are several ways in which the questions and answers in this section of the book might be used by educators. Readers of this text who plan to implement compacting in their own classroom or school may find benefit in reviewing these questions prior to planning and implementation in order to avoid pitfalls and to ensure a comprehensive implementation framework. Professional development facilitators may choose to use the questions, by themselves, as the focus of small-group conversation and deliberation during professional learning sessions, professional learning community gatherings, or within graduate education classes. Participants might be asked to work collaboratively to develop their own responses to the question, later comparing their answers to those of the book's authors. Or, participants could be asked to review both the questions and the responses and to revise the response to align better with their own perspectives and situations.

Prerequisites for Successful Curriculum Compacting

Q: What actions are necessary before I begin the compacting process?

A: Four preliminary components are helpful during the preparation, planning, and decision-making phases of compacting. First, educators should have a clear understanding of the rationale and processes involved in the compacting process. Second, teachers should identify the subject area or unit(s) of instruction that they would like to become the focus of their first compacting experience. In many cases, this subject area is also one that has clear learning standards, assessments linked to these learning goals, and varied suggestions and resources for student enrichment and/or acceleration. Third, the individual teacher or teaching team should identify the students who are likely candidates for curriculum compacting in the chosen subject area, and fourth, teachers need to gather the appropriate assessments, enrichment, and acceleration materials necessary for implementing the compacting process. It is also very helpful for both teachers and students to have access to technology for both assessment and extension tasks.

Consultation With School Administration

Q: Can I compact curriculum if my administrator doesn't know about it or agree with it?

A: In order to achieve long-term success with and acceptance for compacting, it is extremely important that school and district administrators both understand and endorse compacting. If compacting, as a differentiation strategy, has not yet been implemented in a given school or district, preliminary planning should begin with administrator awareness and understanding of the purpose, benefits, and processes for compacting.

Teachers who are interested in implementing curriculum compacting but work on a team that has not yet participated in a related schoolwide initiative will find that the vast majority of administrators are highly supportive of the compacting strategy and will usually become a teacher's best advocate. In fact, it is difficult to imagine a situation where an administrator would not be appreciative of a teacher who wants to address the strengths and needs of high-achieving students in his or her classroom. On the other hand, most administrators don't usually appreciate learning about a new initiative in a classroom from a third party, especially when some parents may have questions or concerns.

By all means, inform school administrators about any intention to implement compacting long before the process begins. Their past experiences with other curriculum and instruction innovations and their knowledge of school-wide dynamics and culture will often yield worthwhile advice and suggestions for teachers who are about to undertake a compacting project.

A new administrator, who may not have a strong background in instructional strategies, may need background information and an opportunity to clarify the goals and procedures common with compacting. Time spent explaining and clarifying the compacting process makes it even more likely that the administrators will become a strong advocate for compacting both now and in the future.

District and School Policies

Q: *Can districts or schools enact policies that would support the adoption and implementation of compacting?*

A: Yes! When compacting is regarded as one of several differentiation strategies that may be a part of some teachers' practices, awareness is increased. When curriculum compacting is adopted by a board of education or school committee as an educational initiative or as policy, it is more likely to be implemented than when it is left to the discretion of volunteers. And, of course, when administrators support the compacting process, there is usually more effort expended to learn how to use its strategies in a meaningful and effective manner.

In the best of all worlds, any initiative or policy adoption related to curriculum compacting is more likely to succeed if teachers, parents, board of education members, and administrators work together to craft the details of the policy and the goals it is intended to achieve. Rather than assuming that compacting is a "them-against-us" mandate, a public and transparent task force, comprised of all stakeholders, usually stands the best chance of achieving acceptance of and attention to the policy.

Student, Teacher, and Parent Orientation, Communication, and Collaboration

Q: *Should students be provided with an orientation to the compacting process?*

A: In the same way in which a teacher makes students aware of differentiation, its strategies, and the reasons behind it, all students in a classroom should be introduced to the compacting process. It should be explained in very general and simple terms, as in the following example:

> Today you will take a pretest on material that will be introduced in class over the next several weeks. The results will help me understand how much you already know about the topics in this unit. I can use this information to decide if you can skip some of the material or if you will need extra time with me to be able to master it.
>
> Some of you may have already learned about the topic on your own outside of school. Some of you may find that this is all brand new, but another topic may be your area of expertise. You should all do your very best on this pretest.
>
> For those of you who already know some of the concepts and skills in this unit, you might wonder what else you could do. Many options exist. In some cases you may have time to spend in the library working on your independent reading. In other cases, some of you may be spending time in the enrichment center or you may be able to start an independent study project that you select yourself. Once the pretest results have been determined, I will be meeting with small groups of students to talk about the results and decide on our next steps for this unit of study.

We also suggest that additional time be provided time for all students to pursue various types of enrichment within the classroom. If only the students whose curriculum can be modified or compacted have the opportunity to work on interest-based tasks or participate in enrichment experiences, students who need much more time to master basic skills will never be provided with that option. This strategy also serves as a motivator to some students to do their best work in class, in order to be rewarded by receiving time to participate in enrichment opportunities. After all, the decision to compact for a student does not only have to be made at the beginning of a new unit.

Q: What procedures should I teach my students prior to beginning the compacting process?

A: Students whose curriculum may be compacted should receive an orientation about that process. They should also be taught the guidelines for classroom behavior when compacting is being implemented for some students. Norms and expectations such as the following may be helpful:

1. Students who are working independently should work silently. Students working in small groups should, as needed, whisper quietly to others or their partner. Loud talk is distracting and hurts learning by others.
2. If you have a question while you are working and you notice that the teacher is busy working with other students, do not interrupt. Use the silent signal strategy that your class has adopted to let your teacher know that you need help. While waiting for the teacher to be free, try to answer your question with your own thinking or by asking a classmate.
3. In order to prove that you can work independently, watch the clock to make sure that you can finish your work in the time you have available.
4. If you need to move around the room to get materials, put things away, or to use the bathroom, remember to keep the shelves and racks orderly and neat. Pick up after yourself.

Q: Should I inform parents when their child's curriculum is compacted?

A: Compacting is an instructional strategy and part of the overall differentiation process that most schools espouse as part of their mission statement. Because it is part of the grade-level and subject-area curriculum and instruction process, there is no legal obligation to obtain parent permission for compacting.

However, it is in everyone's best interests to communicate with parents and to let them know that compacting is part of the instructional framework used in a given classroom. Parents should also be informed of the decision to compact a particular subject area or unit for specific students.

We recommend that a parent letter, similar to the one printed in Figure 14, be sent to parents. They should be told that the compacting process has been started because it may cause noticeable differences in the amount and type of classwork and homework that their child brings home daily. For example, the number of "perfect" papers that were consistently being brought home by a high-achieving student may decrease because work on previously mastered content and skills has been replaced with new learning tasks and more cognitively challenging expectations. Parents should be active partners with teachers in the compacting process, and as you can imagine, are generally very supportive of the compacting process.

Q: What is the typical parent's reaction to curriculum compacting?

A: As stated earlier, most parents have supported it enthusiastically. They are often appreciative and say that they wish that this had been done much earlier in their child's school career. Other parents miss the parade of outstanding papers with stars, grades of 100s, and multiple points of praise. This is a legitimate concern for teachers who want to use, and parents who want to receive, this type of

TO: Parents of (Students' Names)
FROM: Classroom or Enrichment Teacher's Name
RE: Your Child's Participation in Curriculum Compacting
    and Differentiated Instruction

As you may know from our previous correspondence and meetings, your child is involved in enrichment and accelerated learning opportunities both in the classroom and as part of a schoolwide group. I want to assure you that the time spent participating in these enrichment and acceleration tasks will not result in students missing essential work in the regular classroom.

A careful assessment of your son's/daughter's strengths has resulted in an agreement with his or her classroom teacher to "compact" the curriculum in that strength area so that your child will not be repeating work that he or she has already mastered. Time saved by eliminating previously mastered concepts and skills will be used instead to provide enrichment and acceleration experiences. These alternative learning opportunities may take place in the classroom, in the library, or with our school's gifted education teacher.

The report and form that accompanies this letter is called a Compactor. You will notice his or her academic strengths listed in the first column of the form. In the second column, we have listed the assessment strategies used to ensure mastery of the content that is being replaced by the enrichment and acceleration alternatives. The third column contains a description and summary of some of the enrichment and/or acceleration activities that your child will pursue during the time that he or she is not participating in work already mastered.

Please contact me if you have any questions. I will be glad to meet with you about your child's involvement in the compacting process. Thank you for your continued interest in and support of differentiated and enriched learning. Please sign this form to indicate that you have received this completed Compactor and return it to your child's school as soon as possible.

Student's Name: _____

School: _____

Parent or Guardian's Signature: _____

Date: _____

Comments:

Figure 14. Sample letter/e-mail explaining curriculum compacting enrichment program.

positive reinforcement. However, once they have been oriented to the process of compacting, parents soon understand that the substitution of more challenging work that is not quickly mastered or memorized is a key feature of compacting. Most come to appreciate the importance of tasks that help to instill an appreciation for effort and critical thinking.

Q: How might I increase ownership and responsibility as it relates to curriculum compacting?

A: Parents and administrators can be both a student's and a teacher's greatest advocate when it comes to curriculum compacting. In fact, a team approach that includes the combined efforts of the students, teachers, parents, and administrators, usually achieves the best results.

One way to enhance the collaborative nature of a compacting initiative is to clarify the roles of each of the team members. A version of Figure 15 can be crafted by a task force, a PTA, or a professional learning community as they are about to embark on a compacting endeavor.

Getting Started With Curriculum Compacting

Q: Which content areas are the easiest to compact?

A: Subject areas with highly sequential curricular organization such as spelling, grammar, mathematics, reading, and writing are usually the easiest to compact. Many high-achieving students tend to master this content more quickly than some of their age-mates. This is not to say that science, social studies, and the arts can't be compacted. However, in these latter subject areas, it is likely that the teacher will need more preparation time to locate or create the preassessments, plan the related enrichment tasks, and identify the appropriate enrichment resources.

Q: Should I compact for a set period of time (such as a month or a marking period) or by curriculum standards and objectives?

A: Compacting is best managed by focusing on curriculum units and their related standards and learning objectives. If a teacher is already using a standards-based approach to instruction, then it is likely that the district's curriculum is organized to support this practice.

However, if a secondary curriculum is organized and based on topics, time periods, or mentor text, rather than by standards, then compacting can only occur when pretesting demonstrates that a student has already read and under-

Teamwork for Curriculum Compacting

Responsibilities of the Student
- Share your learning questions, strengths, and interests with your parents and teachers.
- Develop good organizational skills.
- Develop a value for effort, curiosity, and independence.

Responsibilities of the Parent
- Become your child's advocate.
- Share your child's interests, strengths, and special learning opportunities with your child's teacher.
- Take responsibility for developing your child's talents.
- Have realistic expectations for yourself, your child, and the school community.

Responsibilities of the Classroom Teacher
- Continually reflect on the teaching and learning process.
- Identify or develop measureable learning goals for each unit of study in the grade-level curriculum or subject area.
- Adjust the level of challenge for individuals or small groups of students.
- Conduct regular and systematic reviews of students' mastery of academic standards.
- Prescribe learning tasks that align with each student's challenge level.
- Work with the enrichment specialists in your school or district to plan enrichment and acceleration experiences for students.
- Employ pretesting, choice and interest-based learning strategies, standards-based teaching and assessment, and flexible grouping as part of a repertoire of instructional strategies necessary to implement compacting effectively.

Responsibilities of the Enrichment Specialist or Teacher of the Gifted
- Organize and implement teacher training about compacting.
- Provide support for teachers who are implementing curriculum compacting.
- Assist teachers in locating and planning enrichment and acceleration experiences.

Responsibilities of the Administrator
- Develop a sound understanding of the purpose and process for curriculum compacting.

Figure 15. Teamwork for curriculum compacting.

- Facilitate professional learning opportunities related to curriculum compacting.
- Provide support to teachers who are implementing curriculum compacting.
- Budget funds for the purchase of enrichment and acceleration resources.
- Collaboratively plan for compacting with teachers.
- Support teachers' professional reflections about their use of the compacting process.

Figure 15. Continued.

stands the novel, or already has an understanding of the historical time period or science topic.

Q: How much extra time does compacting take for an already busy classroom teacher?

A: Educators who consider compacting often assume that the process is going to take inordinate amounts of time to plan and execute. This is surely the case when the existing curriculum units in a given subject area don't already include clear learning objectives and related assessments, or when enrichment and acceleration alternatives are not already listed within the curriculum guides.

Alternatively, when these learning standards, assessment, and enrichment alternatives are already listed in the curriculum guide, teachers often find that compacting, especially for a small group of students, often relieves them from having to correct many homework and test papers. Of course, some additional effort is needed to substitute appropriately challenging material, but most teachers who have learned to compact effectively tell us that it takes no more time than their previous teaching practices. In many cases, department heads, gifted education specialists, librarians, and instructional coaches are willing to help with this component of the compacting process. They also tell us that the rewards and benefits for all students make the process very worthwhile.

Q: Will I have more success if I start with one student or should I start with a group of high-ability students?

A: Some teachers have had success compacting for one student, but many others are able to compact for a small group without much more effort than that expended for one student. Success compacting depends on several factors: the amount of classroom space, the amount of available enrichment resources, the availability of a library, help from other faculty including the teacher of the gifted or media specialist, and the degree of administrative support. It may be easier to begin compacting with one extremely bright student, but it is often better for that student to be a member of a small group that can support each other when they engage in tasks and projects that are different from those assigned to the rest of the class.

Q: Do you recommend compacting to accelerate the content of an entire semester, leaving the last 2 months free for student self-selected projects, or providing accelerated content for a few days a week, leaving the rest of the week open for enrichment?

A: Most teachers prefer to provide compacted, accelerated work 2 or 3 days a week, and set aside the remaining 1 or 2 days or short blocks of time throughout the unit for enrichment or problem-solving options. When you compact the content of a semester into just a few months, it demands tremendous time and energy to plan the remaining 2 full months of enrichment options.

Q: What kinds of staff development will help my colleagues and I begin compacting successfully?

A: The most effective staff development begins with a general overview of compacting. A sample presentation can be found on our website: http://gifted.uconn. edu/wp-content/uploads/sites/961/2015/01/Curriculum_Compacting.pdf. After participating in the general overview session, classroom teachers should meet to discuss how they can begin compacting. The major learning standards and necessary preassessments need to be identified. Additionally, interested teachers should be given the option of observing and conferencing with colleagues who have implemented compacting in the past. Grade-level meetings and planning time to locate or revise preassessments and replacement activities is also extremely helpful for teachers who are beginning the process.

Q: You have said that students whose curriculum is compacted in language arts can use that time to engage in more advanced work in that subject area, to participate in challenging work in other content areas, to complete independent research or inquiry, or work on interest-based learning questions and explorations. What if the enrichment or gifted/talented teacher can't work with this student during his or her compacted time?

A: If an enrichment specialist or gifted education teacher's schedule is aligned to students' compacted time or subject area, so much the better. Unfortunately, this is not always the case. When schedules conflict, we must remember that the classroom teacher is chiefly responsible for providing an appropriate and challenging alternative for students who have already mastered the grade-level learning standards. However, in many cases, the curriculum specialist or gifted education teacher will be more than willing to help the classroom teacher locate the appropriate resources during collegial planning time.

Q: How can I find appropriately challenging substitute materials? For example, what if my students only want to read relatively unchallenging, recreational fiction?

A: Finding appropriately challenging substitute materials is one of the biggest challenges within the compacting process, especially for upper grade levels. When compacting for students in first and second grade, it is much easier to substitute challenging work because many of these youngsters have not yet mastered the basic phonics, comprehension, and math fluency skills.

As stated earlier, student interest is one of the most important criteria for evaluating the appropriateness of substitute resources and tasks. If the selection of substitute work is made only by the teacher, student ownership may become a problem. Some students may choose not to get involved in the compacting process. For example, consider the situation in which a small group of exceptionally able third-grade math students are assigned more challenging math standards. These accelerated math standards will require more work and effort than completing the grade-level curriculum. In these situations, it is important that the students choose to participate in acceleration rather than having it foisted upon them.

Q: Do I have to substitute math work if I am compacting math or should I consider other content options?

A: Many teachers who compact the grade-level math curriculum assume that the time saved should be used for advanced math work. For some highly capable math students, this is their wish as well. In other cases, the student may perform well in math but prefer to use enrichment time to pursue other topics. Students' interests should certainly be considered before a teacher makes such a decision.

Q: What if you are trying to replace compacted curriculum with work in students' interest areas only to discover that your students have no interests?

A: Unfortunately, as students get older and reach adolescence, we find that their academic interests often dissipate. A respectful, sincere, and private conversation and conference with the student often promotes rapport and helps the student develop a sense of trust for the teacher's intentions and goodwill. In these situations, hidden or unspoken interests often emerge.

It is also advisable to assess students' interests using an instrument such as the Interest-A-Lyzer. This constructed survey helps students focus or discover their interests, and suggests a viable direction for exploratory experiences or inquiry-based research or investigations. If students indicate they really have no idea about the nature of their academic interests, a variety of exciting, challenging classroom activities or interest-developing experiences and websites should be substituted. Interests develop at various times and in various ways, and as teachers, we need to be aware that not all of our students currently have a strong understanding of their own goals and strengths.

Q: Can compacting be considered a part of an academically talented student's IEP (Individualized Education Program) in states in which gifted education is considered a part of special education?

A: Yes. In fact, many state department gifted education consultants have indicated that the Compactor form provides an ideal record for documenting enrichment and acceleration decisions.

Compacting in Specific Content or Skill Areas

Q: Can teachers compact in other content areas such as art, home economics, industrial arts, or music?

A: Teachers have shared outstanding compacting examples in all content areas. Technology, music, art, and personal finance are just a few of the subject areas that provide fertile ground for compacting, enrichment, and acceleration. A career and technology education teacher recently provided a marvelous example of compacting: A student entering his workshop class had spent the summer building a case for a grandfather clock. He brought photographs of the clock case and proudly displayed them. At that time, the teacher decided to eliminate the first three simple assignments in woodshop from this youngster's curriculum, deciding that it would be inappropriate for him to have to make a simple bookshelf when his talents were obviously so much further developed. This is a perfect example about how work can be compacted or eliminated within a specific area and be replaced with independent project time.

Q: Am I correct in assuming that if I teach process writing and use writing workshop, compacting is unnecessary?

A: Not necessarily. In this situation, the decision to compact depends on the mastery of grade-level writing standards, including the writing process standards. If students can demonstrate that they can independently and successfully apply the major writing standards for their grade level, they should be able to choose what they pursue during the time set aside for the writing curriculum.

Many teachers who use the process writing approach believe that high-achieving students should become responsible for learning the writing standards in the next grade level. Others expect college prep work from students who demonstrate grade-level mastery. Still others assume that allowing interest-based writing topics is the answer to the compacting decision.

Again, it is important to conference with the student who has demonstrated mastery and provide several alternatives for enrichment and acceleration, providing time for the student to ponder these options and make a relevant and personal choice. If the student expresses a strong desire to conduct science research or pursue math acceleration, or work on his or her capstone project during compacting writing time, grade-level competency in process writing should allow for those opportunities.

Q: Am I correct in assuming that if I teach using a reading workshop approach, compacting is unnecessary?

A: Not necessarily. Alternative reading approaches, such as reading workshop, work well with curriculum compacting, but they do not replace it. Quite often teachers who use these approaches have at their disposal mostly grade-level trade books or alternative reading assignments. For a youngster who is outstanding in reading or language arts, these books may not be appropriately challenging. Therefore, when these reading workshop approaches are used, independent reading text and text analysis tasks should still be geared to the students' individual levels of challenge.

Grouping and Classroom Management Strategies

Q: Is compacting more challenging in a heterogeneous class than in a homogeneous class?

A: Compacting is easier to accomplish with a group of students who are at similar levels of achievement. It isn't always accurate to say that compacting is more difficult in a heterogeneous class because a wide range of abilities, interests, and motivation exist even within homogeneous classes. For example, students in an accelerated English class may have very different backgrounds, achievement levels, and interests in the subject area. Some students may be exceptional in interpreting literature, while others are there simply because they have high state test scores, but don't like to read. Field-test results suggest that compacting is easier to implement for small groups, whether they are enrolled in a heterogeneous or a homogeneous class setting.

Q: Can I compact curriculum for my highest achievers if I don't have help from a department head, instructional coach, or enrichment specialist?

A: Yes! Working with an enrichment specialist or instructional coach can make compacting a little easier because they can often provide access to resources or enrichment materials not available to individual teachers. However, the wealth of open source materials currently available on the Internet to all educators often supplants the need for collaboration with other educators. The selection of key search terms and the time to vet the wealth of resources that result from such a search is a requirement.

Q: How do you manage the rest of the students in the classroom when the students who have had their curriculum compacted start to "act up"?

A: Students whose curriculum has been compacted should receive an orientation to the process and their responsibilities within it. Students should receive frequent, initial feedback about their behaviors during compacted time. They should also be asked to evaluate their productivity and provide related evidence. Without both internal judgments and external feedback, students will have a difficult time learning how to become independent learners who are respectful of the other learners within their classroom community. When students still fail to manage compacted time effectively, the teacher should work with them and their parents to determine the reason for the behavior and to teach appropriate self-regulation strategies to help these students be successful. It is extremely important that classroom teachers be firm in their expectations about how students use their time.

Q: How can I organize classroom space to make compacting easier?

A: Many teachers who use compacting extensively have provided space in their classroom for both small-group and individual work. A small table with two or more chairs and access to laptops or tablets becomes extremely beneficial for students with a compacted curriculum. A small library corner with some pillows or alternate seating arrangements can also be extremely helpful.

Q: At what grade level should compacting begin?

A: Curriculum should be compacted as soon as youngsters enter school. We have conducted professional development sessions with Montessori preschools in which curriculum is modified beginning at age 3 or 4. When the compacting process begins in kindergarten, students learn to use independent time more effectively and demonstrate greater responsibility in their choices and time management.

Q: If I compact for my advanced students and let them leave the classroom to participate in alternate activities, won't the quality of classroom discussions suffer? What if I really believe that students who are compacted would benefit from a particular discussion or special lesson?

A: Many teachers have expressed this concern, and it has merit, to some degree. However, it is also true that less able students are sometimes intimidated by the presence of brighter students, and, consequently, stop contributing to the discussions. The self-efficacy of lower achieving students is often decreased when their higher achieving peers are responding with sophisticated answers when the lower achieving students have no answers at all. Students who are less able to do well in school often feel inferior to or threatened by the precocious verbal ability and intelligence of the higher achieving youngsters.

To resolve the problem, teachers might try some classroom sessions with their most academically able students and some without them; if the discussions are more effective or successful with the more advanced students, then it makes sense to include them some of the time and let the focus be on the less successful students during other times.

Q: What type of flexible grouping allows compacting to be achieved most easily?

A: Flexible small groups work best for compacting. These types of groups are not synonymous with tracking. Such tracking has been defined as the grouping of students for all subject-area instruction based on a single achievement or aptitude test score. This practice is not advised.

Instead, students whose curriculum has been compacted should be flexibly grouped for instruction, practice, research, and problem solving based on mastery, interests, and the need for explicit instruction. In some situations, the creation of a cluster group of high-achieving students within a heterogeneous class makes curriculum compacting easier to facilitate.

Q: If we use ability grouping in math and reading, do we still need to compact the curriculum?

A: Yes. Even with high-ability grouping within specific subjects, students will demonstrate differences in learning rates, effort, and interests. Curriculum compacting can address these needs.

Q: What is the difference between compacting curriculum in an elementary class-room and in a secondary content class? Is it more challenging for middle or high school teachers?

A: Compacting in an elementary classroom is often easier than it is in a secondary content class. Generally, elementary teachers have students in their classrooms for longer blocks of time and are able to use that extended time to learn the best methods for measuring proficiency with individual students. Elementary teachers can usually gain a clearer picture of student ability and achievement levels earlier in the school year than secondary teachers can because they interact with fewer students each day.

Secondary teachers often have to base their compacting decisions on their observations during a 50-minute class, once a day. Secondary teachers work with more students, for less time, and the pace of their schedule makes attention to individual needs and differences more difficult to manage. In this type of secondary school situation, small-group compacting is advisable.

Q: What is the difference between basic skills compacting and content compacting?

A: Basic skills compacting usually occurs at the elementary level. It involves subject areas such as math, reading, and writing. It is often easier to accomplish because of the large percentage of time allocated to these subject areas, the clarity of the standards, and the wealth of assessments currently available. Content compacting usually occurs in science and social studies. In many cases, preassessment and data analysis for content compacting suggests the substitution of enrichment tasks for a portion of a given curriculum unit, not necessarily the entire unit.

Q: What about compacting in an honors or an accelerated class?

A: Yes. Even though students are assumed to be in a homogeneous group, educators who have taught in those situations realize that there is really no such thing as group homogeneity. Despite the variables that led to the grouping pattern, students in these classes still differ widely with regard to their prior knowledge, engagement, effort, and cognitive strategies. Some students are more interested in the subject, some are more motivated, and some have a better background in one particular component of the subject than others. For these reasons, compacting is as appropriate in an honors or accelerated class as it is in a heterogeneous class situation.

Q: What's the difference between compacting curriculum in an honors class and a class based on the Enrichment Triad model?

A: The difference between compacting curriculum in an honors class and a Triad-based class depends on the type of curriculum presented in those classes. An honors class generally deals with a more advanced curriculum. A class such as those advocated in the SEM or the Enrichment Triad model presents the regular curriculum with additional time reserved for interest-based options. Honors classes that offer compacting typically replace learned content with questions, tasks, and resources that provide greater depth or breadth with the topic.

Assessment, Mastery, and Grades

Q: Who is responsible for administering the preassessment?

A: The person responsible for pretesting students is usually the person who teaches the regular curriculum. In some cases, classroom teachers who have implemented curriculum compacting seek and receive help from a reading or math consultant, or the teacher of the gifted, if one is available. During the beginning phases of a curriculum compacting initiative, content and enrichment specialists, or instructional coaches, often volunteer to model the pretesting process or implement it collaboratively with the teacher, followed by feedback and coaching.

Q: Define mastery. *How do I know if my students really know the content and skills that are being assessed?*

A: For most educators, *mastery* is synonymous with the independent application of learned concepts and skills to new situations, contexts, and problems. In a similar vein, "really know" is comparable to being able to accurately analyze, communicate and describe one's understandings. Other educators define mastery as proficiency with at least 80% of the learning standards or objectives within a unit or chapter. Still others expect that 80% of the assessment criteria for each standard can be demonstrated reliably and in a valid fashion.

It seems advisable for a faculty, with the assistance of a facilitator, to discuss the concept of mastery, read related articles from experts in the field of assessment and standards-based grading, and develop their own set of common expectations.

Q: What other ways can I measure mastery if no preassessment suggestions or postassessment tests are included with the curriculum unit, guide, or textbook?

A: We have made several suggestions in this book about how to measure mastery if pretests or posttests are not included with the regular curricular materials. Teachers can, for example, conduct an individual student conference, using prompts and standards-based questions as conference and assessment guides. Assigning a writing prompt, together with related text or video clip evidence, is another strategy for measuring a student's understanding of content and essential concepts and principles.

Mastery can be assessed in many ways, several of which are often more effective than the use of pretests or posttests provided by a publisher. Teachers are encouraged to think flexibly and use their professional expertise to develop alternative assessment formats. In general, whatever standards-based method a teacher plans to use to assess mastery at the end of a unit of study can be modified to assess the same standards at the beginning of the unit.

Q: How should I grade when I compact curriculum?

A: Students should be graded on the regular curriculum that has been compacted. Grades should reflect mastery of grade-level standards *rather than the time spent* in a subject or the nature of the replacement tasks. In most cases, this means that a student who demonstrates mastery of a significant portion of the subject-area standards would receive a mark on a standards-based report card that is consistent with the data that indicates that they have exceeded grade-level expectations. Communication with parents about student work on enrichment projects or investigations are best provided with a narrative, evidence of student work, and the student's own reflection about learning and academic growth.

Q: What if a group of students who have their curriculum compacted do not want to do any other work? Can their grades reflect this?

A: No. There are other ways to handle this. If you find that students are not using their time for alternative study wisely, you should talk about the problem with them. You might reiterate the concept of compacting, and explain what the next step would be if behavior doesn't change (such as a parent meeting).

Compacting represents an educational departure for most students. Some students have never been given any enrichment options before, never had the responsibility for planning their own learning, or never learned how to work independently. It takes time for them to adjust. If there is a need to communicate their current performance with self-directed learning, it should be recorded in the section of the progress report that deals with work habits.

Compacting for Nonidentified Students

Q: Do students who demonstrate average grade-level achievement ever benefit from curriculum compacting?

A: Yes, most definitely. According to our field tests, many different kinds of students can benefit from curriculum compacting in one or more content areas. The purpose of compacting is to alleviate repetition and buy time for enrichment or acceleration options for individual students. We believe that this process actually encourages some students to demonstrate more effort and responsibility for their own learning—especially when they understand that their demonstrated achievement triggers enrichment and interest-based learning options of their own choosing.

Consider the student who doesn't demonstrate mastery during the unit preassessment. Might it be possible for that student to learn the content and achieve mastery of the grade-level standards in that unit at a faster rate than is likely with an overreliance on large-group instruction and practice? It is if that student's teacher has also adopted other best practices, such as those explained in John Hattie's 2009 *Visible Learning* text.

At the beginning of each curriculum unit, students must have an opportunity to review and understand the unit's learning goals and the performances necessary to demonstrate mastery. In addition, the criteria used to measure mastery should be public information for both students and parents. Teachers also support compacting for all students when they adopt a continuous progress, or "move on when ready" approach to curriculum by incorporating learning contracts, small-group teaching, conferences, formative assessment, feedback, and intervention.

Imagine a classroom where every subject area, not just reading and writing, is based on an instructional framework much like a studio or workshop where students work under the watchful eye of a mentor, coach, and content expert. When this happens, the teacher's role is transformed from that of a knowledge dispenser to a facilitator. Students' own intrinsic interests in mastery or the pursuit of enrichment alternatives spurs them to demonstrate the effort needed to reach grade-level proficiency.

Q: Should curriculum be compacted for underachievers?

A: Underachievers, students whose prior academic record suggests the potential for greater achievement, should absolutely be considered for compacting. Students who underachieve are often academically able or talented students who have stopped trying to do all of the work that is required of them because they know that they already mastered it many years earlier. Some students learn to underachieve because they are bored with the regular curriculum and we have found in many of our studies that compacting has an impact on the underachievement problem facing so many bright youngsters in our schools today.

In many instances, these students have also discovered that finishing their lessons before their classmates only means that they will be assigned more of the same work. By orienting them to the compacting process, we can give them an incentive to do better in their classwork. For example, if a student can demonstrate proficiency in grammar, he or she may then earn the opportunity to select a novel to read, access online information about famous authors, write original short stories, compose poetry, or select an area of interest in language arts. Being allowed to select what may be done during time in which the student demonstrates curriculum mastery often encourages an underachieving student to demonstrate mastery.

Q: What about my lower achieving students? Can they participate in enrichment opportunities?

A: All students, regardless of current achievement levels or cognitive ability, should be given time to enjoy enrichment opportunities. Although it is true that some students may not be eligible for curriculum compacting per se, every student should learn the problem solving and creative thinking skills and other facets of process training that alternative activities provide. Teachers could schedule a special time for these activities, such as during enrichment clusters, STEM time, or problem-based learning tasks.

REFERENCES

Archambault, F. X., Westberg, K. L., Brown, S., Hallmark, B. W., Zhang, W., & Emmons, C. (1993). *Regular classroom practices with gifted students: Findings from the Classroom Practices Survey* (RM32102). Storrs: University of Connecticut, National Research Center on the Gifted and Talented.

Assouline, S. G., Colangelo, N., VanTassel-Baska, J., & Lupkowski-Shoplik, A. (Eds.). (2015). *A nation empowered: Evidence trumps the excuses holding back America's brightest students* (Vols. 1–2). Iowa City: The University of Iowa, The Connie Belin & Jacqueline N. Blank International Center for Gifted Education and Talent Development.

Bauerlein, M. (2009). *The dumbest generation: How the digital age stupefies young Americans and jeopardizes our future (Or, don't trust anyone under 30)*. New York, NY: Tarcher.

Baum, S. M., Renzulli, J. S., & Hébert, T. P. (1995). Reversing underachievement: Creative productivity as a systematic intervention. *Gifted Child Quarterly, 39,* 224–235.

Betts, G. T. (1986). The autonomous learner model. In J. S. Renzulli (Ed.), *Systems and models for developing programs for the gifted and talented* (pp. 27–56). Mansfield Center, CT: Creative Learning Press.

Betts, G. T., & Kercher, J. J. (2009). The autonomous learner model for the gifted and talented. In J. S. Renzulli, E. J. Gubbins, K. S. McMillen, R. D. Eckert, & C. A. Little (Eds.), *Systems and models for developing programs for the gifted and talented* (2nd ed., pp. 49–103). Waco, TX: Prufrock Press.

Bridgeland, J., DiIulio, J., & Morison, K. (2006). *The silent epidemic: Perspectives of high school dropouts*. Washington, DC: Civic Enterprises, Peter D. Hart Research Associates, and Bill and Melinda Gates Foundation.

Clark, B. R. (1985). *The school and the university: An international perspective.* Berkeley: University of California Press.

Colangelo, N., Assouline, S. G., & Gross, M. U. M. (2004). *A nation deceived: How schools hold back America's brightest students* (Vol. 1). Iowa City: The University of Iowa, The Connie Belin & Jacqueline N. Blank International Center for Gifted Education and Talent Development.

Feldhusen, J. F., & Kolloff, M. B. (1986). The Purdue three-stage enrichment model for gifted education at the elementary level. In J.S. Renzulli (Ed.), *Systems and models for developing programs for the gifted and talented* (pp. 126–152). Mansfield Center, CT: Creative Learning Press.

Field, G. (2009). The effects of the use of Renzulli Learning on student achievement in reading comprehension, reading fluency, social studies, and science. *International Journal of Emerging Technologies in Learning (iJET), 4*(1), 29–39.

Finn, C. E., Jr., & Wright, B. L. (2015). *Failing our brightest kids: The global challenge of educating high-ability students.* Cambridge, MA: Harvard Education Press.

Firmender, J. M., Reis, S. M., & Sweeny, S. M. (2013). Reading comprehension and fluency levels ranges across diverse classrooms: The need for differentiated reading instruction and content. *Gifted Child Quarterly, 57*(1), 3–14.

Gavin, M. K., Casa, T. M., Adelson, J. L., Carroll, S. R., Sheffield, L. J., & Spinelli, A. M. (2007). Project M^3: Mentoring mathematical minds—A research-based curriculum for talented elementary students. *Journal of Advanced Academics, 18,* 566–585.

Gentry, M. (with K. A. Paul, J. McIntosh, C. M. Fugate, & E. Jen). (2014). *Total school cluster grouping and differentiation: A comprehensive research-based plan for raising student achievement and improving teacher practices* (2nd ed.). Waco, TX: Prufrock Press.

Gentry, M., & Owen, S. V. (1999). An investigation of the effects of total school flexible cluster grouping on identification, achievement, and classroom practices. *Gifted Child Quarterly, 43,* 224–243.

Gubbins, E. J., Housand, B., Oliver, M., Schader, R., de Wet, C. F., Moon, T. R., . . . Brighton, C. M. (2008). *Unclogging the mathematics pipeline through access to algebraic understanding* (RM08236). Storrs: University of Connecticut, The National Research Center on the Gifted and Talented.

Hattie, J. (2009). *Visible learning: A synthesis of over 800 meta-analyses relating to achievement.* London, England: Routledge.

Hofstadter, R. (1963). *Anti-intellectualism in American life.* New York, NY: Knopf.

Kulik, J. A. (1992). *An analysis of the research on ability grouping: Historical and contemporary perspectives* (RBDM9204). Storrs: University of Connecticut, National Research Center on the Gifted and Talented.

Loveless, T., Parkas, S., & Duffett, A. (2008) *High-achieving students in the era of NCLB*. Washington, DC: Thomas B. Fordham Institute.

Michener, J. A. (1996). *This noble land: My vision for America*. New York, NY: Random House.

Moon, T., Tomlinson, C. A., & Callahan, C. M. (1995) *Academic diversity in the middle school: Results of a national survey of middle school administrators and teachers* (RM95124). Storrs: University of Connecticut, National Research Center on the Gifted and Talented.

Reis, S. M. & Boeve, H. (2009). How academically talented students respond to challenge in an enriched and differentiated reading program. *Journal for the Education of the Gifted, 33,* 203–240.

Reis, S. M., Eckert, R. D., Fogarty, E. A., Little, C. A., Housand, A. M., Sweeny, S. M., . . . Sullivan, E. E. (2009). *The joyful reading resource kit: Teaching tools, hands-on activities, and enrichment resources (Grades K–8).* Hoboken, NJ: Jossey-Bass.

Reis, S. M., Eckert, R. D., McCoach, D. B., Jacobs, J. K., Coyne, M. (2008). Using enrichment reading practices to increase reading fluency, comprehension, and attitudes. *Journal of Educational Research, 101,* 299–315.

Reis, S. M., Gentry, M., & Maxfield, L. R. (1998). The application of enrichment clusters to teachers' classroom practices. *Journal for Education of the Gifted, 21,* 310–324.

Reis, S. M., Gubbins, E. J., Briggs, C. J., Schreiber, F. J., Richards, S., Jacobs, J. K., . . . Renzulli, J. S. (2004). Reading instruction for talented readers: Case studies documenting few opportunities for continuous progress. *Gifted Child Quarterly, 48,* 315–338.

Reis, S. M., Hébert, T. P., Díaz, E. I., Maxfield, L. R., & Ratley, M. E. (1995). *Case studies of talented students who achieve and underachieve in an urban high school* (RM95120). Storrs: University of Connecticut, National Research Center on the Gifted and Talented.

Reis, S. M., & Housand, A. M. (2009). The impact of gifted education pedagogy and enriched reading practices on reading achievement for urban students in bilingual and English-speaking classes. *Journal of Urban Education: Focus on Enrichment, 6*(1), 72–86.

Reis, S. M., McCoach, D. B., Coyne, M., Schreiber, F. J., Eckert, R. D., & Gubbins, E. J. (2007). Using planned enrichment strategies with direct instruction to improve reading fluency, comprehension, and attitude toward reading: An evidence-based study. *Elementary School Journal, 108*(1), 3–24.

Reis, S. M., McCoach, D. B., Little, C. A., Muller, L. M., & Kaniskan, R. B. (2011). The effects of differentiated instruction and enrichment pedagogy on reading achievement in five elementary schools. *American Educational Research Journal, 48,* 462–501.

Reis, S. M., & Purcell, J. H. (1993). An analysis of content elimination and strategies used by elementary classroom teachers in the curriculum compacting process. *Journal for the Education of the Gifted, 16,* 147–170.

Reis, S. M., & Renzulli, J. S. (2003). Research related to the Schoolwide Enrichment Triad Model. *Gifted Education International, 18*(1), 15–39.

Reis, S. M., Westberg, K. L., Kulikowich, J., Calliard, F., Hébert, T., Purcell, J., . . . Plucker, J. (1993). *Why not let high ability students start school in January? The curriculum compacting study* (RM93106). Storrs: University of Connecticut, National Research Center on the Gifted and Talented.

Reis, S. M., Westberg, K. L., Kulikowich, J. M., & Purcell, J. H. (1998). Curriculum compacting and achievement test scores: What does the research say? *Gifted Child Quarterly, 42,* 123–129.

Renzulli, J. S. (1977). *The Enrichment Triad Model: A guide for developing defensible programs for the gifted.* Mansfield Center, CT: Creative Learning Press.

Renzulli, J. S. (1988). The Multiple Menu Model for developing differentiated curriculum for the gifted and talented. *Gifted Child Quarterly, 32,* 298–309.

Renzulli, J., Gentry, M., & Reis, S. (2013). *Enrichment clusters: A practical plan for real-world, student-driven learning* (2nd ed.). Waco, TX: Prufrock Press.

Renzulli, J. S., Gubbins, E. J., McMillen, K. S., Eckert, R. D., & Little, C. A. (2009). *Systems and models for developing programs for the gifted and talented* (2nd ed.). Waco, TX: Prufrock Press.

Renzulli, J. S., & Park, S. (2000). Gifted dropouts: The who and the why. *Gifted Child Quarterly, 44,* 261–271.

Renzulli, J. S., & Reis, S. M. (1985). *The Schoolwide Enrichment Model: A comprehensive plan for educational excellence.* Mansfield Center, CT: Creative Learning Press.

Renzulli, J. S., & Reis, S. M. (1994). Research related to the Schoolwide Enrichment Model. *Gifted Child Quarterly, 38,* 7–20.

Renzulli, J. S., & Reis, S. M. (1997). *The Schoolwide Enrichment Model: A comprehensive plan for educational excellence* (2nd ed.). Mansfield Center, CT: Creative Learning Press.

Renzulli, J. S., & Reis, S. M. (2014). *The Schoolwide Enrichment Model: A how-to guide for talent development* (3rd ed.). Waco, TX: Prufrock Press.

Renzulli, J. S., & Smith, L. H. (1979*). Guidebook for developing individualized educational programs (IEP) for gifted and talented students.* Mansfield Center, CT: Creative Learning Press.

Rogers, K. B. (1991). *The relationship of grouping practices to the education of the gifted and talented learner* (RBDM9102). Storrs: University of Connecticut, National Research Center on the Gifted and Talented.

Tannenbaum, A. J. (1983). *Gifted children: Psychological and educational perspectives.* New York, NY: Macmillan.

Tieso, C. L. (2002). *The effects of grouping and curricular practices on intermediate students' mathematics achievement*. Storrs: University of Connecticut, National Research Center on the Gifted and Talented.

Tomlinson, C. (2000). Reconcilable differences: Standards-based teaching and differentiation. *Educational Leadership, 58*(1), 6–11.

U.S. Department of Education, Office of Educational Research. (1993). *National excellence: A case for developing America's talent*. Washington, DC: U.S. Government Printing Office.

VanTassel-Baska, J., Zuo, L., Avery, L. D., & Little, C. A. (2002). A curriculum study of gifted-student learning in the language arts. *Gifted Child Quarterly, 46*, 30–44.

Vygotsky, L., & Cole, M. (1978). *Mind in society: The development of higher psychological processes*. Cambridge: Harvard University Press.

Westberg, K. L., Archambault, F. X., Jr., Dobyns, S. M., & Salvin, T. J. (1993). *An observational study of instructional and curricular practices used with gifted and talented students in regular classrooms* (RM93104). Storrs: University of Connecticut, National Research Center on the Gifted and Talented.

Wolniak, G. C., Neishi, K. M., Rude, J. D., & Gebhardt, Z. (2012, August). *The state of our nation's youth: 2012–2013*. Alexandria, VA: Horatio Alger Association of Distinguished Americans.

Wyner, J., Bridgeland, J., & DiIulio, J. (2007). *Achievement trap: How America is failing millions of high- achieving students from lower-income families*. Lansdowne, VA: Jack Kent Cooke Foundation.

APPENDIX A
Total Talent Portfolio

My Teachers' Names	Year _____ Grade _____
_____	_____
_____	_____
_____	_____
_____	_____

Preferences & Strengths

Subject Areas	My Five Choices	My Five Strengths
Reading		
Writing		
Spelling		
Mathematics		
Social Studies		
Science		
Art		
Music		
PE		
Other:		

Showing What I've Learned	My Five Choices	My Five Strengths
Reports, Stories		
Talking		
Projects		
Artwork		
Pictures/Charts		
Displays		
Acting		
Helping Others		
Media		
Other:		

Special Topics That I Like:

_____

_____

_____

_____

Note: Students can complete this form in one color pen or pencil. Subsequently, teachers and/or parents may wish to complete the document with a different color to highlight similarities and differences between the student's and adult's perceptions about student strengths.

Ways To Learn	I Like This	I Am Good At This
Talking With Others		
Listening to a Speaker		
Reading		
Watching/Viewing		
Games		
Computers		
Reliving/ Pretending		
Centers		
Making/Doing/ Moving Activities		
Working Alone		
Working With a Partner		
Working in a Group		
Working With an Adult		
Choices and Options		
Detailed Directions		

General Interests

Performing Arts	
Creative Writing & Journalism	
Mathematics	
Business/Management	
Athletics	
History	
Social Action	
Fine Arts & Crafts	
Science	
Technology	
Other	

Specific Interests

_____
_____
_____
_____

Activities, Clubs, and Lessons I Do Outside of School:

Family Activities, Special Experiences, and Projects I Do at Home:

My Talents Are:

This Year, I Would Like to:

Modification, Differentiation, & Enrichment Provided

		Reading	Writing	Spelling	Grammar	Hand Writing	Math	Social Studies	Science	Music	Art	PE	Library
1.	Identify students' interests, styles, etc.												
2.	Categorize objectives												
3.	Evaluate curriculum components												
4.	Brainstorm real-world connections												
5.	Connect to knowledge fields												
6.	Escalate objective(s)												
7.	Create enhanced introductory activities												
8.	Choose active learning opportunities												
9.	Incorporate authentic components												
10.	Involve parents												
11.	Use diagnostic tools												
12.	Identify relevant differences among students												
13.	Use open-ended activities												
14.	Provide options to broaden the curriculum												
15.	Telescope instruction												
16.	Offer small-group learning activities												
17.	Provide whole-group enrichment												
18.	Teach cognitive skills												
19.	Use centers & contracts												
20.	Organize simulations												
21.	Debrief students												
22.	Propose extensions												
23.	Offer enrichment clusters												
24.	Connect students to talent development opportunities												

Learning and Talent Development Recommendations

		Reading	Writing	Spelling	Grammar	Hand Writing	Math	Social Studies	Science	Music	Art	PE	Library
1.	Identify students' interests, styles, etc.												
2.	Categorize objectives												
3.	Evaluate curriculum components												
4.	Brainstorm real-world connections												
5.	Connect to knowledge fields												
6.	Escalate objective(s)												
7.	Create enhanced introductory activities												
8.	Choose active learning opportunities												
9.	Incorporate authentic components												
10.	Involve parents												
11.	Use diagnostic tools												
12.	Identify relevant differences among students												
13.	Use open-ended activities												
14.	Provide options to broaden the curriculum												
15.	Telescope instruction												
16.	Offer small-group learning activities												
17.	Provide whole-group enrichment												
18.	Teach cognitive skills												
19.	Use centers & contracts												
20.	Organize simulations												
21.	Debrief students												
22.	Propose extensions												
23.	Offer enrichment clusters												
24.	Connect students to talent development opportunities												

TOTAL TALENT PORTFOLIO
Status Information for

	K	1	2	3	4	5
Abilities						
Grades (above average or better):						
Reading						
Language Arts						
Mathematics						
Social Studies						
Science						
Art						
Music						
Physical Education						
Other:						
Standardized Tests:						

	K	1	2	3	4	5
Style Preferences						
Instructional Style Preferences:						
Discussion						
Lecture						
Learning Games						
Computer Software						
Simulations						
Independent Study						
Peer Tutoring						
Learning Centers						
Mentorship						
Interactive Videos						
Electronic Distance Learning						
Other:						

Interests:						
General Areas:						
Fine Arts and Crafts						
Physical Science						
Musical Performance						
Musical Composition						
Life Science						
Creative Writing and Journalism						
Social Action						
Mathematics						
Logic						
Business/Management						
Technology						
Film/Video						
Computers						
History						
Athletics						
Performing Arts						
Other:						

Expression Style Preferences:						
Written						
Oral/Discussion						
Manipulative						
Artistic						
Display						
Graphic						
Performance						
Dramatization						
Service/Leadership						
Multi-media						
Other:						

Specific interests:

_____

_____

_____

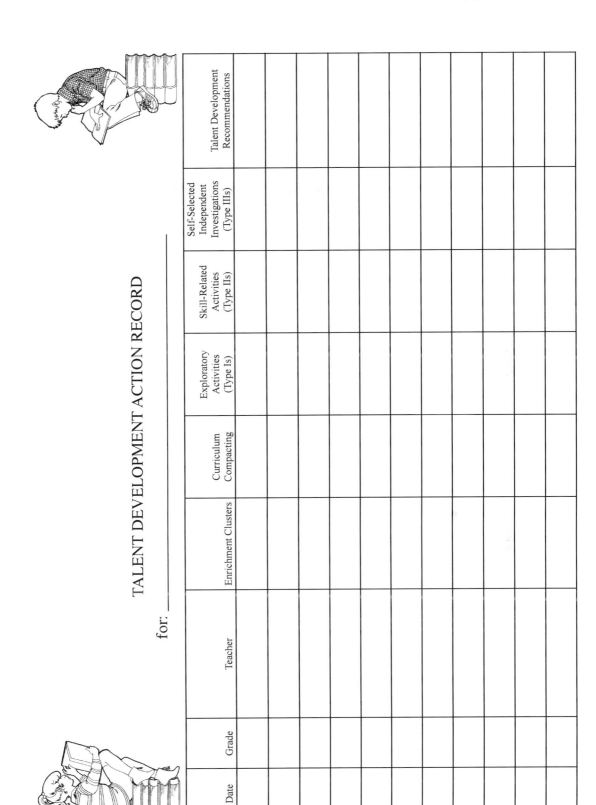

TALENT DEVELOPMENT ACTION RECORD

for: _____

Date	Grade	Teacher	Enrichment Clusters	Curriculum Compacting	Exploratory Activities (Type Is)	Skill-Related Activities (Type IIs)	Self-Selected Independent Investigations (Type IIIs)	Talent Development Recommendations

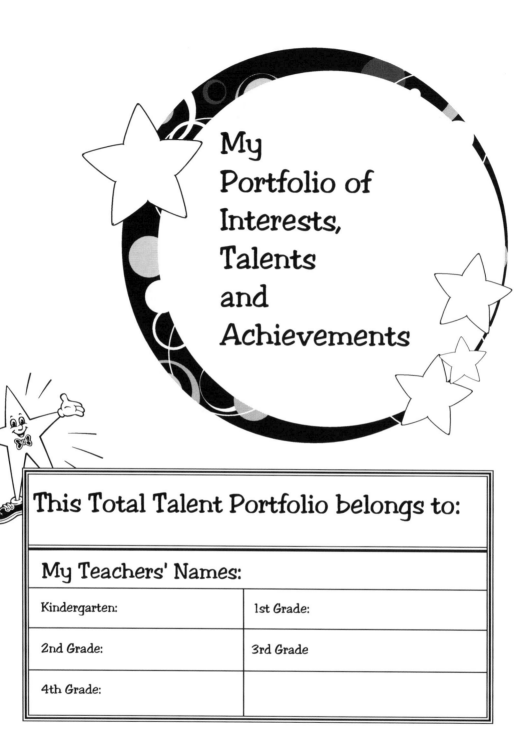

My
Portfolio of
Interests,
Talents
and
Achievements

This Total Talent Portfolio belongs to:	
My Teachers' Names:	
Kindergarten:	1st Grade:
2nd Grade:	3rd Grade
4th Grade:	

TOTAL TALENT PORTFOLIO For:	Status Information									
	K		1		2		3		4	
Subject Areas:	I Like This	I am Good at This	I Like This	I am Good at This	I Like This	I am Good at This	I Like This	I am Good at This	I Like This	I am Good at This
Reading										
Writing										
Spelling										
Mathematics										
Social Studies										
Science										
Art										
Music										
Physical Education										
Other:										
Class Activities I Like:										
Talking With Others										
Listening to the Teacher										
Answering Questions										
Simulations										
Games										
Doing Worksheets										
Doing Projects										
Computers										
Working in a Group										
Pretending										
Working Alone										
Peer Tutoring										
Learning Centers										
Mentorship										
Other:										
Assignments I Like:										
Writing										
Talking										
Hands-on Activities										
Art projects										
Displays										
Drama/Performing										
Helping Others										
Multimedia: video, audio, computer, overhead										
Other:										

TOTAL TALENT PORTFOLIO For:	My Interests and Talents				
	K	1	2	3	4
Interests:					
Performing Arts					
Creative Writing & Journalism					
Mathematics					
Business/Management					
Athletics					
History					
Social Action					
Fine Arts & Crafts					
Science					
Technology					
Other:					
Specific Interests:					

Talents	K	1	2	3	4
This year my talents/ interests were:					
Next year I would like to investigate:					

TOTAL TALENT PORTFOLIO
For:

TALENT DEVELOPMENT ACTION RECORD

DIRECTIONS: Clusters: Record the date and title of the cluster the student participated in. If the title is not descriptive of the cluster subject, include a brief description as well.

Compacting: Be sure to include the date and curriculum area compacted, as well as the replacement activities substituted.

K

ENRICHMENT CLUSTERS	CURRICULUM COMPACTING

1

ENRICHMENT CLUSTERS	CURRICULUM COMPACTING

2

ENRICHMENT CLUSTERS	CURRICULUM COMPACTING

3

ENRICHMENT CLUSTERS	CURRICULUM COMPACTING

4

ENRICHMENT CLUSTERS	CURRICULUM COMPACTING

TOTAL TALENT PORTFOLIO For:

Action Information

	Activities & Lessons I Do Outside of School	Type IIIs & Projects I Did at Home
K		
1		
2		
3		
4		

APPENDIX B
Interest-A-Lyzers

PRIMARY INTEREST-A-LYZER

By
Joseph S. Renzulli
and Mary G. Rizza
University of Connecticut

Name:_____ **Age:**_____

Teacher:_____ **Date:**_____

Note to Teachers & Parents:

This Interest-A-Lyzer is designed for students in grades K-3.
It is intended for whole classroom use but some students, especially
those who cannot read, may need some individual attention for proper
completion. Picture cues are provided for each question to help keep
new readers on task and to facilitate with group administration. It
is suggested that an adult consult with students and annotate the
responses, particularly when students use inventive spelling. This will
facilitate interpretation and ensure proper identification later on.
Interpretation of this instrument is similar to other versions of the
Interest-A-Lyzer and will look at individual responses within the context
of broader categories. The more information obtained from the child, the
easier it will be to interpret. Whenever necessary, the student should
be asked to provide more information by asking questions like "Why?"
or "How long?" or "Is that all?" It is hoped that teachers will view
this instrument as an opportunity to interact with their students on a
positive and enjoyable activity. We feel it is a great way to get to know
your students and their non-academic interests.
Remember that there are no right or wrong answers to this instrument
and special attention should be given to ensure that each response is
true to the student's own unique interests. There are no time limits for
completion. In fact, students should be encouraged to think about their
answers before filling out this instrument.

What kinds of books do you like to read?

_____

_____

_____

_____

What is your favorite book?

_____

_____

Do you belong to any clubs or teams?

Tell about them here:

_____

_____

_____

_____

Imagine that you can travel to any time in history.

Where would you go?

_____

_____

_____

_____

_____

The Interest-A-Lyzer

by
Joseph S. Renzulli
University of Connecticut

Name _____   Age _____

School _____   Grade _____

Date _____

The purpose of this questionnaire is to help you become more familiar with some of your interests and potential interests. The questionnaire is not a test and there are no right or wrong answers. Your answers will be completely confidential. You may want to talk them over with your teacher or other students, but this choice is entirely up to you.

Some of the time that you spend on enrichment activities will be devoted to working on individual or small-group projects. We would like you to work on projects that are of interest to you, so it is necessary for you to do a little thinking to know what some of your interests might be.

A good way for you to get in touch with your interests is to think about some of the things you like to do now and also some of the things you might like to do if the given the opportunity. Some of the questions that follow will be "Imagine if..." questions, but keep in mind that their only purpose is to have you think about the choices you would make in an imaginary situation.

As you read the questions try not to think about the kinds of answers that your friends might write or how they might feel about your answers. Remember, no one will see your answers if you want to keep them confidential.

Do not try to answer the questions now. Read them over and think about them for a few days and then write your answers. Please do not discuss the questionnaire with others at this time. Sometimes we can be influenced by the opinions of others and this influence may prevent you from exploring some of your own interests. Remember, the purpose of The Interest-A-Lyzer is to get YOU to THINK about YOUR OWN INTERESTS.

1. Imagine that your class has decided to create its own Video Production Company. Each person has been asked to sign up for his or her first, second or third choice for one of the jobs listed below. Mark your first choice with a 1, second choice with a 2, and third choice with a 3.

_____ Actor/Actress

_____ Director

_____ Musician

_____ Business Manager   _____ Costume Designer

_____ Computer Effects Specialist   _____ Scenery Designer

_____ Prop Person   _____ Light/Sound Person

_____ Advertising Agent   _____ Camera Operator

_____ Script Writer   _____ Dancer

2. Imagine that you have become a famous author of a well-known book. What is the general subject of your book? Circle One.

Fine Arts	Business	Science
Writing	History	Social Action
Athletics	Mathematics	
Performing Arts	Technology	

What will it be about?

_____

_____

_____

_____

What would be a good title for your book?

_____

Secondary

Interest-A-Lyzer

Thomas P. Hébert
The University of Alabama

Michele F. Sorensen
Farmington, Connecticut Public Schools

Joseph S. Renzulli
The University of Connecticut

This is an informal interest inventory which will serve as a foundation for developing your specific areas of interest throughout the school year. The information you provide is completely confidential. As a result of this survey, we hope to provide you with meaningful educational experiences that will further develop your interests, nurture your talents, and challenge your learning potential.

Read each question carefully and provide us with as much detailed information as possible so we may obtain a clear understanding of your interests.

Name _____

Grade _____   Date _____

School _____

1
☐
You are fed up with the course offerings at your high school. Your principal has asked you to design the perfect course for people with your same interests. What would the course be called? What would be taught?

2
☐
Rather than provide money for a class trip, the board of education has decided to give money to each individual student for a trip of his or her choice! Where would you go? List three (3) places you would visit and explain what you would do while visiting there. Why?

3
☐
You have written your first book which you are ready to submit for publication. What is the title? What is the book about?

4
☐
You have been asked to plan a concert for your high school. You have an unlimited budget! List three (3) choices of musical performances that you would schedule for that evening's program.

Primary
Art Interest -A- Lyzer

By Vidabeth Bensen

Name: _____ **Age:** _____ **Grade:** _____

School: _____ **Date:** _____

These questions will help you learn how you feel about Art. There are no right or wrong answers.

We want you to work on projects that you like in Art. Please take your time answering the questions. Think about them before you put down the answers. Make sure you answer them according to the way you feel, not the way your friends or classmates feel. This is to learn how YOU feel about ART.

1. Check the following things you like to do in your spare time:

_____ Color in coloring books	_____ Look at books or magazines about art
_____ Draw pictures	_____ Go to a museum
_____ Paint pictures	_____ Try different art materials
_____ Others	

_____   _____   _____
_____   _____   _____

2. If you could choose an art project to work on, what would it be?

_____ Paint a picture	_____ Work on a sculpture
_____ Take photographs	_____ Make a silk screen print
_____ Make a collage	_____ Work on a sculpture
_____ Paint a picture	_____ Others

_____   _____

3. Which of the following careers in art would you like to know more about?

_____ Art teacher	_____ Illustrator
_____ Painter	_____ Fashion designer
_____ Cartoonist	_____ Fashion illustrator
_____ Greeting card designer	_____ Photographer
_____ Stage set designer	_____ Costume designer
_____ Architect	_____ Museum worker
_____ Art historian	

4. List below some of the subjects you like to draw and paint.

_____   _____   _____
_____   _____   _____

By Vidabeth Bensen

Name: _____ **Age:** _____

School: _____ **Grade:** _____

                                            Date: _____

ART is a very personal subject. In order for you to become more familiar with the way you feel about art, we would like you to answer the questions in this ART INTEREST-A-LYZER. This is not a test and there are no right or wrong answers.

Some of the time you spend in art will be devoted to small group or individual projects. We want you to work on projects that are of interest to you, but sometimes you have to do some thinking before you know what really interests you.

Take your time when answering this questionnaire. Think about how YOU feel, not how your friends or classmates may feel. Do not discuss the questions with anyone until you have finished it. Your answers will be completely confidential, but if you want to discuss them later with your teacher or classmates, feel free to do so.

The **ART INTEREST-A-LYZER** is for **YOU** to think about **YOUR** interests in **ART**.

1. Check the following things that you like or would like to do in your spare time:

_____Draw pictures
_____Paint pictures
_____Read about famous artists
_____Read magazines about art
_____Visit an art museum or gallery
_____Experiment with different arts and crafts
_____Work with clay
_____Watch videos or films about art or crafts
_____Visit an artist's or sculptor's studio
_____Others _____
_____

2. Pretend that an art group to which you belong wants to raise money to buy art supplies. Each member has been asked to sign up for his or her first, second, and third choices for a project to work on or make and sell at an art fair. Mark your first, second, and third choices below:

_____ Paint a picture
_____ Make a sculpture
_____ Take photos for publicity
_____ Make a linoleum block print
_____ Make a silk screen print
_____ Make a T-shirt design to print
_____ Make a collage
_____ Make jewelry
_____ Mat and/or frame pictures
_____ Set up the display or exhibit
_____ Make posters to advertise the fair
_____ Others _____
_____

3. Your teacher has assigned the class to read a biography and write a report about a famous artist. List below the artists about whom you might like to read:

_____
_____
_____

ABOUT THE AUTHORS

Sally M. Reis, Ph.D., is the Interim Vice Provost for Academic Administration, a Board of Trustees Distinguished Professor, and Teaching Fellow in Educational Psychology at the University of Connecticut, where she also serves as Principal Investigator of The National Research Center on the Gifted and Talented. She was a teacher for 15 years, 11 of which were spent working with gifted students in the elementary, junior high, and high school levels. She has authored more than 130 articles, 14 books, 60 book chapters, and numerous monographs and technical reports. Dr. Reis serves on several editorial boards and is the past president of the National Association for Gifted Children.

Joseph S. Renzulli, Ed.D., is a long-time faculty member of the Department of Educational Psychology at the University of Connecticut and was selected by the university as one of its Distinguished Professors. He holds dual directorships at the Neag Center for Gifted Education and Talent Development and the federally funded The National Research Center for the Gifted and Talented.

Deborah E. Burns, Ph.D., has 43 years of experience in the field of education. She has worked in Michigan, Ohio, and Connecticut as a remedial reading and math teacher, a classroom teacher, a language arts specialist, a gifted education teacher and program coordinator, and as a university professor and program administrator. For the last 15 years, Deb has served as a central office curriculum coordinator for Cheshire Public Schools in Connecticut. She also serves as an adjunct professor for New Haven University and works as a member of the ASCD faculty and consultant team. Deb's current projects include the development of K–8 Common Core, Next Generation Science Standards, and National Council of Social Studies C3 curriculum and assessments. She is also busy implementing a mastery learning initiative that incorporates blended and personalized learning. Curriculum compacting is a major aspect of both of these initiatives.